HARDPRESS.NET
HOME OF HARD-TO-FIND BOOKS

Distinguished Men of Modern Times
by Henry Malden

Address:
HardPress
8345 NW 66TH ST #2561
MIAMI FL 33166-2626
USA
Email: info@hardpress.net

DISTINGUISHED MEN

OF

MODERN TIMES.

IN TWO VOLUMES.

VOL. II.

NEW-YORK:

PUBLISHED BY HARPER & BROTHERS,

NO. 82 CLIFF-STREET.

1842

Entered, according to Act of Congress, in the year 1840, by
HARPER & BROTHERS,
In the Clerk's Office of the Southern District of New-York.

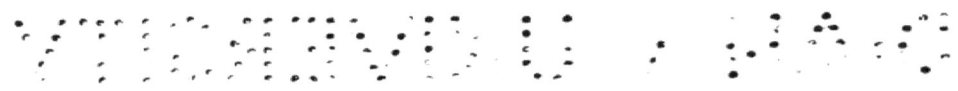

CONTENTS

or

THE SECOND VOLUME.

LIVES

OF

DISTINGUISHED MEN

OF

MODERN TIMES.

SOBIESKI.

So rapid and complete has been the decay of the Ottoman empire as an aggressive power, that any person now living, unacquainted with history anterior to the date of his own birth, would treat the notion of danger to Christian Europe from the ambition of Turkey as the idle fear of an over-anxious mind. Yet there was a time, and that within a century and a half, when popes summoned the princes of Europe to support the Cross, and the Eastern frontier of Christendom was the scene of almost constant warfare between Christian and Moslem. That period of danger was to Poland a period of glory, and the brightest part of it is the reign of the warrior-king, John Sobieski. It proved, indeed, no better than an empty glitter, won at a vast expense of blood and treasure, the benefits of which were chiefly reaped by the faithless and ungrateful Austria.

A 2

Sobieski was the younger son of a Polish noble-man, high in rank and merit. He was born in 1629. The death of his brother, slain in warfare with the Cossacks of the Ukraine in 1649, placed him in possession of the hereditary titles and im-mense estates of his house. To these distinctions he added high personal merits, an athletic body, a powerful, active, and upright mind, and, as the re-sult proved, the qualities which make a general and a statesman. It is no wonder, therefore, that, in the wars carried on by Poland during his youth against Tartars, Cossacks, and Swedes, he won laurels, though the republic gained neither honour nor advantage. At an early age he acquired the confidence of Casimir, the reigning king of Poland, and was employed in various services of impor-tance. On the revolt of Lubomirski, grand mar-shal of Poland, Sobieski was invested with that office, and soon after made lieutenant-general (if we may so translate it) of the Polish army. In that capacity he led the royal troops against Lubo-mirski. The king's obstinacy forced him to give battle at a disadvantage, and he was defeated, July 13, 1666; but the blame of this mishap was uni-versally thrown on the right person, while the skill of Sobieski in conducting the retreat obtained for him general admiration.

He married Marie de la Grange d'Arquien, a French lady of noble birth, who had accompanied the queen into Poland. She was a woman of wit and beauty, who exercised throughout life a great and unhappy influence over a husband devotedly attached to her. Aided by her favour with her mistress, Sobieski obtained the highest military office, that of grand general, in 1667. Happy for Poland that in this instance favour and merit went hand in hand ; for a host of fourscore thousand Tartars broke into the kingdom when its exhausted finances could not maintain an army, and its exhausted population could hardly supply one. By draining his private purse, pledging his resources, and levying recruits on his immense estates, the general raised his troops from twelve to twenty thousand, and marched fearlessly against a force four times his own. The scheme of his campaign was singularly confident, so much so as to excite the disapprobation even of the intrepid Condé. He detached eight thousand men in several corps, with secret orders, and took post with the remaining twelve thousand in a fortified camp at Podahiecz, a small town in the Palatinate of Russia, to stand the attack of eighty thousand Tartars, while his detachments were converging to their assigned stations. The assault was renewed for sixteen successive days ; and day after day the assailants were repulsed with great slaughter. On the seventeenth, Sobieski offered battle in the open field. A bloody contest ensued ; but, while victory was doubtful, the Polish detachments appeared on the Tartar flanks, and decided the victory. Disheartened by their loss, the Tartars made overtures of peace, which was concluded, equally to the satisfaction of both belligerants, October 19, 1667.

The circumstances attendant on the abdication of Casimir, in 1668, and the election of his successor, Michael Wiesnowieski, do not require to be noticed, since Sobieski took little part in the intrigues of the candidates or the deliberations on the Diet. The new king wept and trembled as he mounted a throne to which he had never aspired, and which he protested himself incapable to fill ; and the event proved that he was right. Yet, when he had tasted the sweets of power, he looked jealously on the man most highly esteemed and most able to do his country service, and, therefore, most formidable to a weak and suspicious prince. The Ukraine Cossacks had been converted by oppression from good subjects into bad neighbours, and on the accession of Michael they again raised the standard of revolt. Partly by negotiation and partly by force, the grand general reduced all the country from the Bog to the Dniester in the campaign of 1671, and he received the thanks of the republic for performing such eminent services with such scanty means. It is still more to his credit that he interfered, not for the first time, in favour of the revolted Cossacks, and insisted on their being received back to allegiance with kindness, and encouraged to good behaviour by equitable and friendly treatment.

King Michael, however, was of a very different mind in this matter. Determined on the subjugation of the whole Ukraine, he intrigued to hinder the Diet from confirming the peace, and thus induced the Cossacks to call in the help of Turkey, by threatening which they had stopped the progress of Sobieski. This brought on a fresh discussion in the Diet, in which Sobieski warmly urged the expediency of concession. But Michael still persisted in his course ; and from this period we may date the commencement of a league to dethrone him. In this, at first, Sobieski took no active, certainly no open part. When compelled to declare himself, he asserted with zeal the right of the republic to depose a prince who had shown himself unfit to reign. The consequences of this discord were very serious. At a Diet held in the spring of 1672, Michael was openly required to abdicate. To avoid this, he summoned the minor nobility, who had no seats in the Diet, and with whom, having formerly been of their body, he was more popular, to meet in the field of Golemba, on the bank of the Vistula; and he thus raised a sort of militia, to the number of a hundred thousand, ready to uphold him as their king. Sobieski, encamped at Lowicz with an army devotedly attached to him, maintained the cause of the confederate nobles. Neither party, however, was in haste to appeal to arms; and, in the interim. Mohammed IV., with 150,000 Turks and 100,000 Tartars, invaded Poland. The king, instead of marching against the enemy, contented himself with setting a price on the head of Sobieski, in whom alone the hope of Poland rested. Too weak to oppose the Turks, he sought the Tartars, who had dispersed to carry ruin through his country: he routed them in five successive battles, and recovered an immense booty and thirty thousand prisoners from their hands. Meanwhile the Turks overran Podolia, and took its capital town, the strong fortress of Kaminiec, the bulwark of Poland. Incapable himself of action, and apprehensive alike of the failure or success of Sobieski, Michael hastily concluded an ignominious peace, by which the Ukraine and part of Podolia were ceded to Turkey, and the payment of an annual tribute was agreed upon.

This treaty of Boudchaz, signed October 8, 1672, prevented Sobieski from continuing the war, and he returned indignantly to his camp at Lowicz. Before the end of the year, the king found it necessary to adopt conciliatory measures; and Sobieski, and other nobles who had been outlawed with him, were restored to their civil rights and the enjoyment of their property. At the Diet held in February, 1673, he inveighed against the scandalous peace of Boudchaz, which, in truth, was void, having been concluded without the sanction of that body, and it was resolved to renounce the treaty and to renew the war. Eighty thousand Turks were stationed in a fortified camp at Choczim, to overawe the newly-conquered provinces. On the 12th of November, 1673, Sobieski stormed their camp. Observing that the infantry wavered, he dismounted his own regiment of dragoons and led them to the ramparts, which they were the first to scale. The infantry now rushed forward to support their general; the intrenchments were won, and the Turks routed with great slaughter, and entirely disorganized. This victory was disgraced by the massacre of a great number of prisoners in cold blood. Soon after it the death of Michael relieved Poland from the burden of a weak king, and the Interrex stopped the victorious general's progress, by requiring his attendance in Poland.

The Diet of election commenced its sittings on the first of May, 1674. As before, there were a number of foreign candidates, but none who commanded a decisive majority among the electors; and at last the election of the assembly fell on Sobieski, who, whatever his secret wishes or intrigues may have been, had never openly pretended to the crown. This choice was received with general rejoicing. The new king's first care was to follow up the blow struck at Choczim, and wrest the Ukraine from Turkey. During this and the two following years, that unhappy country was again the scene of bloodshed and rapine. There is little in the history of the war to claim our attention. It was concluded at the memorable seige of Zurawno, where, with a policy somewhat similar to that which he pursued at Podahiecz, he advanced to meet an invading army outnumbering his own six to one. Fortunately, the Turkish government stood in need of peace, and their general had authority and orders to put an end to the war in the best manner he could ; and, after investing the Polish camp for five weeks, he consented to a treaty, signed October 29, 1676, the terms of which were far more favourable than could have been anticipated by Poland. Two thirds of the Ukraine, and part of Podolia, were restored to her, and the tribute imposed by the treaty of Boudchaz was given up. These terms were ratified by the Porte, and seven years of peace succeeded to a previous state of almost constant war.

This interval of rest from arms is not important in the history of Sobieski's life. As he had anticipated, he found the throne no easy seat ; and his criminal weakness in admitting the queen, who never scrupled at disturbing public affairs to gratify her own passions or prejudices, to an undue weight in his counsels, lessens our sympathy with his vexations, and casts a shade over his brilliant qualities. In 1680 greater matters began to be moved.

Ever watchful of the Porte, Sobieski knew through
his spies that Mohammed was preparing for war
with Austria as soon as the existing truce should
expire ; and he conceived the project of uniting the
money of Rome, and the arms of Austria and Venice, with those of Poland ; and, by thus distracting
the power of Turkey, to regain more easily the
much-coveted fortress of Kaminiec, and the rem-
nant of Podolia. He had, indeed, sworn solemnly
to maintain a treaty, which the Turks, on their
part, religiously observed ; but the pope was prepared to absolve him from his oath, and this the
morality of the age thought quite sufficient. For
a time his views were frustrated, both at home and
abroad ; but, as the political storm which was collecting grew darker and darker, both pope and emperor entered more heartily into his scheme, and
an offensive and defensive treaty was concluded
between Austria and Poland.

The Turkish troops assembled in the plains of
Adrianople in May, 1683, in number, according to
the calculations of historians, upward of 200,000
fighting men. The brave Hungarians, heretofore
the bulwark of Austria against the Ottoman, but
now alienated by oppression and misgovernment,
revolted under the celebrated Tekeli, and thus
opened a way into the heart of the Austrian empire. Kara Mustapha commanded the immense
army destined by the Porte for this warfare, and
for once he showed judgment and decision in neg-
lecting small objects, and pushing forward at once
to Vienna. Leopold fled in haste with his court :
the Imperial general, the brave Charles of Lorraine, threw in part of his small army to re-enforce

the garrison, but was unable to oppose the progress of the besiegers. The trenches were opened on the 14th of July, and the heavy artillery of the Turks crumbled the weak ramparts, and carried destruction into the interior of the city. Unhappy is the country which trusts to foreign aid in such an emergency! The German princes had not yet brought up their contingents; and even Sobieski, the last man to keep back in such a cause, could not collect his army fast enough to meet the pressing need of the occasion. Letter after letter reached him, entreating that he would at least bring the terror of his name and his profound military skill to the relief of Austria; and he set off at length to traverse Moravia with an escort of only two thousand horse, leaving the Grand-general Jablonowski to bring up the army with the utmost speed. After all, the Polish troops reached Tuln, on the Danube, the place of rendezvous, before the Bavarians, Saxons, and other German auxiliaries were collected. On the 7th of September the whole army was assembled, in number about 74,000. Vienna was already in the utmost distress. Stahremberg, the brave commandant, had written to the Duke of Lorraine a letter, containing only these pithy words: "No more time to lose, my lord; no more time to lose." Incapable of resisting, with its enfeebled garrison, a general assault, the place must have fallen but for the avarice and stupid pride of Mustapha, who believed that the Imperial capital must contain immense treasures, which he was loath to give up to indiscriminate plunder; and never so much as dreamed that any one would be hardy enough to contest the prize with his multitudes before it should fall into his hands from mere exhaustion.   There was, in truth, no more time to lose ; for it was calculated, on the 22d of August, that Vienna could only hold out three days against a general assault ; and the 9th of September arrived before the Christian army moved from Tuln. Five leagues of mountain road still separated it from Vienna, in any part of which its progress might have been stopped by such a detachment as the immense Turkish army could well have spared.

The battle of deliverance, fought on the 12th of September, 1683, was short and decisive ; the Turks had been both disgusted and disheartened by their general's misconduct.   Sobieski was not expected to command in person : but the Tartars had seen him lead his cavalry to the charge too often to overlook the signs which marked his presence, and the knowledge of it sunk their hearts still more.   " Allah !" said the brave Khan of the Tartars, as he pointed out to the vizier the pennoned lances of the Polish Horse Gaurds, " Allah ! but the wizard is among them, sure enough."   The vizier attempted to atone by a higher courage for his past errors : but despair or disaffection had seized on both soldiers and officers.   Even the veteran Tartar chief replied to his entreaties, " The Polish king is there.   I know him well.   Did I not tell you all we had to do was to get away as fast as possible ?"   The Polish cavalry pushed forward to the vizier's tent, and cut their way through the Spahis, who alone disputed the victory ; and, with the capture of their great standard, the consternation and confusion of the Turks became final and complete.   Entering Vienna the next day, Sobieski was received with an enthusiasm little agreeable to the jealous temper of the emperor, who manifested his incurable meanness of disposition, not only in his cold reception and ungracious thanks of the deliverer of his kingdom, but in the ingratitude and perfidy of all his subsequent conduct.

Whether from pure love of beating the Turks, or from a false hope that Leopold might be induced to perform his promises, Sobieski, contrary to the wishes of the republic, pursued the flying enemy into Hungary. Near Gran, on the Danube, he met with a severe check, in which his own life had nearly been sacrificed to the desire of showing the Imperialists that he could conquer without their help. This he acknowledged after his junction with the Duke of Lorraine. " Gentlemen," he said, " I confess I wanted to conquer without you, for the honour of my own nation. I have suffered severely for it, being soundly beat ; but I will take my revenge both with you and for you. To effect this must be the chief object of our thoughts." The disgrace was soon wiped off by a decisive victory gained nearly on the same spot. Gran capitulated, and the king led his army back to Poland in the month of December.

The glory of this celebrated campaign fell to Poland, the profit accrued to Austria. Kaminiec was still in the possession of Turkey, and continued so during the whole reign of Sobieski : not from want of effort, for the recovery of that important fortress was the leading object of the campaigns of 1684, 5, and 7 ; but the Polish army was better fitted for the open field than for the tedious and expensive process of a siege. In 1686, Leopold, apprehensive lest Sobieski should break off an alliance distasteful to his subjects and unsatisfactory to himself (for the emperor had broken every promise, and failed in every inducement which he had held out to the Polish sovereign), threw out another bait, which succeeded better than the duplicity and ingratitude of the contriver deserved. He suggested the idea of wresting from the Turks Moldavia and Wallachia, to be held as an independent and hereditary kingdom by Sobieski and his family, and promised a body of troops to assist in the undertaking. The great object of Sobieski's ambition, by pursuing which he lost much of his popularity and incurred just censure, as aiming at an unconstitutional object by unconstitutional means, was to hand the crown of Poland to his son at his own decease, and render it, if possible, hereditary in his family. As a step to this, the possession of the above-named provinces was most desirable; or, if this wish should be frustrated, it was still desirable, in placing his posterity among the royal houses of Europe ; and, with a preference of private to public interest, which is not the less censurable for being common, he rejected an offer made by Mohammed to restore Kaminiec, and pay a large sum to indemnify Poland for the expenses of the war, in order that he might pursue his favourite scheme of family aggrandizement. Satisfied, however, with having engaged him in this new diversion of the Turkish power, Leopold had not the smallest intention of sending the promised troops ; and the King of Poland was involved in great danger from their non-appearance at the expected place. This campaign, however, was so far satisfactory, that Moldavia yielded without resistance or bloodshed : but a second and a third expedition, undertaken in 1688 and 1691, to consolidate and extend his conquests, were unsuccessful, and the sovereignty soon passed back into the hands of Turkey. The campaign of 1691 was the last in which Sobieski appeared in the field.

The reader will see, from this brief account, that he gained few laurels after the campaign of Vienna. Indeed, he scarcely deserved to do so ; for, great and disinterested as his conduct often was, in this juncture he sacrificed national to family interests, and consumed the blood and riches of his countrymen in a needless and fruitless war.

Sobieski's internal policy has little to recommend it or to exalt his fame. Devoted to his wife, who proved herself unworthy of his affection by the most harassing demands upon his time and attention, and still more by a pernicious, unwise, and unconstitutional interference in state affairs, the king lowered his popularity and reputation by thus weakly yielding to an unworthy influence, and, as the natural consequence, he was continually thwarted by a harassing and often factious opposition. Civil discord, family quarrels, and the infirmities of a body worn out prematurely by unsparing exposure for more than forty years to the toils of war, combined to imbitter the decline of his life. During the five years which elapsed from Sobieski's last campaign to the time of his death, the history of Poland records much of unprincipled intriguing, much personal ingratitude, and some upright opposition to his measures, but nothing of material importance to his personal history. He died June 17, 1696, on the double anniversary, it is said, of

his birth and his accession to the throne ; and, by
another singular coincidence, his birth and death
were alike heralded by storms of unusual violence.

The character of Sobieski is one of great brilliancy and not inconsiderable faults.   As a subject,
he displayed genuine, disinterested patriotism : but
as a king, the welfare of his family seems to have
been dearer to him than that of his country.   Nor
did his domestic government display the vigour and
decision which might reasonably have been expected from his powerful mind.   But his justice was
unimpeachable ; he was temperate, and unrevenge-
ful even when personally affronted, which often occurred in the tumultuous Diets of Poland ; and, in
a bigoted age, he displayed the virtue of toleration.
The constant labours of an active life did not destroy his taste for literature, and his attainments
were considerable ; he spoke several languages,
aspired to be a poet, and loved the company of
learned men.   He was remarkable for the suavity
of his temper and the charms of his conversation.
Such a character, though far from perfection, is entitled to the epithet of GREAT. which he honourably
won and enjoyed ; and as a soldier, he has claims
to our gratitude which not every soldier possesses.
His warfare was almost uniformly waged against an
aggressive and barbarian power, which, in the utmost need of Christian Europe, he stood forward to
resist, and finally broke.   Like other nations, Turkey has had its alternations of success and reverses ; but never, since the campaign of Vienna,
have the arms of the East threatened the repose of
Europe.

The history of Sobieski's life and reign is told at

large in the works of his countryman Zaluski; in a Life of him by the Abbé Coyer, of which there is an English translation; and in a recent publication by M. Salvandy. The same writer has republished a most interesting collection of Letters, written by Sobieski to his queen during the campaign of Vienna, printed for the first time in Poland about ten years ago.

BOSSUET.

THE life of the Bishop of Meaux, a theologian and polemic familiarly known to his countrymen as the oracle of their church, forms an important part of the ecclesiastical history of the seventeenth century. A short personal memoir of such a man can serve only to excite curiosity, and, in some measure, to direct more extended inquiries.

Jacques-Benigne Bossuet, whose father and ancestors were honourably distinguished in the profession of the law, was born at Dijon, September 27, 1627. He was placed in his childhood at the college of the Jesuits in his native town, whence, at the age of fifteen, he was removed to the college of Navarre at Paris. At both these places his progress as a student was so rapid that he passed for a prodigy. It may be mentioned, not more as a proof of precocious intellect than as characteristic of the times, that, soon after his removal to Paris, whither the fame of his genius had preceded him, he was invited to exhibit his powers as a preacher at the Hotel de Rambouillet in his sixteenth year. His performance was received with great approbation.

In the year 1652 he was ordained priest, and, his talents having already made him known, he soon after received preferment in the cathedral church of Metz, of which he became successively canon, archdeacon, and dean. It was here that he published his Refutation of the Catechism of Paul Ferri, a Protestant divine of high reputation. This was the first of that series of controversial writings which contributed, more than all his other works, to procure for him the high authority which he enjoyed in the church. He came forward in the field of controversy at a time when public attention was fixed on the subject, and when the favourite object both with Church and State was the peaceable conversion of the Protestants.

Richelieu, in the preceding reign, had crushed, by the vigour of his administration, the political power of the Protestant party. He, in common with many other statesmen, Catholic and Protestant, had conceived a notion that uniformity of religious profession was necessary to the tranquillity of the state. But, though unchecked in the prosecution of his objects by any scruples of conscience or feelings of humanity, he would have considered the employment of force, where persuasion could be made effectual, to be, in the language of a modern politician, not a crime, but a blunder. When, therefore, the army had done its work, he put in action a scheme for reclaiming the Protestants by every species of politic contrivance. The system commenced by him was continued by others; and of all those who laboured in the cause, Bossuet was indubitably the most able and the most distinguished.

His first effort, the Refutation of the Catechism,

recommended him to the notice of the queen-mother; and the favour which he now enjoyed at court was farther increased by the fame of his eloquence in the pulpit, which he had frequent opportunities of displaying at Paris, whither he was called from time to time by ecclesiastical business. He was summoned to preach at the Chapel of the Louvre before Louis XIV., who was pleased to express, in a letter to Bossuet's father, the great delight which he received from the sermons of his son; for the versatile taste of this monarch enabled him in one hour to recreate himself with the wit and beauty of his mistresses, and in the next to listen with seeming pleasure to the exhortations of a Christian pastor. But Bossuet had still stronger claims on the gratitude of Louis, by converting to the Roman Catholic faith the celebrated Turenne. This victory is said to have been achieved by his well-known Exposition, written in the year 1668, and published in 1671.

So great was his influence at this time, that he was requested by the Archbishop of Paris to interfere in one of those many disputes which the papal decrees against the tenets of Jansenius occasioned. The nuns of Port Royal, who were attached to the doctrine and the discipline of the Jansenists, were required to subscribe the celebrated Formulary, which selected for condemnation five propositions said to be contained in a certain huge work of Jansenius. . Those recluses modestly submitted, that they were ready to accept any doctrine propounded by the Church, and even to affix their names to the condemnation of the obnoxious propositions; but that they could not assert that these propositions were to be found in a book which they had never seen. In this difficulty the assistance of Bossuet was requested, who, after several conferences, wrote a long letter to the refractory nuns, highly commended for its acute logic and sound divinity. Much of the logic and divinity was, however, probably thrown away upon the persons for whose use they were intended ; but there was one part of the letter sufficiently intelligible. He congratulated them on their total exemption from all obligation to examine, and from the task of self-guidance ; and assured them that it was their bounden duty, as well as their happy privilege, to subscribe and assent to everything which was placed before them by authority. The nuns were not convinced. They escaped, however, for the present ; but, in the end, they paid dearly for their passive resistance to the decision of Pope Alexander VII. on a matter of fact.

In the year 1669 Bossuet was promoted to the bishopric of Condon, which he resigned the following year, on being appointed to the important office of preceptor to the dauphin.

History has told us nothing of the pupil, but that his capacity was mean, and his disposition sordid. To him, however, the world is indebted for the most celebrated of Bossuet's performances. The Introduction to Universal History was written expressly for his use ; and this masterly work may serve to confirm an opinion, entertained even by his friends, that Bossuet was not peculiarly qualified for his situation. To compose such a work for such a boy was worse than a waste of power. Though devoted closely and conscientiously to the duties of his new office, he was not altogether withdrawn from what might be called his vocation, the prosecution of controversy. It was during the period of his connexion with the court that his celebrated conference occurred with the Protestant Claude. Mlle. de Duras, a niece of Turenne, had conceived scruples respecting the soundness of her Protestant principles from the perusal of Bossuet's "Exposition." She consulted M. Claude, who promised to resolve her doubts in the presence of Bossuet himself. The challenge was accepted, and the memorable conference was the result. Both parties published an account of it; and their statements, as might be expected, without suspicion of dishonesty on either side, did not entirely agree. The lady was content to follow the example of her uncle.

Bossuet's engagement with the dauphin was concluded in the year 1681, when he was rewarded with the bishopric of Meaux. In so short a memoir of such a man, where only the most prominent occurrences of his life can be noticed, there is danger lest the reader should regard him only in the character of a controversialist, or in the proud station of acknowledged leader of the French Catholic Church. It is the more necessary, therefore, in this place to observe, that to the comparatively obscure but really important duties of his diocese, he brought the same zeal and energy which he had displayed on a more conspicuous theatre ; and that he could readily exchange the pen of the polemic for that of the devout and affectionate pastor.

Louis, however, was not disposed to leave the bishop undisturbed in his retirement. He was

soon called forth to be the advocate of his temporal against his spiritual master.

The kings of France had long exercised certain
powers in ecclesiastical matters, which had rather
been tolerated than sanctioned by the popes.   Louis was determined not only to preserve, but considerably to extend, what his predecessors had enjoyed.   Hence a sharp altercation had been carried
on for many years between him and the See of
Rome.   But in 1682, in consequence of a threatening brief issued by that haughty pontiff, Innocent
XII., he summoned, by the advice of his clergy,
for the purpose of settling the matters in debate, a
general assembly of the church.   Of this famous
assembly Bossuet was deservedly regarded as the
most influential member.   He opened the proceedings with a sermon, having reference to the subjects which were to come under consideration.
In this discourse the reader may find, perhaps,
some marks of that embarrassment which he is
supposed to have felt.   He had the deepest sense
of the unbounded power and awful majesty of kings
in general, and the highest personal veneration for
Louis in particular; but then, on the other hand,
the degree of allegiance which he owed to his spiritual head it was almost impiety to define.   So, after having illustrated, with all the force of his eloquence, the inviolable dignity of the church, and
fully established the supremacy of St. Peter, he
carries up, as it were, in a parallel line, the lof-
tiest panegyric on the monarchy and monarchs of
France.

The discourse was celebrated for its ability; and,
without doubt, the conflicting topics were managed

with great skill. His difficulties did not cease with the dismissal of the assembly. The question of the Régale, or the right of the king to the revenues of every vacant see, and to collate to the simple benefices within its jurisdiction, was settled not at all to the satisfaction of the pope; and the declaration of the assembly, drawn up by Bossuet himself, was fiercely attacked by the transalpine divines. It was, of course, as vigorously defended by its author, who was, in consequence, accused by all his enemies, and some of his friends, of having forgotten his duty to the pope in his subserviency to the king.

Nothing wearied by his exertions in the royal cause, he had scarcely left the assembly, when he resumed his labours in defence of his church against heresy. Several smaller works, put forth from time to time, seemed to be only a preparation for his great effort in the year 1688, when he published his " History of the Variations in the Protestant Churches." In this book he has made the most of what may be called the staple argument of the Catholics against the Protestants.

The course of the narrative has now brought us beyond the period of the memorable revocation of the Edict of Nantes; and it will naturally be asked in what light Bossuet regarded this act of folly and oppression. Neither his disposition nor his judgment would lead him to approve the atrocities perpetrated by the government; but, in a letter to the Intendant of Languedoc, he labours to justify the use of pains and penalties in enforcing religious conformity, that is, he justifies the act of Louis XIV. In this matter he was not advanced

beyond his times; but, whatever may have been
his theory of the lawfulness of persecution, his
conduct towards the Protestants was such as to obtain for him the praise even of his opponents.

Hitherto we have seen Bossuet labouring inces-
santly to reconcile the Huguenots of France to the
established religion. But, about this time, he took
part in a more grand and comprehensive measure,
sanctioned by the emperor, and some other sovereign princes of Germany, for the reunion of the
great body of the Lutherans throughout Europe
with the Roman Catholic Church. They engaged
the Bishop of Neustadt to open a communication
with Molanus, a Protestant doctor of high reputation in Hanover. With these negotiators were
afterward joined Leibnitz on the part of the Protestants, and Bossuet on that of the Roman Catholics. Between these two great men the correspondence was carried on for ten years, in a spirit
worthy of themselves and the cause in which they
were engaged; and it terminated, as probably they
both expected it would terminate, in leaving the
two churches in the same state of separation in
which it found them.

It would have been well for the fame of Bossuet
if the course of his latter days had been marked
only by this defeat; if it had not been signalized,
when gray hairs had increased the veneration which
his genius and services had procured him, by an
inglorious victory over a weak woman and a
friend. The history of Madame Guyon, and the
revival of mysticism under the name of Quietism,
principally by her means, will more properly be
found in a Life of Fenelon. The part which

Bossuet took in the proceedings respecting her must be here briefly noticed. As universal referee in matters of religion, he was called upon to examine her doctrines, which began to excite the jealousy of the church. His conduct towards her in the first instance was mild and forbearing; but either zeal or anger betrayed him at length into a cruel persecution of this amiable visionary. Fenelon, who had partly adopted her views of Christian perfection, and thoroughly admired her Christian character, was required by Bossuet to surrender to him at once his opinions and his feelings. Fenelon was willing to do much, but would not consent to sacrifice his integrity to the offended pride of the irritated prelate. He defended his opinions in print, and the points in debate were, by his desire, referred to the pope; and to him they should, in common decency, have been left: but we are disgusted with a detail of miserable intrigues, carried on in the council appointed by the pope to examine the matter, and of vehement remonstrances with which his holiness himself was assailed, with the avowed object of extorting a reluctant condemnation. The warmest friends of Bossuet do not attempt to defend him on the plea that these things were done without his concurrence: they insist only on his disinterested zeal for religion. But let it be remembered, that this interference with papal deliberation proceeded from one who believed the pontiff to be solemnly deciding, with the aid of the Holy Spirit, a point of faith for the whole Catholic Church. Bossuet triumphed; but from that moment he sunk perceptibly in the general esteem of his countrymen.

During the few remaining years of his life he maintained his wonted activity, and in his last illness we find with pleasure that the Bible was his companion, and that he could employ his intervals of repose from severe suffering in composing a commentary on the 23d Psalm. He died on the 12th of April, 1704, in his 76th year.

The authority which Bossuet acquired was such, that he may be said not only to have guided the Gallican Church during his life, but in some measure to have left upon it the permanent impression of his own character. Of this authority no adequate notion can be formed from the preceding sketch. Few even of his works, which fill twenty volumes quarto, have been noticed. It should, however, be mentioned, that he was employed by Louis XIV. in an attempt to overcome the religious scruples of James II., whose conscience revolted from that exercise of the prerogative in favour of the Protestant Church which his restoration to the throne would have required. The laboured and somewhat extraordinary letter which Bossuet wrote on this occasion is dated May 22, 1693.

His countrymen claim for Bossuet an exalted place among historians, orators, and theologians. The honours bestowed by them on his " Introduction to Universal History" have been confirmed by more impartial judges ; and, even when unsupported by reference to the age in which it was written, it stands forth on its own merits as a noble effort of a comprehensive and penetrating mind. His Funeral Orations come to us recommended by the judgment of Voltaire, who ascribes to Bossuet alone, of all his contemporaries, the praise of real eloquence. The English reader will often be rewarded by passages which in oratorical power have seldom been surpassed, and which may induce him to forgive much that is cold, inflated, and unnatural. But the Orations must be considered also as Christian discourses, delivered by a minister of the gospel from a Christian pulpit. They were composed, for the most part, to grace the obsequies of royal persons, and are, in fact, dedicated to the honour and glory of kings and princes. A text from Scripture is the peg on which is hung everything which can minister to human pride and dignify the vanities of a court; and the effect is but slightly impaired by well-turned phrases, proper to the occasion, on the nothingness of earthly things. But the orator is not content with general declamation, with prostrating himself before his magnificent visions of ancient pedigrees: he descends to the meanest personal flattery of the living as well as the dead. When the Duchess of Orleans was laid in her coffin, her friends might have hoped that her frailties would be buried with her; but they could hardly have expected that a Christian monitor should have held her forth as an exquisite specimen of female excellence, the glory of France, whom Heaven itself had rescued from her enemies to present as a precious and inestimable gift to the French nation. But on this occasion Bossuet was not yet perfect in his art, or perhaps the subject was not sufficiently disgraceful to draw forth all his powers. When afterward called to speak over the dead body of the queen, whose heart had withered under the wrongs which a licentious husband,

C 2

amid the hypocrisy of external respect, had heaped
upon her, he finds it a fitting opportunity to pro-
nounce, at the same time, a panegyric on the king.
He recounts the victories won by the French arms,
and ascribes them all to the prowess of his hero.
But Louis is not only the taker of cities, he is the
conqueror of himself; and the royal sensualist is
praised for the government of his passions, the
despot for his clemency and justice, and the grasping conqueror for his moderation.

The controversial writings of Bossuet deserve
more regard than either his History or his Orations, if the importance of a book is to be measured by the extent and permanency of its effects.
The Exposition of the Doctrines of the Roman
Catholic Church, one of the shortest, but, perhaps,
most notable of his theological works, was published under circumstances which gave occasion to a
story of mysterious suppression and alteration.
But a more serious charge has been brought against
the author, of having misrepresented the doctrines
of his church, in order to entrap the Protestants.
So grave an accusation ought not to be lightly
entertained; and though suspicion is excited by
symptoms of disingenuous management in the controversy to which the publication gave birth; and
though it appears to be demonstrable that the Roman Catholic religion, as commonly professed, and
many of its doctrines, as expressed or implied in
some of its authorized formularies, differ essentially
from the picture which Bossuet has drawn, yet it
should at least be remembered that the book itself
was eventually, though tardily, sanctioned by the
highest authority in the Romish Church.   It is pos-

sible that Bossuet may, by his Exposition, have converted others besides Turenne ; but there can be no doubt that he has wrought an extensive, though a less obvious, change within the bosom of his own church. The high authority of his name would give currency to his opinions on any subject connected with the Catholic faith ; and many sincere Romanists, who had felt the objections urged against certain practices and dogmas of their own church, would rejoice to find, on the authority of Bossuet, that they were not obliged to own them.

The charge of insincerity has been extended beyond this particular instance to the general character of the bishop ; and it has been asserted that he held, in secret, opinions inconsistent with those which he publicly professed. This charge, however, is apparently destitute of all proof.

Enough has been shown to justify us in concluding that he was not one of those rare characters which can break loose from all the obstacles that oppose themselves to the simple love and uncompromising search of truth. Some men, like his illustrious countryman Du Pin, struggle to be free. It should seem that Bossuet, if circumstances fettered him, would be unconscious of his thraldom ; and that he would exert all the energies of his powerful mind, not to escape from his prison, but to render it a tenable fortress or a commodious dwelling. It would be foolish and unjust to infer from this that he would persevere through life in deliberately maintaining what he had discovered to be false on the most momentous of all subjects.

A complete catalogue of his works may be found at the end of the Life of Bossuet in the Biographie

Universelle. The Life itself, which is obviously written by a partial friend, contains much information in a small compass. The affair of Quietism, and the contest between Bossuet and Fenelon, are minutely detailed, with great accuracy, in the Life of Fenelon by the Cardinal de Bausset, whose impartiality seems to have been secured by the profound veneration which he entertained for each of the combatants, though the impression left on the reader's mind is not favourable to the character of Bossuet.

LOCKE.

JOHN LOCKE was born August 29, 1632, at Wrington, a village of Somersetshire, about eight miles from Bristol. He was the eldest of two sons of John Locke, a man of some property, who had been bred to the law, but became afterward a captain under Cromwell. In those turbulent times he met with losses which diminished his fortune, and he left an inconsiderable inheritance to his son. Locke received his education at Westminister School, and Christ Church, Oxford. While an under-graduate he was chosen to write a welcome on the occasion of a visit which Cromwell paid to that university, just after the conclusion of his peace with the Dutch. This he did in a laudatory copy of verses in English and Latin, comparing the great Protector to Julius for warlike, and to Augustus for peaceful, accomplishments. This and some Latin verses prefixed to a work of Sydenham's, are Locke's only poetical attempts. There is little merit in either. He was a great admirer of the meager verse of Sir Richard Blackmore, which is no great evidence of his poetical taste. Between the degrees of Bachelor and Master of Arts he was elected student of his college. From that time he applied himself diligently, for many years, to the study of medicine, without, however, practising it as a matter of gain. The weakness of his health probably gave this turn to his thoughts; his brother died of consumption; and he himself was apprehensive through life of falling a victim to the same disease. In 1664 he went abroad as secretary to Sir W. Swan, envoy to the court of Brandenburg; and on his return to Oxford the year following, he applied himself to the discovery of the effects of the air on the human frame. His first work, published in 1667, was a register of the variations in the atmosphere, determined between certain periods by the common instruments, as a supplement to a work by Boyle.

He was amusing himself with such inquiries, when one of the slight but important accidents of life brought him an acquaintance whose influence determined his future course. A friend, being obliged to take a journey, desired Locke to make his excuses to Lord Ashley (afterward Earl of Shaftesbury) for not having procured for him some mineral waters against his arrival in Oxford. When Lord Ashley arrived, Locke carried this message to him. They were mutually pleased with each other, and an acquaintance, thus casually commenced, speedily grew up into a strict friendship.

Locke's advice determined Lord Ashley to submit
to a surgical operation, by which, it is said, the life
of the patient was saved; and he was received into
the house, and practised his profession in the family and among a few private friends of his noble
patron. While living in this way, his thoughts
were turned into the channel of politics by the advice of his new associates; and, taking up that
study earnestly, he was soon able to advise and
assist Ashley in all his plans of state, becoming at
the same time the referee of his private affairs.
This warm friendship is singular, considering the
purity of Locke's life and the notoriously bad character, public and private, of his patron. But the
latter was an eloquent orator and an admirable
talker; and it was probably this latter quality
which attached Locke so much. He had so great
an esteem for good conversation, as to assign it a
first place in the formation of a man's mind, calling
books the raw material, and social talk, with medi-
tation, the true architects of our mental construc-
tions. In 1668 Locke attended the Earl and
Countess of Northumberland to France. But some
accident caused him soon to return to his old residence with Shaftesbury, for whom he drew up the
fundamental laws of Carolina, which had just been
granted to him and other lords. Two of the articles of this settlement gave great offence to the
clergy, and were expunged. They are somewhat
remarkable, and should be mentioned. One was,
" That no man that doth not acknowledge a God,
and that God publicly worshipped, should be a freeman or inhabitant of Carolina." The other was a
proposition, that any seven persons agreeing in a

form of worship should be esteemed a church, and be supported by the state. The Church of England, however, was alone established in that colony. In 1671 Locke commenced his great Essay on the Human Understanding, but his engagements with Shaftesbury prevented its immediate completion. The year following, his patron becoming chancellor, Locke was made secretary of presentations, which office he speedily lost on the partial disgrace of the earl, who, still remaining President of the Board of Trade, appointed him secretary to a Commission of Inquiry into the state of Trade and of the Colonial Plantations. This office he also lost in the same manner, upon Lord Shaftesbury's total disgrace in 1674.

Having retained his studentship, Locke then retired to Oxford, partly for his health's sake, and partly to pursue his old medical studies. He took the degree of Bachelor of Medicine in this year. It appears that he continued to pay some attention to these studies until an advanced age ; for in 1697 he communicated to the Royal Society the history of a curious case which he had seen at the great hospital of La Charité, during his residence at Paris. In 1675, with the hope of obtaining relief from an asthmatical complaint, he went to Montpellier. There was also another reason for this journey. He had just published an anonymous pamphlet for Shaftesbury, blaming the conduct of the House of Lords in the matter of the Test Act, containing a vehement abuse of the bishops, and of what he called their favourite doctrine, " the divine right" of kings and priests. This pamphlet does not appear in the folio edition of his works : it was anonymous, like most of his other productions. The odium consequent upon this publication made his absence from England expedient, if not necessary. During his stay abroad Locke kept a journal of what he saw, did, and thought. In it we find the heads of many of his future works, which are very concise and valuable; but the narrative is dry, and the attempts at humour not very successful; he seems, however, to have been as observant of what relates to the external world as he was of the intellectual. In 1679, Shaftesbury, on being made president of the council, summoned Locke to England. But the old statesman's favour was short-lived; he was committed to the Tower in July, 1681, and, soon after his release, retired to Holland, where he died in January, 1683. Locke accompanied him, and continued his faithful services until death. For seventeen years he had been Shaftesbury's constant partisan and adviser; and the odium attached to that nobleman clung to himself, and prevented his return to England for many years. In 1683 he was reported by the English envoy at the Hague to be on terms of intimacy with the malecontents in Holland; upon which the secretary (Sunderland) wrote to Dr. Fell, the dean of Christ Church, ordering his expulsion from college. This mandate was not immediately complied with: the dean declared that for many years he had watched the conduct of Locke, and even tried to entrap him into an exposure of his political sentiments, but had always found him too wary. He allowed Locke time to come and defend himself, which he would not do, and then expelled him from his studentship.

On the accession of James II., William Penn, the Quaker of Pennsylvania, being in some favour with the king, would have procured a pardon for Locke, but he refused the offer, through a friend, as having been guilty of no crime. In May, 1685, the English ambassador demanded him of the States-General, on the pretext that he had been concerned in the unsuccessful expedition of the Duke of Monmouth. It is supposed that he owed this bad turn partly to the malice of the envoy himself, as his name did not appear in the list of those required which was sent from England. He never liked the person nor the invasion of the duke, and was at Utrecht when the army of that unfortunate nobleman sailed from the Texel. Locke was not given up, but he was obliged to hide himself for about a year in the house of his friend M. Veen, at Amsterdam, receiving assurance from the local authorities that timely warning should be given him of pressing danger. He was obliged to conceal himself so closely as only to be able to take exercise during the night. It is probable that the real cause of this persecution was his first Letter on Toleration, written in Latin about this time, and addressed to his friend Limborch, the sentiments of which were peculiarly offensive to the English court.

Locke had now time to attend to his own affairs, being no longer taken up with those of a patron. He busied himself in the completion of his Essay concerning the Human Understanding, which was not, however, printed till 1689. The extracting of passages from various works for reviewal in Le Clerc's literary journal, the Bibliothèque Univer-

selle, the formation and continuation of a small society for the weekly discussion of all subjects, the
members of which were his friends Le Clerc, Limborch, Guenelon, and others, and the abridgment
of his Essay, served to fill up his time during the
remainder of his stay in Holland. In 1689 he
published a second letter on Toleration, and early
in the same year returned to his native country, in
the fleet which conducted the Princess of Orange
to the throne of England. The revolution had
completely changed the face of affairs in Locke's
favour : he was considered a martyr to its principles, and was esteemed accordingly by its authors.
On his return he immediately petitioned William
to cause him to be reinstated in his studentship :
but the college refused to restore him, offering, at
the same time, to make him a supernumerary student. This he would not accept, for the reason
that he felt it not to be a full reparation for the injustice he had suffered, and he allowed the matter
to drop.

If Locke had been ambitious, his path to political advancement was now open. William offered
him the ambassadorship to the Imperial court or
to that of Brandenburg. He refused both these
high appointments ; but accepted a commissionership of appeals from his friend Lord Mordaunt,
afterward Earl of Peterborough. This office was
worth only £200 a year. His friends, Sir Francis
and Lady Masham (a daughter of the celebrated
Cudworth), prevailed on him to take apartments in
their house at Oates in Essex, between which place
and his office in London he spent the remainder of
his life. In 1690 Locke published his Treatise on

Civil Government. The folio edition of his Essay, and a Letter on Education, appeared in the latter part of the same year. In 1692 he produced a third Letter on Toleration. The state of the coinage being a subject of great importance at that time, he took it into consideration, and published " Certain Thoughts on the State of English Silver Money, &c.," in a letter to a Member of Parliament. This treatise was thought so good, that, when the matter was inquired into by the government, Locke was consulted, and his advice taken with respect to the new coinage. In consequence of this important assistance, he received from William III. a Commissionership of Foreign Trade and Plantations, the value of which was £1000 a year. The king was exceedingly desirous of a reconciliation with the dissenters, and to forward his views Locke wrote his " Reasonableness of Christianity. This book involved him in a religious controversy with Dr. Edwards, who attacked his opinions in his " Socinian Unmasked," to which Locke replied by two vindications, each of them longer than the original work. No sooner had he finished this labour than he was called upon to encounter a fresh and more able antagonist. Toland and some other Unitarians having turned to their own use some of the arguments in Locke's Essay, Dr. Stillingfleet, the learned Bishop of Worcester, confounded Locke with that party. In his defence of the doctrine of the Trinity, the bishop severely censured various passages of Locke's great work, as tending to subvert some of the fundamental doctrines of Christianity : Locke replied, and there was an exchange of answers between them till the bishop's death.

That event took place soon after Locke's third answer, which was the last thing he ever published.
These replies of Locke are reputed to be most finished specimens of a grave and subtle irony, too
refined, perhaps, to be generally perceived by the
uninitiated eye.

In 1700 Locke's weak state of health induced
him to retire from public life. He resigned his situation in a personal interview with the king, giving
no previous notice of his intention to the conductors
of the government, and refusing the pension which
his sovereign wished him to accept. He took up
his residence at Oates, where he passed the remainder of his life in reading and contemplating
the Scriptures. He often regretted that he had
not occupied himself more with this study. The
piety of his latter years was without formality or
ostentation, not arising from that sense of disappointment or those feelings of irksomeness for want
of employment which sometimes lead men to seek
refuge in a late devotion. Neither his mental nor
bodily senses failed him to the last moment, though
the year previous to his death was passed in extreme weakness. On taking the sacrament he declared "that he was in peace with all men, and in
sincere union with the Church of Christ, by whatever name distinguished." The affectionate atten-
tions of Lady Masham softened the pains of his last
illness, and he died gently in his chair while she was
reading to him one of the Psalms of David, on the
28th of October, 1704, and in his seventy-third
year. He died from the natural decay of an originally weak constitution, and was buried in the
churchyard at High Laver, near Oates, under a de-

cent monument. He left behind him many unpublished works, among which his "Conduct of the
Understanding" stands highest. "An Examination of Malebranche's opinion of seeing all things
in God;" "A Discourse of Miracles;" part of a
fourth letter on the subject of Toleration; some
imperfect memoirs of the life of the Earl of Shaftesbury; a new method for a commonplace-book;
and paraphrases of several of the epistles of St.
Paul, make up the list of his posthumous works, almost all of which were translated into French by
Le Clerc and others, and appeared (together with
those published by himself) in three folio volumes
not many years after his death. A great many of
his letters to his friends Molyneux and Limborch
are also published in this edition. There remain
many more, which have been given to the world by
various hands, addressed to the Earl of Peterborough, Dr. Mapletoft, &c., and to Newton. In
Lord King's life of Locke, his correspondence with
the latter is given at full length, and is very curious, chiefly relating to subjects they were both engaged in, the prophecies and miracles.

That which has assured to Locke imperishable
fame is the "Essay concerning the Human Understanding." This great work, however, met with
considerable opposition; the heads of colleges at
Oxford even endeavoured to prevent its being read
in their University. Whatever differences of opinion there may be in relation to its views, it will be
generally admitted, that in it Locke laid the foundation of modern metaphysical philosophy.

Two of Locke's principal works, the "Treatise
on Civil Government," and "Essay on Education,"

are more capable of a short analysis. The former may be taken as an expression of his own opinions in defence of the Revolution. It is divided into two parts. The first contains an exposure of the fallacies of Sir Robert Filmer's "Patriarcha," arguing that Adam had not such natural or gifted right of dominion as Filmer pretends; that if he had, his heirs had not; that if they had, yet there is no general law, divine or human, which determines the right of succession, much less of bearing rule; lastly, that if such right had been determined, yet the eldest line from Adam being unknown, no man can pretend more than another to that right of inheritance; consequently, that some other source of political power must be found than "Adam's private dominion and paternal jurisdiction." Locke proceeds in the second part to declare his opinion as to what this other source may be. He argues, that originally the executive power was in the hands of each individual; but, by mutual consent, for mutual benefit, as men grew into societies, political power was created, and given to persons chosen from the whole body by the major part of such societies. He protests against absolute power, as not expressing the will of the majority; but defends prerogative, as a discretionary power lodged in the hands of the executive government. He maintains that this compact must be held sacred; but that it reverts to the society upon the misconduct of rulers or delegates, or where its duration has been previously declared temporary. When so forfeited, the will of the society may create new forms of government, or, under the old form, continue it in other hands.

In his Essay on Education, he says that the child should have much air and exercise, and should be accustomed to little sleep and early habits. That superstitious terrors and the frequent use of the rod should be carefully avoided; that the boy should be used to suffer pain gradually, to harden him, but not as a punishment; that the parents' authority should be perfect over the child, and be gradually taken off, till the relation between them becomes at length a confiding friendship; and that particular attention should be paid to his manners, so that his courage, learning, wit, plainness, and good-nature do not turn to brutality, pedantry, buffoonery, rusticity, and fawning. He says, that the children's curiosity should be encouraged; that they should learn by pleasant means, and that their attainments should never be forced; that they should not be left to flounder in difficulties, but helped through them. Locke prefers a careful tutor to a public school; he says that a boy stands a better chance of being both virtuous and well-bred under the instruction of the former. What he would have him know is Latin, Greek, and a little mathematics, and how to keep accounts; the less of logic, he thinks, the better; he should write a good hand; and a virtuous youth, he declares, so bred, "one may turn loose into the world with great assurance that he will find employment and esteem everywhere." He farther recommends that the boy should travel between the ages of eight and sixteen rather than between sixteen and twenty-one; and that, when he comes of age, he had better not marry according to the usual custom, but wait some years, that his children "may not tread too closely on his heels."

The habit of Locke's mind was, perhaps, originally severe; but, from constant social intercourse
with men of all characters and opinions, was rendered mild and equable.   Nothing seems to have
provoked him into a loss of temper so much as
being forced into argument with professed logicians.
He calls the logical method taught at Oxford an
ill, if not the worst, way of acquiring knowledge
and seeking truth.   He was intrusted by his patron
with the education and marriage of his son, who
was the father of the author of the "Characteristics."   The latter nobleman (the third Earl of
Shaftesbury) owed much to Locke's care, and was
his eulogist.

Locke was of a cautious if not timid disposition.
This appears from many of his letters, and may be
inferred from the anonymous publication of most
of his writings.   His weak health, the political
persecution to which he was exposed during a
great part of his life, and the discipline to which he
was subjected in childhood, which was strict and severe, account in some measure for this failing.   His
friendships were steady, as is evinced by his close
adherence to his patron Shaftesbury.   Sydenham's
contemporary and friendly character of Locke is
remarkable : he says, in a prefatory letter to one
of his works, that " if we consider his genius, his
penetrating and exact judgment, and the strictness
of his morals, he has scarcely any superior, and
few equals now living."

FENELON.

FRANCOIS DE SALIGNAC DE LAMOTHE-FENELON was born August 6, 1651, at the castle of Fenelon, of a noble and ancient family in the province of Perigord.

Early proofs of talent and genius induced his uncle, the Marquis de Fenelon, a man of no ordinary merit, to take him under his immediate care and superintendence. By him he was placed at the seminary of St. Sulpice, then lately founded in Paris for the purpose of educating young men for the church.

The studies of the young abbé were not encouraged by visions of a stall and mitre. It seems that the object of his earliest ambition was, as a missionary, to carry the blessings of the Gospel to the savages of North America, or to the Mohammedans and heretics of Greece and Anatolia. The fears, however, or the hopes of his friends, detained him at home ; and, after his ordination, he confined himself for several years to the duties of the ministry in the parish of St. Sulpice.

At the age of twenty-seven he was appointed superior of a society which had for its object the instruction and encouragement of female converts to the Church of Rome ; and from this time he took up his abode with his uncle. In this house he first became known to Bossuet, by whose recommendation he was intrusted with the conduct of a mission, charged with the duty of reclaiming the

Protestants in the province of Poitou, in the memorable year 1685, when the Huguenots were wri-
thing under the infliction of the severe measures employed by the government to give full effect to the
revocation of the Edict of Nantes. Fenelon had
no mind to have soldiers for his coadjutors, and requested that all show of martial terror might be
removed from the places which he visited. His
future proceedings were in strict conformity with
this gentle commencement, and consequently exposed him to the harassing remonstrances of his
superiors.

His services in Poitou were not acknowledged
by any reward from the government, for Louis
XIV. had begun to look coldly upon him; but it
was not his fortune to remain long in obscurity.
Among the visiters at his uncle's house, whose
friendship he had the happiness to gain, was the
Duke de Beauvilliers, a man who could live at the
court of Louis without ceasing to live as a Christian.
This nobleman was appointed, in the year 1689,
governor of the Duke of Burgundy, the grandson
of Louis, and heir, after his father the dauphin, to
the throne of France. His first act was to ap-
point Fenelon preceptor to his royal charge, then
in his eighth year, and already distinguished for the
frightful violence of his passions, his insolent demeanour, and tyrannical spirit. The child had,
however, an affectionate heart and a quick sense
of shame. Fenelon gained his love and confidence, and used his power to impress upon him the
Christian's method of self-government. His headstrong pupil was subdued, not by the fear of man,
but by the fear of God. In the task of instruction

less difficulty awaited him, for the young prince was remarkably intelligent and industrious. The progress of a royal student is likely to be rated at his full amount by common fame ; but there is reason to believe that in this case it was rapid and substantial.

In 1694 he was presented to the Abbey of St. Valery, and two years afterward promoted to the Archbishopric of Cambray, with a command that he should retain the office of preceptor, giving personal attendance only during the three months of absence from his diocese which the Canons allowed. In resigning his abbey, which, from conscientious motives, he refused to keep with his archbishopric, he was careful to assign such reasons as might not convey an indirect censure of the numerous pluralists among his clerical brethren. Probably this excess of delicacy, which it is easy to admire and difficult to justify, was hardly requisite in the case of many of the offenders. One of them, the Archbishop of Rheims, when informed of the conscientious conduct of Fenelon, made the following reply : " M. de Cambray, with his sentiments, does right in resigning his benefice, and I, with my sentiments, do very right in keeping mine." This mode of defence is capable of very general application, and is, in fact, very generally used, being employed for other cases besides that of pluralities.

This preferment was the last mark of royal favour which he received. Louis was never cordially his friend, and there were many at court eager to convert him into an enemy. An opportunity was afforded by Fenelon's connexion with Madame Guyon.

It is well known that this lady was the great apostle of the Quietists, a sect of religionists, so called, because they studied to attain a state of perfect contemplation, in which the soul is the passive recipient of divine light. She was especially noted for her doctrine of pure love ; she taught that Christian perfection consisted in a disinterested love of God, excluding the hope of happiness and fear of misery, and that this perfection was attainable by man. Fenelon first became acquainted with her at the house of his friend the Duke de Beauvilliers, and, convinced of the sincerity of her religious views, was disposed to regard her more favourably from a notion that her religious opinions, against which a loud clamour had been raised, coincided very nearly with his own. It has been the fashion to represent him as her convert and disciple. The truth is, that he was deeply versed in the writings of the later Mystics ; men who, with all their extravagance, were perhaps the best representatives of the Christian character to be found among the Roman Catholics of their time. He considered the doctrine of Madame Guyon to be substantially the same with that of his favourite authors ; and, whatever appeared exceptionable in her expositions, he attributed to loose and exaggerated expressions natural to her character.

The approbation of Fenelon gave currency to the fair Quietist among orthodox members of the church. At last the bishops began to take alarm ; the clamour was renewed, and the examination of her doctrines solemnly intrusted to Bossuet and two other learned divines. Fenelon was avowedly her friend; yet no one hitherto had breathed a suspicion of any flaw in his orthodoxy. It was even during the examination, and towards the close of it, that he was promoted to the Archbishopric of Cambray. The blow came, at length, from the hand of his most valued friend. He had been altogether passive in the proceedings respecting Madame Guyon. Bossuet, who had been provoked into vehement wrath, and had resolved to crush her, was sufficiently irritated by this temperate neutrality. But when Fenelon found himself obliged to publish his "Maxims of the Saints," in which, without attacking others, he defends his own views of some of the controverted points, Bossuet, in a tumult of zeal, threw himself at the feet of Louis, denounced his friend as a dangerous fanatic, and besought the king to interpose his royal arm between the church and pollution. Fenelon offered to submit his book to the judgment of the pope. Permission was granted in very ungracious terms, and it was presently followed by a sentence of banishment to his diocese. This sudden reverse of fortune, which he received without whispering even a complaint, served to show the forbearance and meekness of his spirit, but it deprived him of none of his powers. An animated controversy arose between him and Bossuet, and all Europe beheld with admiration the boldness and success with which he maintained his ground against the renowned and veteran disputant; and that, too, in the face of fearful discouragement. The whole power of the court was arrayed against him, and he stood alone; for his powerful friends had left his side. The Cardinal de Noailles and others,

VOL. II.—E

who had in private expressed unqualified approbation of his book, meanly withheld a public acknowledgment of their opinions. While his enemy enjoyed every facility, and had Louis and his
courtiers and courtly bishops to cheer him on, it
was with difficulty that Fenelon could find a printer who would venture to put to press a work which
bore his name. Under these disadvantages, harassed in mind, and with infirm health, he replied to
the deliberate attacks of his artful adversary with
a rapidity which, under any circumstances, would
have been astonishing. He was now gaining
ground daily in public opinion. The pope, also,
who knew his merit, was very unwilling to condemn him. His persecutors were excited to additional efforts. He had already been banished from
court ; now he was deprived of his name of preceptor, and of his salary ; of that very salary which
some time before he had eagerly offered to resign,
in consideration of the embarrassed state of the
royal treasury. The flagging zeal of the pope
was stimulated by threats conveyed in letters from
Louis, penned by Bossuet. At length the sentence
of condemnation was obtained, but in too mild a
form to satisfy altogether the courtly party. No
bull was issued. A simple brief pronounced certain propositions to be erroneous and dangerous,
and condemned the book which contained them,
without sentencing it in the usual manner, to the
flames.

It is needless to say that Fenelon submitted.
He published without delay the sentence of condemnation, noting the selected propositions, and
expressing his entire acquiescence in the judgment

pronounced ; and prohibited the faithful in his diocese from reading or having in their possession
his own work, which, up to that moment, he had defended so manfully. Protestants, who are too apt,
in judging the conduct of Roman Catholics, to for-
get everything but their zeal, have raised an outcry
against his meanness and dissimulation. Fenelon
was a sincere member of a church which claimed
infallibility. We may regret the thraldom in which
such a mind was held by an authority from which
the Protestant happily is free ; but the censure
which falls on him personally for this act is certainly misplaced.

The faint hopes which his friends might have
cherished, that, when the storm had passed, he would
be restored to favour, were soon extinguished by
an event which, while it closed against him for ever
the doors of the palace, secured him a place in history, and without which it is probable that he would
never have become the subject even of a short
memoir.

A manuscript which he had intrusted to a servant to copy was treacherously sold by this man
to a printer in Paris, who immediately put it to the
press, under the title of " Continuation of the Fourth
Book of the Odyssey, or Adventures of Telemachus, son of Ulysses, with the royal privilege,"
dated April 6, 1699. It was told at court that the
forthcoming work was from the pen of the obnoxious archbishop ; and, before the impression of the
first volume was completed, orders were given to
suppress it, to punish the printers, and seize the
copies already printed. A few, however, escaped
the hands of the police, and were rapidly circula-

ted. One of them, together with a copy of the remaining part of the manuscript, soon after came into the possession of a printer at the Hague, who could publish it without danger.

So eager was the curiosity which the violent proceedings of the French court had excited, that the press could hardly be made, with the utmost exertion, to keep pace with the demand. Such is the history of the first appearance of Telemachus.

Louis was persuaded to think that the whole book was intended to be a satire on him, his court, and government; and the world was persuaded for a time to think the same. So, while the wrath of the king was roused to the uttermost, all Europe was sounding forth the praises of Fenelon. The numerous enemies of Louis exulted at the supposed exhibition of his tyranny and profligate life. The philosophers were charmed with the liberal and enlightened views of civil government which they seemed to discover. It is now well-known that the anger and the praise were alike undeserved. The book was probably written for the use of the Duke of Burgundy, certainly at a time when Fenelon enjoyed the favour of his sovereign, and was desirous to retain it. He may have forgotten that it was impossible to describe a good and a bad king, a virtuous and a profligate court, without saying much that would bear hard upon Louis and his friends. As for his political enlightenment, it is certain that he had his full share of the monarchical principles of his time and nation. He wished to have good kings, but he made no provision for bad ones. It is difficult to believe that Louis was seriously alarmed at his notions of political economy. That science was not in a very advanced state ; but no one could fear that a prince could be induced by the lessons of his tutor to collect all the artificers of luxury in his capital, and drive them in a body into the fields to cultivate potatoes and cabbages, with a belief that he would thus make the country a garden, and the town a seat of the Muses.

Nothing was now left to Fenelon but to devote himself to his episcopal duties, which he seems to have discharged with equal zeal and ability. The course of his domestic life, as described by an eye-witness, was retired, and, to a remarkable degree, uniform. Strangers were courteously and hospitably received ; but his society was confined, for the most part, to the ecclesiastics who resided in his house. Among them were some of his own relations, to whom he was tenderly attached, but for whose preferment, it should be noticed, he never manifested an unbecoming eagerness. His only recreation was a solitary walk in the fields, where it was his employment, as he observes to a friend, to converse with his God. If in his rambles he fell in with any of the poorer part of his flock, he would sit with them on the grass and discourse about their temporal as well as their spiritual concerns ; and sometimes he would visit them in their humble sheds, and partake of such refreshment as they offered him.

In the beginning of the 18th century we find him engaged at once in controversy and politics. The revival of the old dispute with the Jansenists, to whom he was strongly opposed, obliged him to take up his pen ; but, in using it, he never forgot

E 2

his own maxim, that "rigour and severity are not of the spirit of the Gospel." For a knowledge of his political labours we are indebted to his biographer, the Cardinal de Bausset, who first published his letters to the Duke de Beauvilliers on the subject of the war which followed the grand alliance in the year 1701. In them he not only considers the general questions of the succession to the Spanish monarchy, the objects of the confederated powers, and the measures best calculated to avert or soften their hostility, but even enters into details of military operations, discusses the merits of the various generals, stations the different armies, and sketches a plan of the campaign. Towards the close of the war he communicated to the Duke de Chevreuse heads of a very extensive reform in all the departments of government. The reform did not suppose any fundamental change of the old despotism. It was intended, doubtless, for the consideration of the Duke of Burgundy, to whose succession all France was looking forward with sanguine hopes, founded on the acknowledged excellence of his character, which Fenelon himself had so happily contributed to form. But among the other trials which visited his latter days, he was destined to mourn the death of his pupil.

Fenelon did not long survive the general pacification. After a short illness and intense bodily suffering, which he seems to have supported by calling to mind the sufferings of the Saviour, he died February 7th, 1715, in the sixty-fourth year of his age. No money was found in his coffers. The produce of the sale of his furniture, together with the arrears of rent due to him, were appropriated, by his direction, to pious and charitable purposes.

The calumnies with which he was assailed during the affair of Quietism were remembered only to the disadvantage of their authors. The public seem eventually to have regarded him as a man who was persecuted because he refused to be a persecutor; who had maintained, at all hazards, what he believed to be the cause of truth and justice; and had resigned his opinion only at the moment when conscience required the sacrifice.

Universal homage was paid by his contemporaries to his talents and genius. In the grasp and power of his intellect, and in the extent and completeness of his knowledge, none probably would have ventured to compare him with Bossuet; but in fertility and brilliancy of imagination, in a ready and dexterous use of his materials, and in that quality which his countrymen call esprit, he was supposed to have no superior. Bossuet himself said of him, " Il brille d'esprit, il est tout esprit, il en a bien plus que moi"—(He shines with genius, he is all genius, he has far more of it than I).

It is obvious that his great work, the Adventures of Telemachus, was, in the first instance, indebted for some portion of its popularity to circumstances which had no connexion with its merits; but we cannot attribute to the same cause the continued hold which it has maintained on the public favour. Those who are ignorant of the interest which attended its first appearance, still feel the charm of that beautiful language which is made the vehicle of the purest morality and the most ennobling sentiments. In the many editions through which it

passed between its first publication and the death
of the author, Fenelon took no concern. Publicly
he neither avowed nor disavowed the work, though
he prepared corrections and additions for future
editors. All obstacles to its open circulation were
removed by the death of Louis ; and in the year
1717, the Marquis de Fenelon, his great-nephew,
presented to Louis XV. a new and correct edition,
superintended by himself, from which the text of
all subsequent editions has been taken.

The best authority for the life of Fenelon accessible to the public is the laborious work of his biographer, the Cardinal de Bausset, which is rendered particularly valuable by the great number of
original documents which appear at the end of each
volume. Its value would be increased if much of
the theological discussion were omitted, and the
four volumes compressed into three.

PENN.

WILLIAM PENN was born in London, October
14, 1644. He was the son of a naval officer of
the same name, who served with distinction both
during the Protectorate and after the Restoration,
and who was much esteemed by Charles II. and
the Duke of York. At the age of fifteen he was entered as a gentleman-commoner at Christ Church,
Oxford. He had not been long there when he received from the preaching of Thomas Loe his first
bias towards the doctrines of the Quakers ; and,

in conjunction with some fellow-students, he began to withdraw from attendance on the Established Church, and to hold private prayer-meetings. For this conduct Penn and his friends were fined by the college as nonconformists. He was soon after involved in still more serious censure by his ill-governed zeal, in relation to an order from the king, that the ancient custom of wearing surplices should be revived. This seemed to Penn an infringement of the simplicity of Christian worship: whereupon he, with some friends, tore the surplices from the backs of those students who appeared in them. For this act of violence, totally inconsistent, it is to be observed, with the principles of toleration which regulated his conduct in after life, he and they were very justly expelled.

Admiral Penn, who, like most sailors, possessed a quick temper, and high notions of discipline and obedience, was little pleased with this transaction, and still less satisfied with his son's grave demeanour, and avoidance of the manners and ceremonies of polite life. Arguments failing, he had recourse to blows, and even turned his son out of doors; but he soon relented so far as to equip him, in 1662, for a journey to France, in hopes that the gayety of that country would cure him of his new-fashioned, and, as he regarded them, fanatical notions. Paris, however, soon became wearisome to William Penn, and he spent a considerable time at Saumur, for the sake of the instruction and company of Moses Amyrault, an eminent Protestant divine. Here he confirmed and improved his religious impressions; and, at the same time, insensibly acquired, from the influence of those around him, an increased polish and courtliness of demeanour, which greatly pleased the admiral on his return home in 1664.

Admiral Penn went to sea in 1664, and was absent two years on service. During which time the external effects of his son's residence in France had worn off, and he had returned to those grave habits, and that rule of associating only with religious people, which had before given his father so much displeasure. To try the effect of absence and change of associates, Admiral Penn sent William to manage his estates in Ireland : a duty which he performed with satisfaction both to himself and his father. But it chanced that, on a visit to Cork, he again attended the preaching of Thomas Loe, by whose exhortations he was deeply impressed. From that time he began to frequent the Quakers' meetings ; and in September, 1667, he was imprisoned, with others, under the persecuting laws which then disgraced the English statute-book. Upon application to the higher authorities, he was soon, however, released.

On receiving tidings that he had connected himself with the Quakers, the admiral immediately summoned him to England ; and he was soon made certain of the fact, among other peculiarities, by his son's pertinacious adherence to the Quakers' notions concerning what they called Hat Worship. This led him to a violent remonstrance. William behaved with all due respect ; but in the main point, that of forsaking his associates and rule of conduct, he yielded nothing. The father at last confined his demands to the simple point that his son should sit uncovered in the presence of himself, the king, and the Duke of York. Still William felt bound not to make even this concession; and, on his refusal, the admiral again turned him out of doors.

Soon after, in 1668, he began to preach, and in the same year published his first work, "Truth Exalted," &c. We cannot here notice his very numerous works, of which the titles run, for the most part, to an extraordinary length: but "The Sandy Foundation Shaken," published during the same year, claims notice as having led to his first public persecution. In it he was induced not to deny the doctrine of the Trinity, which in a certain sense he admitted, but to object to the language in which it is expounded by the English Church; and for this offence he was imprisoned for some time in the Tower. During his confinement he composed "No Cross, No Crown," one of his principal and most popular works, of which the leading doctrine, admirably exemplified in his own life, was, that the way to future happiness and glory lies not through a course of misery and needless mortification in this world, but rather through labour, watchfulness, and self-denial, and a continual striving against corrupt passions and inordinate indulgences. This is enforced by copious examples from profane as well as sacred history; and the work gives evidence of an extent of learning very creditable to its author, considering his youth, and the circumstances under which it was composed. He was detained in prison for seven months, and treated with much severity. In 1669 he had the satisfaction of being reconciled to his father.

William Penn was one of the first sufferers by the passing of the Conventicle Act in 1670. He

was imprisoned in Newgate, and tried for preaching to a seditious and riotous assembly in Grace-
church-street ; and this trial is remarkable and
celebrated in criminal jurisprudence for the firmness with which he defended himself, and still more
for the admirable courage and constancy with which
the jury maintained the verdict of acquittal which
they had pronounced.   He showed on this, and on
all other occasions, that he well understood and
appreciated the free principles of the English Constitution, and that he was resolved not to surrender
one iota of that liberty of conscience which he
claimed no less for others than for himself.   "I
am far from thinking it fit," he said, in addressing
the House of Commons, "because I exclaim against
the injustice of whipping Quakers for papists, that
papists should be whipped for their consciences.
No : for though the hand pretended to be lifted up
against them hath lighted heavily upon us, and we
complain, yet we do not mean that any should take
a fresh aim at them, or that they should come in
our room ; for we must give the liberty we ask,
and would have none suffer for a truly sober and
conscientious dissent on any hand."   His views
of religious toleration and civil liberty he has well
and clearly explained in the treatise entitled "England's Present Interest," &c., published in 1674,
in which it formed part of his argument, that the
liberties of Englishmen were anterior to the settlement of the English Church, and could not be affected by discrepances in their religious belief.
He maintained, that "to live honestly, to do no injury to another, and to give every man his due,
was enough to entitle every native to English priv-

lleges. It was this, and not his religion, which gave him the great claim to the protection of the government under which he lived. Near three hundred years before Austin set his foot on English ground, the inhabitants had a good constitution. This came not in with him; neither did it come in with Luther; nor was it to go out with Calvin. We were a free people by the creation of God, by the redemption of Christ, and by the careful provision of our never-to-be-forgotten, honourable ancestors: so that our claim to these English privileges, rising higher than Protestantism, could never be justly invalidated on account of nonconformity to any tenet or fashion it might prescribe."

In the same year died Sir William Penn, in perfect harmony with his son, towards whom he now felt the most cordial regard and esteem, and to whom he bequeathed an estate computed at £1500 a year: a large sum in that age. Towards the end of the year he was again imprisoned in Newgate for six months: the statutable penalty for refusing to take the oath of allegiance, which had been maliciously tendered to him by a magistrate. This appears to have been the last absolute persecution for religion's sake which he endured. Religion in England has generally met with greater toleration in proportion as it has been backed by the worldly importance of its professors; and though his poor brethren continued to suffer imprisonment in the stocks, fines, and whipping, as the penalty of their peaceable meetings for divine worship, the wealthy proprietor, notwithstanding that he travelled largely, both in England and abroad, and laboured both in writing and in preaching as the missionary of his sect, both escaped injury, and acquired reputation and esteem by his self-devotion. To the favour of the king and of the Duke of York he had a hereditary claim, which appears always to have been cheerfully acknowledged; and an instance appears in his being admitted to plead, before a Committee of the House of Commons, the request of the Quakers, that their solemn affirmation should be admitted in the place of an oath. An enactment to this effect passed the Commons in 1678, but was lost, in consequence of a prorogation, before it had passed the Lords. It was on this occasion that he made that appeal in behalf of general toleration, of which a passage is quoted in a preceding page.

Penn married in 1672, and took up his abode at Rickmansworth in Hertfordshire. In 1677 we find him removed to Worminghurst in Sussex, which long continued to be his place of residence. His first engagement in the colonization of America was in 1676, in consequence of being chosen arbitrator in a dispute between two Quakers, who had become jointly interested in the colony of New-Jersey. Though nowise concerned, by interest or proprietorship (until 1681, when he purchased a share in the eastern district of New-Jersey), he took great pains in this business; he arranged the terms upon which colonists were invited to settle; and he drew up the outline of a simple constitution, reserving to them the right of making all laws by their representatives, of security from imprisonment or fine, except by the concurrence of twelve men of the neighbourhood, and perfect freedom in the exercise of their religion : " regulations," he said, "by an adherence to which they could never be brought into bondage but by their own consent." In these transactions he had the opportunity of contemplating the glorious results which might be hoped from a colony founded with no interested views, but on the principles of universal peace, toleration, and liberty; and he felt an earnest desire to be the instrument in so great a work, more especially as it held out a prospect of deliverance to the prosecuted Quaker brethren in England, by giving them a free and happy asylum in a foreign land. Circumstances favoured his wish. The crown was indebted to him £16,000 for money advanced by the late admiral for the naval service. It was not unusual to grant, not only the property, but the right of government, in large districts in the unsettled parts of America, as in the cases of New-York and New-Jersey, which had thus been granted to the Duke of York and Lord Baltimore respectively; and though it was hopeless to extract money from Charles, yet he was ready enough, in acquittal of this debt, to bestow on Penn, whom he loved, a tract of land from which he himself could never expect any pecuniary return. Accordingly, in 1681, Penn received a grant by charter of that extensive province, named Pennsylvania by Charles himself, in honour of the admiral: by which charter he was invested with the property in the soil, and with the power of ruling and governing the same; of enacting laws, with the advice and approbation of the freemen of the territory assembled for the raising of money for public uses; of appointing judges, and of administering justice. He immediately drew up and published "Some Account of

Pennsylvania," &c. ; and then "Certain Conditions or Concessions," &c., to be agreed on between himself and those who might wish to purchase land in the province. These having been accepted by many persons, he proceeded to frame the rough sketch of a constitution, on which he proposed to base the charter of his newly-acquired domain. The price fixed for land was forty shillings, with the annual quit-rent of one shilling, for one hundred acres ; and it was provided that no one should, in word or deed, affront or wrong the Indian, without incurring the same penalty as if the offence had been committed against a fellow-planter ; that strict precautions should be taken against fraud in the quality of goods to sold them ; and that all differences between the two people should be adjudged by twelve men, six of each. And he declares his intention to be, "to leave myself and my successors no power of doing mischief; that the will of one man may not hinder the good of a whole country."

The government under this constitution, as originally organized by Penn, consisted, says Mr. Clarkson, " of a governor, a council, and an assembly ; the last two of which were to be chosen by, and therefore to be the representatives of, the people. The governor was to be perpetual president, but he was to have but a treble vote. It was the office of the council to prepare and propose bills, to see that the laws were executed, to take care of the peace and safety of the province, to settle the situation of ports, cities, market-towns, roads, and other public places, to inspect the public treasury, to erect courts of justice, to institute schools for the virtuous education of youth, and to reward the authors of useful discovery. Not less than two thirds of these were necessary to make a quorum, and the consent of not less than two thirds of such quorum in all matters of moment. The assembly were to have no deliberative power; but when bills were brought to them from the governor and council, were to pass or reject them by a plain yes or no. They were to present sheriffs and justices of the peace to the governor; a double number, for his choice of half. They were to be chosen annually, and to be chosen by secret ballot." This groundwork was modified by Penn himself at later periods, and especially by removing that restriction which forbade the assembly to debate or to originate bills; and it was this, substantially, which Burke, in his "Account of the European Settlements in America," describes as "that noble charter of privileges, by which he made them as free as any people in the world, and which has since drawn such vast numbers of so many different persuasions and such various countries to put themselves under the protection of his laws. He made the most perfect freedom, both religious and civil, the basis of his establishment; and this has done more towards the settling of the province, and towards the settling of it in a strong and permanent manner, than the wisest regulations could have done on any other plan.

In 1682 a number of settlers, principally Quakers, having been already sent out, Penn himself embarked for Pennsylvania, leaving his wife and children in England. On occasion of this parting, he addressed to them a long and affectionate letter, which presents a very beautiful picture of his domestic character, and affords a curious insight into the minute regularity of his daily habits. He landed on the banks of the Delaware in October, and forthwith summoned an assembly of the freemen of the province, by whom the frame of government, as it had been promulgated in England, was accepted. Penn's principles did not suffer him to consider his title to the land as valid without the consent of the natural owners of the soil. He had instructed persons to negotiate a treaty of sale with the Indian nations before his own departure from England ; and one of his first acts was to hold that memorable assembly, to which the history of the world offers no parallel, at which the bargain was ratified, and a strict league of amity established. We do not find specified the exact date of this meeting, which took place under a gigantic elm-tree, near the site of Philadelphia, and of which a few particulars only have been preserved by the uncertain record of tradition. Well and faithfully was that treaty of friendship kept by the wild denizens of the woods : "a friendship," says Proud, the historian of Pennsylvania, "which for the space of more than seventy years was never interrupted, or so long as the Quakers retained power in the government."

Penn remained in America until the middle of 1684. During this time much was done towards bringing the colony into prosperity and order. Twenty townships were established, containing upward of 7000 Europeans ; magistrates were appointed ; representatives, as prescribed by the constitution, were chosen, and the necessary public business transacted. In 1683 Penn undertook a journey of discovery into the interior; and he has given an interesting account of the country in its wild state, in a letter written home to the Society of Free Traders to Pennsylvania. He held frequent conferences with the Indians, and contracted treaties of friendship with nineteen distinct tribes. His reasons for returning to England appear to have been twofold; partly the desire to settle a dispute between himself and Lord Baltimore concerning the boundary of their provinces, but chiefly the hope of being able, by his personal influence, to lighten the sufferings and ameliorate the treatment of the Quakers in England. He reached England in October, 1684. Charles II. died in February, 1685. But this was rather favourable to Penn's credit at court; for, besides that James appears to have felt a sincere regard for him, he desired for his own church that toleration which Penn wished to see extended to all alike. This credit at court led to the renewal of an old and assuredly most groundless report, that Penn was at heart a papist—nay, that he was in priest's orders, and a Jesuit: a report which gave him much uneasiness, and which he took much pains, in public and in private, to contradict. The same credit, and his natural and laudable affection and gratitude towards the Stuart family, which he never dissembled, caused much trouble to him after the Revolution. He was continually suspected of plotting to restore the exiled dynasty; was four times arrested, and as often discharged, in the total absence of all evidence against him. During the years 1691, 1692, and part of 1693, he remained in London, living, to avoid offence, in great seclusion: in the latter year he was heard in his own defence before the king and council, and informed that he need apprehend no molestation or injury.

The affairs of Pennsylvania fell into some confusion during Penn's long absence. Even in the peaceable sect of Quakers there were ambitious, bustling, and selfish men; and Penn was not satisfied with the conduct either of the representative Assembly, or of those to whom he had delegated his own powers. He changed the latter two or three times, without effecting the restoration of harmony; and these troubles gave a pretext for depriving him of his powers as governor in 1693. The real cause was probably the suspicion entertained of his treasonable correspondence with James II. But he was reinstated in August, 1694, by a royal order, in which it was complimentarily expressed, that the disorders complained of were produced entirely by his absence. Anxious as he was to return, he did not find an opportunity till 1699: the interval was chiefly employed in religious travel through England and Ireland, and in the labour of controversial writing, from which he seldom had a long respite. His course as a philanthropist, on his return to America, is honourably marked by an endeavour to ameliorate the condition of negro slaves. The society of Quakers in Pennsylvania had already come to a resolution, that the buying, selling, and holding of men in slavery was inconsistent with the tenets of the Christian religion; and, following up this honourable declaration, Penn had no difficulty in obtaining for them free admission into the regular meetings for religious worship, and in procuring that other meetings should be held for their particular benefit. The Quakers therefore merit our respect as the earliest, as well as some of the most zealous emancipators. Mr. Clarkson says, " When Penn procured the insertion of this resolution in the monthly meeting book of Philadelphia, he sealed as assuredly and effectually the abolition of the slave trade, and the emancipation of the negroes within his own province, as, when he procured the insertion of the minute relating to the Indians in the same book, he sealed the civilization of the latter ; for, from the time the subject became incorporated into the discipline of the Quakers, they never lost sight of it. Several of them began to refuse to purchase negroes at all ; and others to emancipate those which they had in their possession, and this of their own accord, and purely from the motives of religion ; till at length it became a law of the society that no member could be concerned, directly or indirectly, either in buying or selling, or in holding them in bondage ; and this law was carried so completely into effect, that in the year 1780, dispersed as the society was over a vast tract of country, there was not a single negro as a slave in the possession of an acknowledged Quaker. This example, soon after it had begun, was followed by others of other religious denominations."

In labouring to secure kind treatment, to raise the character, and to promote the welfare of the Indians, Penn was as active and constant during this visit to America as before. The legislative measures which took place while he remained, and the bickerings between the Assembly and himself, we pass over, as belonging rather to a history of Penn-

sylvania than to the biography of its founder.   For
the same reason, we omit the charges preferred
against him by Dr. Franklin.   The union in one
person of the rights belonging both to a governor and
a proprietor, no doubt is open to objection : but this
cannot be urged as a fault upon Penn ; and we believe
that it would be difficult to name any person who
has used more disinterested views.   That he was
indifferent to his powers or his emoluments is not
to be supposed, and ought not to have been expected.   He spent large sums, he bestowed much pains
upon the colony ; and he felt and stated it to be a
great grievance, that, whereas a provision was voted to the royal governor during the period of his
suspension, not so much as a table was kept for
himself ; and that, instead of contributing towards
his expenses, even the trivial quit-rents which he
had reserved remained unpaid : nay, it was sought
by the Assembly, against all justice, to divert them
from him towards the support of the government.
It is to be recollected that Franklin wrote for a
political object, to overthrow the privileges which
Penn's heirs enjoyed.

The governor returned to England in 1701, to
oppose a scheme agitated in Parliament for abolishing the proprietary governments, and placing the
colonies immediately under royal control : the bill,
however, was dropped before he arrived.   He enjoyed Queen Anne's favour, as he had that of her
father and uncle ; and resided much in the neighbourhood of the court, at Kensington and Knights-
bridge.   In his religious labours he continued constant, as heretofore.   He was much harassed by a
lawsuit, the result of too much confidence in a dis-

honest steward : which having been decided against him, he was obliged for a time to reside within the Rules of the Fleet Prison. This, and the expenses in which he had been involved by Pennsylvania, reduced him to distress, and in 1709 he mortgaged the province for £6600. In 1712 he agreed to sell his rights to the government for £12,000, but was rendered unable to complete the transaction by three apoplectic fits, which followed each other in quick succession. He survived, however, in a tranquil and happy state, though with his bodily and mental vigour much broken, until July 30, 1718, on which day he died, at his seat at Rushcomb, in Berkshire, where he had resided for some years.

His first wife died in 1693. He married a second time in 1696, and left a family of children by both, to whom he bequeathed his landed property in Europe and America. His rights of government he left in trust to the Earls of Oxford and Powlett, to be disposed of; but no sale having been made, the government, with the title of proprietaries, devolved on the surviving sons of the second family.

Penn's numerous works were collected, and a life prefixed to them, in 1726. Select editions of them have been since published. Mr. Clarkson's " Life," Proud's " History of Pennsylvania," and Franklin's " Historical Review, &c., of Pennsylvania," for a view of the exceptions which have been taken to Penn's character as a statesman, may be advantageously consulted.

NEWTON.

Isaac Newton was born on Christmas-day, 1642, Old Style, at Woolsthorpe, a hamlet in the parish of Colsterworth, in Lincolnshire. In that spot his family had possessed a small estate for more than a hundred years; and his father died there a few months after his marriage to Harriet Ayscough, and before the birth of his son. The widow soon married again, and removed to North Witham, the rectory of her second husband, Mr. Smith, leaving her son, a weakly child, who had not been expected to live through the earliest infancy, under the charge of her mother.

Newton's education was commenced at the parish school, and at the age of twelve he was sent to Grantham for classical instruction. At first he was idle, but soon rose to the head of the school. The peculiar bent of his mind soon showed itself in his recreations. He was fond of drawing, and sometimes wrote verses; but he chiefly amused himself with mechanical contrivances. Among these was a model of a windmill turned either by the wind or by a mouse enclosed in it, which he called the miller; a mechanical carriage, to be kept in motion by the person who sat in it; and a water-clock, which was long used in the family of Mr. Clarke, an apothecary, with whom he boarded at Grantham. This was not his only method of measuring time; the house at Woolsthorpe, whither he returned at the age of fifteen, still contains dials made by him during his residence there.

Mr. Smith died in 1656, and his widow then returned to Woolsthorpe with her three children by her second marriage. She brought Newton himself there also, in the hope that he might be useful in the management of the farm. This expectation was fortunately disappointed. When sent to Grantham on business, he used to leave its execution to the servant who accompanied him, and passed his time in reading, sometimes by the wayside, sometimes at the house of Mr. Clarke. His mother no longer opposed the evident tendency of his mind. He returned to school at Grantham, and was removed thence, in his eighteenth year, to Trinity College, Cambridge.

The 5th of June, 1660, was the day of his admission as a sizer* into that distinguished society. He applied himself eagerly to the study of mathematics, and mastered its difficulties with an ease and rapidity which he was afterward inclined almost to regret, from an opinion that a closer attention to its elementary parts would have improved the elegance of his own methods of demonstration. In 1664 he became a scholar of his college, and in 1667 was elected to a fellowship, which he retained beyond the regular time of its expiration in 1675, by a special dispensation, authorizing him to hold it without taking orders.

It is necessary to return to an earlier date, to trace the series of Newton's discoveries. This is

* A sizer in this University is next in degree below a pensioner; the name given to such under-graduates as support themselves entirely at their own expense.--*Am. Ed.*

not the occasion for a minute enumeration of them,
nor for any elaborate discussion of their value or
explanation of their principles ; but their history
and succession require some notice.　The earliest
appear to have related to pure mathematics.　The
study of Dr. Wallis's works led him to investigate
certain properties of series, and this course of research soon conducted him to the celebrated Bino-
mial Theorem.　The exact date of his invention
of the method of Fluxions is not known ; but it
was anterior to 1666, when the breaking out of the
plague obliged him for a time to quit Cambridge,
and, consequently, when he was only about twenty-
three years old.

This change of residence interrupted his optical
researches, in which he had already laid the foundation of his great discoveries.　He had decompo-
sed light into the coloured rays of which it is com-
pounded ; and, having thus ascertained the principal cause of the confusion of the images formed
by refraction, he turned his attention to the construction of telescopes which should act by reflec-
tion, and be free from this evil.　He had not, however, overcome the practical difficulties of his undertaking, when his retreat from Cambridge stopped for a time this train of experiment and invention.

On quitting Cambridge Newton retired to Woolsthorpe, where his mind was principally employed
upon the system of the world.　The theory of Co-
pernicus, and the discoveries of Galileo and Kepler, had at length furnished the materials from
which the true system was to be deduced.　It was,
indeed, all involved in Kepler's celebrated laws.

The equable description of areas proved the existence of a central force; the elliptical form of the planetary orbits, and the relation between their magnitude and the time occupied in describing them, ascertained the law of its variation. But no one had arisen to demonstrate these necessary consequences, or even to conjecture the universal principle from which they were derived. The existence of a central force had indeed been surmised, and the law of its action guessed at; but no proof had been given of either, and little attention had been awakened by the conjecture.

Newton's discovery appears to have been quite independent of any speculations of his predecessors. The circumstances attending it are well known: the very spot in which it first dawned upon him is ascertained. He was sitting in the garden at Woolsthorpe, when the fall of an apple called his attention to the force which caused its descent, to the probable limits of its action and the law of its operation. Its power was not sensibly diminished at any distance at which experiments had been made: might it not, then, extend to the moon, and guide that luminary in her orbit? It was certain that her motion was regulated in the same manner as that of the planets round the sun; if, therefore, the law of the sun's action could be ascertained, that by which the earth acted would also be found by analogy. Newton therefore proceeded to ascertain, by calculation from the known elements of the planetary orbits, the law of the sun's action. The great experiment remained: the trial whether the moon's motions showed the force acting upon her to correspond with the theoretical amount of terrestrial

gravity at her distance. The result was disap
pointment. The decision was to be made by as-
certaining the exact space by which the earth's action turned the moon aside from her course in a
given time. This depended on her actual distance
from the earth, which was only known by comparison with the earth's diameter. The received estimate of that quantity was very erroneous; it proceeded on the supposition that a degree of latitude
was only sixty English miles, nearly a seventh part
less than its actual length. The calculation of the
moon's distance, and of the space described by her,
gave results involved in the same proportion of error; and thus the space actually described appeared to be a seventh part less than that which corresponded to the theory. It was not Newton's
habit to force the results of experiments into conformity with hypothesis. He could not, indeed,
abandon his leading idea, which rested, in the case
of the planetary motions, on something very nearly amounting to demonstration. But it seemed
that some modification was required before it could
be applied to the moon's motion, and no satisfactory
solution of the difficulty occurred. The scheme,
therefore, was incomplete; and, in conformity with
his constant habit of producing nothing till it was
fully matured, Newton kept it undivulged for many
years.

On his return to Cambridge Newton again applied himself to the construction of reflecting telescopes, and succeeded in effecting it in 1668. In
the following year Dr. Barrow resigned in his favour the Lucasian professorship of mathematics,
which Newton continued to hold till the year 1703,

when Whiston, who had been his deputy from 1699, succeeded him in the chair. January 11, 1672, Newton was elected a Fellow of the Royal Society. He was then best known by the invention of the reflecting telescope ; but, immediately after his election, he communicated to the society the particulars of his theory of light, on which he had already delivered three courses of lectures at Cambridge, and they were shortly afterward published in the Philosophical Transactions.

It is impossible here to state the various phenomena of light and colours which were first detected and explained by Newton. They entirely changed the science of optics, and every advance which has since been made in it has only added to the importance and confirmed the value of his observations. The success of the new theory was complete. Newton, however, was much vexed and harassed by the discussions which it occasioned. The annoyance which he thus experienced made him even think of abandoning the pursuit of science ; and, although it failed to withdraw him from the studies to which he was devoted, it confirmed him in his unwillingness to publish their results.

The next few years of Newton's life were not marked by any remarkable events. They were passed almost entirely at Cambridge, in the prosecution of the researches in which he was engaged. The most important incident was the communication to Oldenburgh, and, through him, to Leibnitz, that he possessed a method of determining maxima and minima, of drawing tangents, and performing other difficult mathematical operations. This was the method of fluxions, but he did not announce its name or its processes. Leibnitz, in return, explained to him the principles and processes of the Differential Calculus. This correspondence took place in the years 1676 and 1677; but the method of fluxions had been communicated to Barrow and Collins as early as 1699, in a tract first printed in 1711, under the title " Analysis per equationes numero terminorum infinitas." Newton had indeed intended to publish his discovery as an introduction to an edition of Kinckhuysen's Algebra, which he undertook to prepare in 1672; but the fear of controversy prevented him, and the method of fluxions was not publicly announced till the appearance of the Principia in 1687. The edition of Kinckhuysen's treatise did not appear; but the same year, 1672, was marked by Newton's editing the Geography of Varenius.

In 1679 Newton's attention was again called to the theory of gravitation, and by a fuller investigation of the conditions of elliptical motion, he was confirmed in the opinion that the phenomena of the planets were referable to an attractive force in the sun, of which the intensity varied in the inverse proportion of the square of the distance. The difficulty about the amount of the moon's motion remained, but it was shortly to be removed. In 1679 Picard effected a new measurement of a degree of the earth's surface, and Newton heard of the result at a meeting of the Royal Society in June, 1682. He immediately returned home to repeat his former calculation with these new data. Every step of the process made it more probable that the discrepance which had so long perplexed him would wholly disappear : and, so great was his excitement at the prospect of entire success, that he was unable to proceed with the calculation, and intrusted its completion to a friend. The triumph was perfect, and he found the theory of his youth sufficient to explain all the great phenomena of nature.

From this time Newton devoted himself unremittingly to the development of his system, and a period of nearly two years was entirely absorbed by it. In 1684 the outline of the mighty work was finished ; yet it is likely that it would still have remained unknown, had not Halley, who was himself on the track of some part of the discovery, gone to Cambridge in August of that year, to consult Newton about some difficulties he had met with. Newton communicated to him a treatise De Motu Corporum, which afterward, with some additions, formed the first two books of the Principia. Even then Halley found it difficult to persuade him to communicate the treatise to the Royal Society ; but he finally did so in April, 1686, with a desire that it should not immediately be published, as there were yet many things to complete. Hooke, whose unwearied ingenuity had guessed at the true law of gravity, immediately claimed to himself the honour of the discovery ; how unjustly, it is needless to say, for the merit consisted, not in the conjecture, but the demonstration. Newton was inclined, in consequence, to prevent the publication of the work, or at least of the third part, De Mundi Systemate, in which the mathematical conclusions of the former books were applied to the system of the universe. Happily, his reluctance was overcome, and the whole work was pub-

lished in May, 1687.   Its doctrines were too novel
and surprising to meet with immediate assent ; but
the illustrious author at once received the tribute
of admiration for the boldness which had formed,
and the skill which had developed his theory, and
he lived to see it become the common philosophical
creed of all nations.

We next find Newton acting in a very different
character.   James II. had insulted the University
of Cambridge by a requisition to admit a Benedictine monk to the degree of Master of Arts, without
taking the oaths enjoined by the constitution of the
University.   The mandate was disobeyed ; and the
vice-chancellor was summoned before the Ecclesiastical Commission to answer for the contempt.
Nine delegates, of whom Newton was one, were
appointed by the University to defend their proceedings ; and their exertions were successful.
He was soon after elected to the Convention Parliament, as member for the University of Cambridge.   That parliament was dissolved in February, 1690, and Newton, who was not a candidate for a seat in the one which succeeded it, returned to Cambridge, where he continued to reside
for some years, notwithstanding the efforts of
Locke, and some other distinguished persons with
whom he had become acquainted in London, to fix
him permanently in the metropolis.

During this time he continued to be occupied
with philosophical research, and with scientific and
literary correspondence.   Chymical investigations
appear to have engaged much of his time ; but the
principal results of his studies were lost to the
world by a fire in his chambers about the year

1692. The consequences of this accident have been very differently related. According to one version, a favourite dog, named Diamond, caused the mischief; and the story has been often told, that Newton was only provoked by the loss of the labour of years, to the exclamation, " Oh, Diamond ! Diamond ! thou little knowest the mischief thou hast done." Another, and probably a better au. thenticated account, represents the disappointment as preying deeply on his spirits for at least a month from the occurrence.

We have more means of tracing Newton's other pursuits about this time. History, chronology, and divinity were his favourite relaxations from science, and his reputation stood high as a proficient in these studies. In 1690 he communicated to Locke his " Historical Account of Two Notable Corruptions of the Scriptures," which was first published long after his death. About the same time he was engaged in those researches which were afterward imbodied in his Observations on the Prophecies : and in December, 1692, he was in correspondence with Bentley on the application of his own system to the support of Natural Theology.

During the latter part of 1692 and the beginning of 1693, Newton's health was considerably impaired, and he laboured in the summer under some epidemic disorder. It is not likely that the precise character or amount of his indisposition will ever be discovered ; but it seems, though the opinion has been much controverted, that for a short time it affected his understanding, and that in September, 1693, he was not in the full possession of his mental faculties. The disease was soon removed, and there is no reason to suppose it ever recurred. But the course of his life was changed; and from this time forward he devoted himself chiefly to the completion of his former works, and abstained from any new career of continued research.

His time, indeed, was less at his own disposal than it had been. In 1696, Mr. Montague, the chancellor of the Exchequer, an early friend of Newton, appointed him to the Wardenship of the Mint, and in 1699 he was raised to the office of Master. He removed to London, and was much occupied, especially during the new coinage in 1696 and 1697, with the duties of his office. Still he found time to superintend the editions of his earlier works, which successively appeared with very material additions and improvements. The great work on Optics appeared for the first time in a complete form in 1704, after the death of Hooke had freed Newton from the fear of new controversies. It was accompanied by some of his earlier mathematical treatises; and contained also, in addition to the principal subject of the work, suggestions on a variety of other subjects of the highest philosophical interest, imbodied in the shape of queries. Among these is to be found the first suggestion of the polarity of light; and we may mention at the same time, although they occur in a different part of the work, the remarkable conjectures, since verified, of the combustible nature of the diamond, and the existence of an inflammable principle in water. The second edition of the Principia appeared under the care of Cotes in 1713, after having been the subject of correspondence between Newton and his editor for nearly four years. Dr. Pemberton published a third edition in 1725, and he frequently communicated about the work with Newton, who was then eighty-two years old.

These were the chief scientific employments of the latter part of Newton's life; and it is not necessary to particularize all its minor details. In 1712 he made some improvements in his Arithmetica Universalis, a work containing his algebraical discoveries, of which Whiston had surreptitiously published an edition in 1707. It is also worthy of remark, that at the beginning of the year 1697, John Bernouilli addressed two problems as a challenge to the mathematicians of Europe, and that Leibnitz in 1716 made a similar appeal to the English analysts; and that Newton in each case undertook and succeeded in the investigation.

This enumeration of Newton's philosophical employments has far outrun the order of time. After his return to London, compliments and honours flowed in rapidly upon him. In 1699 he was elected one of the first foreign associates of the Académie des Sciences at Paris; and in 1701 he was a second time returned to parliament by the University of Cambridge. He did not, however, long retain his seat. At the election in 1705 he was at the bottom of the poll, and he does not appear again to have been a candidate. In 1703 he was chosen President of the Royal Society, and held that office till his death. In 1705 he was knighted by Queen Anne upon her visit to Cambridge.

Newton's life in London was one of much dignity and comfort. He was courted by the distinguished of all ranks, and particularly by the Princess of Wales, who derived much pleasure from her intercourse both with him and Leibnitz. His domestic establishment was liberal, and was superintended during great part of his time by his niece, Mrs. Barton, a woman of much beauty and talent, who married Mr. Conduitt, his assistant and successor at the Mint. Newton's liberality was almost boundless, yet he died rich.

The only material drawback to Newton's enjoyment during this portion of his life seems to have arisen from controversies as to the history and originality of his discoveries; a molestation to which his slowness to publish them very naturally exposed him. There was a long and angry dispute with Leibnitz about the priority of fluxions or the differential calculus; and, after the fashion of most disputes, it diverged widely from the original ground, and it became necessary for Newton to vindicate the religious and metaphysical tendencies of his greatest works. His success was complete on all points. Leibnitz does not appear to have been acquainted with the method of fluxions at the time of his own discovery, but there is now no doubt of Newton's having preceded him by some years; and the attacks made on the tendency of Newton's discoveries have long been remembered only as disgracing their author. But such discussions had always been distasteful to Newton, and this controversy, which was conducted with great rancour by his opponents and some of his supporters, imbittered his later years.

The same fate awaited him in another instance.

His system of chronology had been long conceived, but he had not communicated it to any one until he explained it to the Princess of Wales. At her desire, he afterward, in 1718, drew up a short abstract of it for her use, and sent it to her on condition that no one else should see it. She afterward requested that the Abbé Conti might have a copy of it, and Newton complied, but still on the terms that it should not be farther divulged. Conti, however, showed the manuscript at Paris to Freret, who, without the author's permission, translated and published it with observations in opposition to its doctrines. Newton drew up a reply, which was printed in the Philosophical Transactions for 1725, and this was the signal for a new attack by Souciet. Newton was then roused to his last great exertion, that of fully digesting his system, which as yet existed only in confused papers, and preparing it for the press. He did not live to complete his task, but the work was left in a state of great forwardness, and was published in 1728 by Mr. Conduitt. Its value is well known. As a refutation of the systems of chronology then received, it is almost demonstrative ; and the affirmative conclusions, if not always minutely correct or even generally satisfactory, are yet among the most valuable contributions which science has made to history.

With the exception of the attack of 1693, Newton's health had usually been very good. But he suffered much from stone during the last few years of his life. His mental faculties remained in general unaffected, but his memory was much impaired. From the year 1725 he lived at Kensington, but was still fond of going occasionally to London, and visited it on the 28th of February, 1727, to preside at a meeting of the Royal Society. The fatigue appears to have been too great ; for the disease attacked him violently on the 4th of March, and he lingered till the 20th, when he died. His sufferings were severe, but his temper was never soured, nor the benevolence of his nature obscured. Indeed, his moral was not less admirable than his intellectual character, and it was guided and supported by that religion, which he had studied, not from speculative curiosity, but with the serious application of a mind habitually occupied with its duties and earnestly desirous of its advancement.

Newton died without a will, and his property descended to Mrs. Conduitt and his other relations in the same degree. He was buried with great pomp in Westminster Abbey, where there is a monument to his memory, erected by his relations. His Chronology appeared, as has been already mentioned, almost immediately after his death ; and the Lectiones Opticæ, the substance of his lectures at Cambridge in the years 1669, 1670, and 1671, were published from his manuscripts in 1729. In 1733, Mr. Benjamin Smith, one of the descendants of his mother's second marriage, published the Observations on the Prophecies. These, in addition to the works already mentioned, are Newton's principal writings ; there are, however, several smaller tracts, some of which appeared during his lifetime, and others after his death, which it is not necessary here to specify. They would have conferred much honour on most philosophers ; they are hardly remembered in reckoning up Newton's titles to fame.

It is remarkable, that, until the recent publication of Dr. Brewster's life, no one had thought it worth while to devote an entire work to the history of so remarkable a man as Newton. There is, however, an elaborate memoir of him, written by M. Biot, in the Biographie Universelle, which has been republished in the Library of Useful Knowledge.

DEFOE.

DANIEL, the son of James Foe, citizen and butcher, was born in London, in the parish of Cripplegate, in or about the year 1663; at what time, or on what account he prefixed the syllable De to his paternal name, does not clearly appear. He was a Dissenter himself, and appears to have been of a dissenting family. Early imbued with a dread of papal ascendancy, he took up arms to support the Duke of Monmouth's insurrection, and was fortunate in escaping not only the sword, but the legal consequences of that rash adventure. In 1685 he went into business as a hosier, in Freeman's Yard, Cornhill. He was not successful, probably because his attention was engrossed by affairs foreign to his trade; for he not only mingled in the political and religious dissensions of that stormy time, but was too much occupied, according to his biographer, Mr. Chalmers, by engagements, which became neither the conscientious dissenter nor the steady man of business. " With the usual imprudence of superior genius, he was carried by his vivacity into companies who were gratified by his wit, and he spent those hours in the idle hilarity of the tavern which he ought to have employed in the calculations of the counting-house ; and being obliged to abscond from his creditors in 1692, he attributed those misfortunes to the war which were doutless owing to his own misconduct. He afterward carried on the brick and pantile works near Tilbury Fort, though probably with no success. He was in after times wittily reproached, ' that he did not, like the Egyptians, require bricks without straw, but, like the Jews, required bricks without paying his labourers.' He was born for other enterprises, which, if they did not gain him wealth, have conferred a renown that will descend the current of time with the language wherein his works are written." His misfortunes, however, even if accompanied by some imprudence, did not alienate his friends. " I was invited," he says in his Appeal to Honour and Justice, " by some merchants with whom I had corresponded abroad, and some also at home, to settle at Cadiz, and that with offers of very good commissions ; but Providence, which had other work for me to do, placed a secret aversion in my mind. Some time after I was, without the least application of mine, and being then seventy miles from London, sent for to be accomptant to the commissioners of the glass duty, in which service I continued to the determination of their commission."

Having lost this occupation, Defoe's active mind

expanded itself in a variety of schemes. He wrote, he tells us, many sheets about the coin ; he proposed a law for registering seamen ; he projected county banks ; factories for goods ; a commission of inquiry into the estates of bankrupts ; a pension-office for the relief of the poor ; an academy " to encourage polite learning, and to polish and refine the English tongue ;" and an academy for the education of women, with a view to the improvement of society, by training them to a more exemplary discharge of their social duties. Notices of various of these schemes, and of the use and abuse of a speculative spirit in a mercantile country, will be found in his Essay on Projects, published in January, 1697. In 1701 he produced a satire in verse, called The True-born Englishman, which arose out of a personal and virulent attack by one Tutchen on William III., whose faults were finally summed up in the epithet " foreigner." " This," Defoe says, " filled me with a kind of rage against the book, and gave birth to a trifle, which I never could hope should have met with such general acceptation as it did—I mean, The True-born Englishman. How this poem was the occasion of my being known to his majesty ; how I afterward was received by him ; how employed ; and how, above all my capacity of deserving, rewarded, is no part of the present case :" and history does not supply us with the particulars here left unnoticed. But, whatever were Defoe's services or their rewards, he always expressed his gratitude and affection for King William's memory in ardent terms. In the same year he published two able tracts in support of the principles of the Revolution, one entitled

Vol. II.—H

The Original Power of the Collective Body of the People of England Examined and Asserted ; the other, The Freeholder's Plea against the Stock-jobbing Elections of Parliamentmen. The following pithy sentence may give some notion of the general tenour of the latter : " It is very rational to suppose that those who buy will sell, or, what seems more rational, they who have bought must sell." In these pieces the ultimate resort of all power in the people, and the responsibility of the parliament to the people, inasmuch, to use his own words elsewhere, " as the person sent is less than the sender," are forcibly explained and asserted. The same principles were developed more strongly in what is commonly called The Legion Letter, a remonstrance against certain exercises of the privilege of parliament, by which the subject's right of petitioning was thought to be curtailed. This remarkable paper, which, though never clearly avowed, is believed to have been written by Defoe, and presented by him, dressed in women's clothes, to the speaker, was entitled, A Memorial from the Gentlemen, Freeholders, and Inhabitants of the Counties of ——, in behalf of themselves, and many thousands of the good people of England, to the Knights, Citizens, and Burgesses in Parliament assembled ; and ends in the following words : " For Englishmen are no more to be slaves to parliaments than to kings.

> " Our name is LEGION,
> And we are MANY.

" If you require to have this memorial signed with our names, it shall be done on your first orders, and formally presented."

Of this attempt to intimidate the house, no open notice was taken, nor does it appear to have been known at the time who was the author. But any ill-will which the Tories might have had against Defoe, if suspected, was gratified by the consequences of a pamphlet which he published in 1702, entitled, The Shortest Way with the Dissenters, or Proposals for the Establishment of the Church. In this ironical performance, which ostensibly recommends the total extirpation of Dissenters from England, he intended to satirize the blind prejudices and headstrong zeal of the high Tory faction ; but he had the misfortune to raise up enemies on every side. Some of the Dissenters took it literally, and raised an outcry against him as a persecutor : the Tories understood it better, and had influence enough to get a persecution commenced against him, and a reward offered for his apprehension by the government. The House of Commons voted the book a libel, and ordered it to be burned by the hangman. The printer and the publisher of it were taken into custody, upon which Defoe, who had secreted himself, came forward, "to throw himself upon the favour of government rather than that others should be ruined for his mistakes." He was tried in July, 1703, found guilty of composing and publishing a seditious libel, and, by a very oppressive sentence, was condemned to be imprisoned, to stand in the pillory, to pay a fine of 200 marks, and to find security for his good behaviour during seven years. It is in allusion to this that Pope, who ought to have better appreciated such a man, has made an unworthy attack upon Defoe in the Dunciad,

"Earless on high stood unabash'd Defoe."

He had no reason to be, and was not abashed; and he composed a Hymn to the Pillory, and an Elegy on the Author of a True-born Englishman, esteeming himself defunct as an author when he was obliged to find sureties for good behaviour. These, like all his works, contain the energetic expression of an independent spirit; to poetical merit they have no claim.

Early in 1704, while he was still in prison, Defoe commenced a periodical paper, entitled The Review, which, in addition to the usual topics of news, contained a report of the proceedings of a "Scandal Club, which discusses questions in divinity, morals, war, trade, language, poetry, love, marriage, drunkenness, and gaming. Thus it is easy to see that the Review pointed out the way to the Tatlers, Spectators, and Guardians, which may be allowed, however, to have treated these interesting topics with more delicacy of language, more terseness of style, and greater depth of learning: yet has Defoe many passages, both of prose and poetry, which, for refinement of wit, neatness of expression, and efficacy of moral, would do honour either to Steele or Addison." (Chalmers.) This periodical was published three times a week until May, 1713, when it was brought to a close. Defoe continued in Newgate until August, 1704, when Harley procured his release, and recommended him to Queen Anne, who seems to have thought that he had been hardly used, and contributed generously towards the relief of his family, reduced to poverty by the misfortunes of its head. She employed him, he says, in "several honourable though secret

services ;" and he speaks, in his appeal to Honour
and Justice, of a "special service, in which I ran
as much risk of my life as a grenadier upon the
counterscarp." These seem to have been rewarded by a pension or by some subordinate office ;
but the exact nature of the recompense is not
known. In October, 1706, he was despatched to
Scotland, to assist in promoting the union between
the two kingdoms. In addition to his talents and
readiness as an author, he possessed great practical knowledge of commerce and matters connected
with the revenue : he frequently attended the committees of the Scottish parliament, and made a variety of calculations relative to trade and taxes for
their use ; and he was very serviceable, as a popular writer, in replying to the various attacks which
were made upon that hated measure. His intimate
acquaintance with the transactions of this period
qualified him well for a work, which now, probably,
is known to few readers, but which contains a great
body of minute information concerning the condition
and the history of Scotland at that period—The
History of the Union between England and Scotland : of which Mr. Chalmers says, " The minute-
ness with which he describes what he saw and heard
upon that turbulent stage, where he acted a conspicuous part, is extremely interesting to us, who
wish to know what actually passed, however this
circumstantiality may have disgusted contempora-
neous readers. History is chiefly valuable as it
transmits a faithful copy of the manners and sentiments of every age. This narrative of Defoe is a
drama, in which he introduces the highest peers
and the lowest peasants speaking and acting, ac-

cording as they were each actuated by characteristic passions; and while the man of taste is amused by his manner, the man of business may draw instruction from the documents which are appended to the end and interspersed in every page. This publication had alone preserved his name, had his Crusoe pleased us less." Chalmers naturally makes the most of its merits, for his Life of Defoe was originally prefixed to a reprint of it in 1786: but the author would have been little known if his popularity had depended on this work only.

After his return from Scotland Defoe resided for some time at Newington. He incurred great obloquy, he says, for trying to make the best of the peace of Utrecht after it was concluded, and bore infinite reproaches as having been hired and bribed to defend a bad peace, upon the supposition that he was the author of pamphlets in which he had no share. To escape from this persecution he went to Halifax, in Yorkshire, where he had ample opportunity to observe the confidence of the Jacobite party, and the success with which they laboured to make converts among the lower ranks. To counteract these plottings, he wrote A Seasonable Caution, Reasons against the Succession of the House of Hanover, and some other pamphlets with similar titles; intending, he says, by means of their apparent drift, to put them into the hands of persons whom the Jacobites had deluded. But Defoe was unfortunate as an ironical writer: perhaps the same qualities which gave his fictions such an air of truth, tended to give his irony too much the appearance of being in earnest. On this, as on a former occasion, some persons were foolish or malicious enough to misconstrue his meaning, and to accuse him of writing seditious libels in favour of the Pretender. On this frivolous charge an information was filed against him in the spring of 1713, on which he was taken into custody, and obliged to find bail to a large amount; and the consequences might have been still more serious but for a second intervention of Harley, who procured a free pardon for him in the following November. Speaking of these very publications in his Appeal, he protests that "if the Elector of Hanover had given me a thousand pounds to have written for the interests of his succession, and to expose and render the interests of the Pretender odious and ridiculous, I could have done nothing more effectual to these purposes than these books were."

Well intended and valuable as his labours might be, his only recompense for them was a bare immunity from persecution. After the accession of George I. he was discountenanced and neglected. In 1715 he wrote An Appeal to Honour and Justice, comprising a defence of his character, and a general account of his life, principles, and conduct. He was struck by apoplexy before he had quite completed this work, but recovered the full possession of his faculties, and lived until April 26, 1731. After this attack, whether from the wish to avoid excitement and anxiety, or from the little advantage which his political writings had produced to him, he almost ceased to handle controversial subjects, and devoted himself with unwearying industry to works of a more popular and lucrative kind. Upon the profits of his pen he seems to have depended for his livelihood; and to the necessity of courting popular favour it may probably be attributed that the subjects of some of his works are vulgar, and the style coarse: but even out of vicious and re-volting subjects he had the art of extracting a whole-some moral. The following are the names and dates of the principal productions of his declining years; and it is very remarkable, considering the circumstances under which they were composed, that they should comprise all those fictions to which he owes his imperishable name in British literature : Life and Adventures of Robinson Crusoe, 1719. Life, Adventures, and Piracies of the Famous Cap-tain Singleton, 1720.   Fortunes and Misfortunes of the Famous Moll Flanders, 1721.   Religious Courtship; Journal of the Plague Year, 1722. Life of Colonel Jack, 1723.   Tour through the whole Island of Great Britain, 1724–7.   New Voyage round the World, 1725.   Political History of the Devil, 1726.   Complete English Tradesman, 1727.   Plan of English Commerce, 1728.   Me-moirs of a Cavalier—date uncertain.   But, not-withstanding the unceasing industry which enabled him to produce these, and many other works, in the time specified, he appears to have died insolvent, for a creditor took out letters of administration on his effects.

A catalogue of the numerous works known, or confidently believed by the compiler to be Defoe's, and of those also which are attributed to him on more doubtful evidence, is given by Mr. Chalmers at the end of that edition of his life which is sub-joined to Stockdale's edition of Robinson Crusoe, in 2 vols. 8vo, 1790, hardly one in four of which has been named in this short account.   Defoe was

a very rapid as well as laborious composer; it is
said that he once wrote two shilling pamphlets in a
single day. His controversial works, however,
have long lost their interest; and his principal historical work, that on the Union, is too prolix and
minute to find general acceptance in our days. In
his acquaintance with commerce, and insight into
the principles by which it is governed, he is entitled
to rank with the most skilful of his contemporaries; but the progress of economical science has
of course deprived his commercial writings of most
of their value except as records of the past. Of
his numerous works of fiction, we may notice the
History of the Plague in London in 1765, Memoirs of a Cavalier, and Robinson Crusoe, as the
best known and the most deserving. The first,
which professes to be the journal of a saddler resident in Whitechapel during the awful visitation
which he describes, is said to have been received
as genuine even by Dr. Mead, as no doubt it has
been by very many of those who are unacquainted
with its real history. There is a homely pathos,
a minute and scrupulous adherence to versimilitude
in it, which almost irresistibly persuades the reader
that none but an eyewitness could have written such
an account. The Memoirs of a Cavalier possess
the same air of truth. They relate the campaigns
of a young Englishman of good family, first in
Germany under Gustavus Adolphus, afterward on
the royal side in the civil wars; and depict with
great vividness and fidelity the principal events of
those interesting and stirring times. But, popular
as these works have been and deserve to be, they
sink into obscurity when compared with the uni-

versal acceptation of Robinson Crusoe; the only
thing, according to Dr. Johnson, written by mere
man, that was ever wished longer by its readers,
except Don Quixote and the Pilgrim's Progress.
And Bunyan and Defoe had some points in common.   Both came of the people, and both, without
the advantages or trammels of a learned education,
wrote for and to the people; they slighted no
source of pathos or eloquence as being too humble,
and cared little for homeliness of phrase if it expressed their meaning clearly and strongly.   It is
needless to give any account of a book which in
one shape or other—for in the numerous reprints it
has often been curtailed and mutilated—must be
familiar to every reader.   The story is well-known
to be identical with that of Alexander Selkirk, who,
after a solitary abode of four years on the island
of Juan Fernandez, returned to England in 1709.
Defoe has been charged with surreptitiously obtaining and making an unfair use of this man's
papers; but there seems to be no ground whatever
for the accusation.   Selkirk's story had been made
public in several forms seven years at least before
Robinson Crusoe was written, and it was free to
Defoe, or to any man, to take it as the ground upon
which to build a tale.   And, so far from Selkirk's
papers having been traced into Defoe's hands, it
does not even appear that these pretended papers
were ever in existence: indeed, Selkirk seems, from
the published accounts of him, to have been so
much below the fictitious Crusoe in the extent of
his resources and the fertility of his ingenuity (and
we say this with no desire to undervalue his active
spirit and contented temper), that it is hardly pos-

sible that he should have furnished more than the first hint, which Defoe has expanded into so instructive, fascinating, and varied a story.

The following lively criticism of this remarkable work is extracted from Dunlop's History of Fiction :

"Defoe and Swift, though differing very widely in education, opinions, and character, have, at the same time, some strong points of resemblance. Both are remarkable for the unaffected simplicity of their narratives ; both intermingle so many minute circumstances, and state so particularly names of persons, and dates, and places, that the reader is involuntarily surprised into a persuasion of their truth. It seems impossible that what is so artlessly told should be a fiction, especially as the narrators begin the account of their voyages with such references to persons living, or whom they assert to be alive, and whose place of residence is so accurately mentioned, that one is led to believe a relation must be genuine, which could, if false, have been so easily convicted of falsehood. The incidents, too, are so very circumstantial, that we think it impossible they could have been mentioned except they had been real." . . . . Speaking of the moral of Robinson Crusoe, he continues, " We are delighted with the spectacle of difficulty overcome, and with the power of human ingenuity and contrivance to provide not only accommodation but comfort, in the most unfavourable circumstances. Never did human being excite more sympathy in his fate than this shipwrecked mariner ; we enter into all his doubts and difficulties, and every rusty nail which he acquires fills us with satisfaction. We thus learn to appreciate our own comforts, and we acquire, at the same time, a habit of activity; but, above all, we attain a trust and devout confidence in Divine mercy and goodness. The author, also, by placing his hero in an uninhabited island in the Western Ocean, had an opportunity of introducing scenes which, with the merit of truth, have all the wildness and horror of the most incredible fiction. *That* foot in the sand—*those* Indians who land on the solitary shore to devour their captives—fill us with alarm and terror; and, after being relieved from the fear of Crusoe perishing by famine, we are agitated by new apprehensions for his safety. The deliverance of Friday, and the whole character of that young Indian, are painted in the most beautiful manner; and, in short, of all the works of fiction that have ever been composed, Robinson Crusoe is perhaps the most interesting and attractive."

HANDEL.

GEORGE FREDERIC HANDEL, whom we will venture to call the greatest of musicians, considering the state in which he found his art and the means at his command, was born at Halle, in the Duchy of Magdeburg, February 24, 1684. He was intended, almost from his cradle, for the profession of the civil law; but, at the early age of seven, he manifested so uncontrollable an inclination and so decided a talent for the study of music, that his father, an eminent physician, wisely consented to change his destination, and suffered him to continue under the direction of a master of those studies, which he had been secretly pursuing with no other guide than his own genius.

Friedrich Zachau, organist of the cathedral church of Halle, was the first and, indeed, the chief instructor of Handel. He discharged the duties of his office so well, that his pupil, when not nine years old, had become competent to officiate for his teacher, and had composed, it is said, many motets for the service of the church. A set of sonatas, written by him when only ten years old, was in the possession of George III.

In 1703 Handel went to Hamburg, where the opera was then flourishing under the direction of Reinhard Keiser, a master of deserved celebrity, but whose gayety and expensive habits often compelled him to absent himself from the theatre. On one of these occasions Handel was appointed to fill his place as conductor. This preference of a junior roused the jealousy of a fellow-performer, named Mattheson, to such a degree, that a rencounter took place between the rivals in the street; and Handel was saved from a sword-thrust, which probably would have taken fatal effect, only by the interposition of a music-score which he carried buttoned up under his coat. Till this time he had occupied but a very subordinate situation in the orchestra, that of second *ripieno* violin; for, from the period of his father's death, he had depended wholly on his own exertions, nobly determining not to diminish his mother's rather straitened income by any demands on her for pecuniary assistance. But now an opportunity for making known his powers

had arrived ; for the continued absence of the conductor Keiser from his post induced the manager
to employ Handel in setting to music a drama called Almeria.   So great was the success of this piece,
that it was performed thirty nights without interruption.   The year following he composed Florin-
da ; and, soon after, Nerone, both of which were received in as favourable a manner as his first dramatic effort ; but not one of these is to be found in
the collection formed by George III., and they seem
quite unknown to all writers on music except by
their titles.

The success of his operas at Hamburg produced
a sum which enabled him to visit Italy.   Florence
was the first city in which he made any stay.   He
was there received in the kindest manner by the
Grand-duke Giovanni Gaston de Medicis, and produced the opera of Rodrigo in 1709, for which he
was presented with a hundred sequins and a service of plate.   Thence he proceeded to Venice,
where he brought out Agrippina, which was received with acclamation, and performed twenty-seven
nights successively.   It seems that horns and other
wind instruments were in this opera first used in
Italy as accompaniments to the voice.

On visiting Rome he was hospitably and kindly
entertained by the Cardinal Ottoboni, a person of
the most refined taste and princely magnificence.
Besides his splendid collection of pictures and stat-
ues, he possessed a library of music of great extent, and kept in his service an excellent band of
performers, which was under the direction of the
celebrated Corelli.   At one of the parties made by
the cardinal, Handel produced the overture to Il

Trionfo del Tempo, which was attempted by the band so unsuccessfully, that the composer, in his hasty manner, snatched the violin from Corelli, and played the most difficult passages with his own hand. The Italian, who was all modesty and meekness, ingeniously confessed that he did not understand the kind of music ; and when Handel still appeared impatient, only said, " Ma, caro Sassone, questa musica è nel stilo Francese, di ch'io non m'intendo"——(" But, my dear Saxon, this music is in the French style, which I do not understand"). And so far Corelli was perfectly right ; Handel's overtures are formed after the model of Lully, though it is hardly necessary to add, he improved what he imitated. This anecdote indicates the vast superiority in point of execution possessed by the moderns. A learner of two years' standing would now play the violin part of any of Handel's overtures at first sight without a fault.

At Rome Handel composed his Trionfo del Tempo, the words of which were written for him by the Cardinal Pamphilii, and a kind of *mystery,* or oratorio, La Resurrezione. The former he afterward brought out in London, with English words by Dr. Morell, under the title of the Triumph of Time and Truth. From Rome he went to Naples, where he was treated with every mark of distinction. But he now resolved, notwithstanding the many attempts to keep him in Italy, to return to Germany ; and in 1710 reached Hanover, where he found a generous patron in the elector, who subsequently ascended the English throne as George I. Here he met the learned composer Steffani, who, having arrived at a time of life when retirement

becomes desirable, resigned his office of Maestro
di Capella to the elector, and Handel was appointed his successor, with a salary of 1500 crowns,
upon condition that he would return to the court of
Hanover at the termination of his travels.

Towards the end of 1710 Handel arrived in
London. He was soon introduced at court, and
honoured with marks of Queen Anne's favour.
Aaron Hill was then manager of the Italian opera,
and immediately sketched a drama from Tasso's
Jerusalem, which Rossi worked into an opera under the name of Rinaldo, and Handel set it to music. This was brought out in March, 1711; and
it is stated in the preface that it was composed in
a fortnight; a strong recommendation of a work
to those who delight in the wonderful rather than
in the excellent: but, in fact, there is nothing in this
which could have put the composer to much expense either of time or thought. Handel undoubtedly wrote better operas than any of his contemporaries or predecessors; but he was controlled
by the habits and taste of the day, and knew by
experience that two or three good pieces were as
much as the fashionable frequenters of the Italian
theatre would listen to in his time.

At the close of 1711 he returned to Hanover,
but revisited London late in 1712; and shortly
after was selected, not without many murmurs from
English musicians, to compose a Te Deum and
Jubilate on occasion of the peace of Utrecht. The
queen settled on him a pension of two hundred
pounds as the reward of his labour; and as he
was solicited to write again for the Italian stage,
he never thought of returning to his engagement

at Hanover till the accession of the elector to the British throne reminded him of his neglect of his royal employer and patron. On the arrival of George I. in London, Handel wanted the courage to present himself at court ; but his friend, Baron Kilmansegge, had the address to get him restored to royal favour. The pleasing *Water-music*, performed during an excursion made up the river by the king, was the means by which the German baron brought about the reconciliation ; and this was accompanied by an addition of two hundred pounds to the pension granted by Queen Anne.

From the year 1715 to 1720 Handel composed only three operas. The first three years of this period he passed at the Earl of Burlington's, where he was constantly in the habit of meeting Pope, who, though devoid of any taste for music, always spoke and wrote in a flattering manner of the German composer. The other two years he devoted to the Duke of Chandos, Pope's Timon ; and at Cannons, the duke's seat, he produced many of his anthems, which must be classed among the finest of his works, together with the greater number of his hautbois concertos, sonatas, lessons, and organ-fugues.

A project was now formed by several of the English nobility for erecting the Italian theatre into an Academy of Music, and Handel was chosen as manager, with a condition that he should supply a certain number of operas. In pursuance of this, he went to Dresden to engage singers, and brought back with him several of great celebrity, Senesino among the number. His first opera under the new system was Radamisto, the success of which was

astonishing.   But there were at that time two Italian composers in London, Bononcini and Attilio,
who till then had been attached to the opera-house,
and were not without powerful supporters.   These
persons did not passively notice the ascendency of
Handel, and the insignificance into which they were
in danger of falling ; they persuaded several weak
and some factious people of noble rank to espouse
their cause, and to oppose the German intruder, as
they called the new manager.   Hence arose those
feuds to which Swift has given immortality by his
well-known epigram ; and hence may be traced
Handel's retirement from a scene of cabal, persecution, and loss.   The final result of this, however,
was fortunate, for it led to the production of his
greatest works, his oratorios, which not only amply
compensated him for all the injury which his fortune sustained in this contest, but raised him to a
height of fame which he never could have gained
by his Italian operas.

The two contending parties, wishing to appear
reasonable, proposed something like terms of accommodation : those were, that an opera in three
acts should be composed by the three rivals, one
act by each, and that he who best succeeded should
for ever after take the precedence.   The drama
chosen was Muzio Scevola, of which Bononcini set
the first act, Handel the second, and Attilio the
third.   Handel's " won the cause," and Bononcini's
was pronounced the next in merit.   But, strange
to say, though each no doubt strained his ability to
the utmost in this struggle, not a single piece in
the whole opera is known at the present day, or is.

perhaps, to be found, except in the libraries of curious collectors.

This victory left Handel master of the field for some years, and the Academy prospered. During this period he brought out about fifteen of his best operas. But the genius of discord must always have a seat in the temple of harmony, and a dispute between the German manager and the Italian soprano, Senesino, renewed former quarrels, broke up the Academy, materially damaged the fortune of the great composer, and was the cause of infinite vexation to him during much of his future life.

Dr. Arbuthnot, always a stanch friend of Handel, now became his champion, and his ridicule had more weight with the sensible portion of the public than the futile arguments, if they deserve the name, advanced by the noble supporters of Senesino. But fashion and prejudice were, as usual, too strong for reason: a rival opera-house was opened in Lincoln's Inn Fields; and, after having composed several new operas, comprising some of the best, and having sacrificed nearly the whole of his property and injured his health in a spirited attempt to support the cause of the lyric stage against the presumption of singers and the folly of their abettors, Handel was at last compelled to terminate his ineffectual labours and stop his ruinous expenses by abandoning the contest and the Italian opera together.

The sacred musical drama, or oratorio, was ultimately destined to repair his all but ruined fortune, and to establish his fame beyond the reach of cavil, and for ever. Esther, the words of which, it is said, were the joint production of Pope and

Arbuthnot, was composed for the Duke of Chandos in 1720. In 1732 it was performed ten nights at the Haymarket, or King's Theatre. Deborah was produced in 1733, and in the same year Athalia was brought out at Oxford. These three oratorios were performed at Covent Garden in the Lent of 1734. Acis and Galatea and Alexander's Feast were brought out in 1735; Israel in Egypt in 1738; L'Allegro et il Penseroso in 1739. Saul was produced at the theatre in Lincoln's Inn Fields in 1740. But, up to this period, his oratorios failed to reimburse him for the expenses incurred; and even the Messiah, that sublime and matchless work, was, as Dr. Burney, Sir John Hawkins, and Handel's first biographer, Mr. Mainwaring, all agree in stating, not only ill attended, but ill received, when first given to the public, in the capital of the empire, in 1741.

Such miscarriages, and a severe fit of illness, the supposed consequence of them, determined him to try his oratorios in the sister kingdom, where he hoped to be out of the reach of prejudice, envy, and hostility. Dublin was at that time noted for the gayety and splendour of its court, and the opulence and spirit of its principal inhabitants. Handel therefore judged wisely in appealing to such a people. Pope, in his Dunciad, alludes to this part of his history, introducing a poor phantom as representative of the Italian opera, who thus instructs Dulness:

" But soon, ah soon, rebellion will commence,
If Music meanly borrows aid from sense :
Strong in new arms, lo! giant Handel stands,.
Like bold Briareus, with a hundred hands :

To stir, to rouse, to shake the soul he comes,
And Jove's own thunders follow Mars's drums.
Arrest him, empress, or you sleep no more.—
She heard—and drove him to th' Hibernian shore."

"On his arrival in Dublin," we are told by Dr. Burney, in his Commemoration of Handel, "he, with equal judgment and humanity, began by performing the Messiah for the benefit of the city prison. This act of generosity and benevolence met with universal approbation, as well as his music, which was admirably performed." He remained in Ireland about nine months, where his finances began to mend ; an earnest, as it were, of the more favourable reception which he experienced on returning to London in 1742. He then recommenced his oratorios at Covent Garden ; Sampson was the first performed. And now fortune seemed to wait on all his undertakings ; and he took the tide at the flood. His last oratorio became most popular, and the Messiah was now received with universal admiration and applause. Dr. Burney remarks, " From that time to the present, this great work has been heard in all parts of the kingdom with increasing delight : it has fed the hungry, clothed the naked, fostered the orphan," and, he might have added, healed the sick. Influenced by the most disinterested motives of humanity, Handel resolved to perform his Messiah annually for the benefit of the Foundling Hospital, and, under his own direction and that of his successors, it added to the funds of that charity alone the sum of £10,300 ($50,000). How much it has produced to other benevolent institutions it is impossible to calculate ; the amount must be enormous.

He continued his oratorios till almost the mo-

ment of his death, and derived considerable pecu‑
niary advantage from them, though a considerable
portion of the nobility persevered in their opposi‑
tion to him. George II., however, was his steady
patron, and constantly attended his performances,
when they were abandoned by most of the court.

In the close of life, Handel had the misfortune to
lose his sight, from an attack of gutta serena, in
1751. This evil, for a time, plunged him into deep
despondency ; but when the event was no longer
doubtful, an earnest and sincere sense of religion
enabled him to bear his affliction with fortitude,
and he not only continued to perform, but even to
compose. For this purpose he employed for his
amanuensis Mr. John Christian Smith, a good mu‑
sician, who furnished materials for a life of his
employer and friend, and succeeded him in the
management of the oratorios. " To see him, how‑
ever," Dr. Burney feelingly observes, " led to the
organ after this calamity, at upward of seventy
years of age, and then conducted towards the au‑
dience to make his accustomed obeisance, was a
sight so truly afflicting to persons of sensibility as
greatly diminished their pleasure in hearing him
perform."

His last appearance in public was on the 6th of
April, 1759. He died that day week, on Good Fri‑
day ; thus realizing a hope which he expressed a
very few days before his decease, when aware that
his last hours were approaching. He was buried
in Westminster Abbey : the dean, Dr. Pearce, bish‑
op of Rochester, assisted by all the officers of the
choir, performed the ceremony. A fine monument,
executed by Roubiliac, is placed in the Poet's Cor‑

ner, above the spot where his mortal remains are deposited; but a still more honourable tribute to his memory was paid in the year 1784, by the performances which took place under the roof which covers his dust. A century having then elapsed from the time of his birth, it was proposed that a Commemoration of Handel should take place. The management of it was intrusted to the directors of the ancient concert, and eight of the most distinguished members of the musical profession. The king, George III., zealously patronised the undertaking, and nearly all the upper classes of the kingdom seconded the royal views. A vocal and instrumental band of 525 persons was collected from all parts, for the purpose of performing in a manner never before even imagined, the choicest works of the great master. The principal aisle in Westminster Abbey was fitted up for the occasion with boxes for the royal family, the directors, the bench of bishops, and the dean and prebendaries of the church; galleries were erected on each side, and a grand orchestra was built over the great west door, extending from within a few feet of the ground to nearly half-way up the great window. There were four morning performances in the church: the tickets of admission were one guinea each; and the gross receipts (including an evening concert at the Pantheon) amounted to £12,736. The disbursements rather exceeded £6,000, and the profits were given to the Society for Decayed Musicians and the Westminster Hospital; £6000 to the former, and £1000 to the latter. Such was the success of this great enterprise, that similar performances, increasing each year in magnitude, took place annually till the period of the French Revolution, when the state of public affairs did not encourage their longer continuance.

As a composer, Handel was great in all styles, from the familiar and airy to the grand and sublime. His instinctive taste for melody, and the high value he set on it, are obvious in all his works; but he felt no less strongly the charms of harmony, in fulness and richness of which he far surpassed even the greatest musicians who preceded him; and had he been able to employ the variety of instruments now in use, some of which have been invented since his death, and to command that orchestral talent, which probably has had some share in stimulating the inventive faculty of modern composers, it is reasonable to suppose that the field of his conceptions would have expanded with the means at his command. Unrivalled in sublimity, he might then have anticipated the variety and brilliance of later masters.

Generally speaking, Handel set his words with deep feeling and strong sense. Now and then he certainly betrayed a wish to imitate by sounds what sounds are incapable of imitating; and occasionally attempted to express the meaning of an isolated word, without due reference to the context. And sometimes, though not often, his want of a complete knowledge of our language led him into errors of accentuation. But these defects, though great in little men, dwindle almost to nothing in this "giant of the art;" and every competent judge, who contemplates the grandeur, beauty, science, variety, and number of Handel's productions, will feel for him that admiration which Haydn, and still more Mozart, was proud to avow, and be ready to exclaim in the words of Beethoven, " Handel is the unequalled master of all masters !   Go, turn to him, and learn, with such scanty means, how to produce such effects."

CHATHAM

WILLIAM PITT, the first Earl of Chatham, was born in Westminster, November 15, 1708.   He was sent to Eton at an early age, and admitted a gentleman-commoner of Trinity College, Oxford, in January, 1726.   His father, Robert Pitt, Esq., of Boconnock, in Cornwall, died in the following year, and left to him the scanty inheritance of a younger son.   He quitted Oxford without taking a degree ; spent some time in travelling on the Continent ; and entered the army shortly after his return.   He obtained a seat in Parliament for Old Sarum in 1735, and attached himself to the party in opposition, then headed in the lower house by the Pulteneys, and favoured in the upper by the Prince of Wales.   His known talents and his determined hostility soon drew upon him the anger of Sir Robert Walpole, who is reported to have said, " We must at all events muzzle that terrible cornet of horse."   Failing in this, he had recourse to a method of revenge, which would not have been tolerated in later times, and took away Pitt's commission.   For this injury, however, the sufferer received an ample recompense in the increased estimation of the public.

Pitt spoke with great ability and energy, in 1739, against the proposed convention with Spain, and in 1740, against a bill introduced to facilitate the impressment of seamen, containing very arbitrary and oppressive provisions. Many of his speeches have been preserved, to a certain extent, in the periodical works of the day; though it is probable, from the very imperfect mode of reporting which then prevailed, that little remains of their original garb of words. Walpole was compelled to resign in 1742; but, with his usual dexterity, he contrived, by disuniting the opposition, to secure himself from the consequences of an inquiry into his conduct. Pitt spoke with much heat and eloquence in favour of the inquiry; and two of his speeches on this subject are reported at considerable length. He obtained no share in the ministry upon Walpole's fall, and continued to be a leader in opposition during the years 1742–3–4. More especially was he earnest in reprobation of the Hanoverian policy, which was supposed at that time to have an undue preponderance in the British councils; and his pertinacity on this point engendered in the breast of George II. a strong personal dislike, which is said to have prevented his admission into what was whimsically termed the " broad-bottomed administration," formed at the close of 1744. In that autumn he received a bequest of £10,000 from the celebrated Duchess of Marlborough, "upon account of his merit, in the noble defence he has made for the support of the laws of England, and to prevent the ruin of his country."

Pitt was assured by the Pelhams that, as soon as the king's antipathy could be removed, his services would be secured to the government; and he accordingly received the appointment of Vice-treasurer of Ireland, February 22, 1746, and, May 6, was promoted to the office of Paymaster-general. In the latter capacity he showed his superiority to pecuniary corruption, by foregoing the profit which it had been usual to derive from the large balances retained in that officer's hands, and by rejecting other lucrative perquisites of office. But he has incurred the charge of political dishonesty, by supporting measures as a minister, analogous in character to those which, under former governments, he had so strongly condemned. On this subject we may quote the words of a recent writer on the history of parties in England. "By the absorption into the government of almost all its leaders and chief orators, the opposition was for some time reduced in Parliament to extreme insignificance. Mr. Pitt was now one of the most determined supporters of the very measures which the first ten years of his parliamentary life had been spent in condemning and opposing. Nor did he scruple to avow his change of opinion. In reference, for instance, to the claim of exemption from search for British ships when found near the coast of Spanish America, which, urged by the opposition in the time of Sir Robert Walpole, had involved the country in a war with Spain, and was afterward abandoned at the peace of Aix-la-Chapelle by the government of which Pitt was a member, he said in the House of Commons that he had indeed once been an advocate for that claim; but it was when he was a young man; he was now ten years older, and, having considered public affairs more coolly, was convinced it could not be maintained. In the same manner very much of his old jealousy of military power and of the prerogative appears to have evaporated in the cooler consideration which he had now been enabled to give to such matters. We do not profess to doubt the perfect honesty of Mr. Pitt in this change of sentiment; and we may also think that his more matured opinions were, upon the whole, more rational than those of his fervid and impetuous nonage as a politician; but the facts (which only furnish an instance of what has often happened) are worth recording as a lesson for such as are capable of understanding it." It is to be recollected, that the remarkable events of 1745–6 may very well have modified Mr. Pitt's opinions with respect to the maintenance of a standing army.

On the death of Henry Pelham, March 6, 1754, his brother, the Duke of Newcastle, became First Lord of the Treasury. Pitt's wishes certainly pointed to the office of Secretary of State, vacated by the duke, but he received no promotion. This was excused on the ground of the king's personal dislike; but Pitt felt himself aggrieved; and having neither regard nor respect for the prime minister, he gradually placed himself in decided opposition to the government. Still he retained his place as paymaster until November 20, 1755, on which day, with his friends Legge and George Grenville, he was dismissed. In the opposition he resumed his former activity; and he had abundant ground for invective against the incapacity which led to those reverses in the Mediterranean, in America, and in India, which raised a general cry of indignation through the country. The duke tried in vain to strengthen himself, by making overtures of reconciliation to Mr. Pitt, and at last resigned, November 11, 1756. The Duke of Devonshire received the Treasury, Pitt was made Secretary of State, and Legge and Grenville both were taken into office. This arrangement was, however, short-lived. The king was ill-pleased at the way in which the present ministry had been forced upon him; and he had a personal dislike to some of them, especially to Pitt, and to the first Lord of the Admiralty, Lord Temple, who was dismissed in April, 1757. Upon this Pitt resigned. During the short period of this administration he had displayed his vigour and decision in originating measures to repair the losses which had been sustained in America; and had endeavoured, but in vain, to save the unfortunate Admiral Byng.

A sort of ministerial interregnum succeeded, and lasted until the beginning of June. The king tried in vain to construct an administration. Meanwhile Pitt was at the height of popularity, and addresses of approbation were showered upon him from all parts of the kingdom. At last the king was compelled to recall him; and, after considerable negotiation, he consented to form a government in union with the Duke of Newcastle, whose parliamentary influence conferred on him a degree of importance quite disproportioned to the weakness of his character. Pitt, with the power of Premier, returned to his post as Secretary, and the duke took the office of first Lord of the Treasury.

Pitt found the country engaged in an unsuccessful war, and hampered with a system of continental alliances, against which he had often directed the

full vigour of his eloquence.   By continuing that
system he endangered his popularity, and incurred
the charge of having sacrificed his principles to his
ambition.   There is no doubt (and this ought to
teach us moderation in our censures) that even
honest men, as they are in the administration or
opposition, may view the same measures under very
different aspects.   Objectionable as he had thought
and called that policy, he probably persuaded himself that, under existing circumstances, it was inexpedient to change it ; and he followed it up with
an energy and decision, which at least led to results very different to those which had disgraced
the government of his predecessors.   He is reported to have said to the Duke of Devonshire, " My
lord, I am sure I can save this country, and nobody
else can ;" and the success which attended him
made good one half at least of the boast.   France
was alarmed by frequent, and, on the whole, successful descents upon her shores ; the connexion
with Frederic of Prussia was strengthened and improved ; the plans for the expulsion of the French
from North America, which Pitt had formerly conceived, were now carried into effect ; and the result of his judgment in selecting officers for foreign
service, and of his indefatigable care that no preliminary steps were neglected at home, was seen in
those various successes which were crowned by the
glorious capture of Quebec, and the ultimate cession of Canada by the French.   In three years he
raised England from depression and despondency
into a situation to give laws to Europe ; and during
that time he converted into confidence and favour
that obstinate dislike with which George II. had so

long regarded him. But with the accession of George III., October 25, 1760, a new favourite, Lord Bute, rose into power. Pitt continued at the head of the administration for a time, but he found that his counsels had ceased to be the mainspring of government ; and, having been outvoted in the cabinet when he urged the necessity of immediately declaring war against Spain, he resigned, October 5, 1761, to use his own words, "in order not to remain responsible for measures which he was no longer allowed to guide." The king bestowed on him a pension of £3000, and raised his wife to the rank of Baroness Chatham.

Not many months elapsed before the new ministers found it absolutely necessary to declare war against Spain, the very point upon which Pitt had resigned. A general peace was effected by the treaty of Paris, signed February 10, 1763, by which Canada and the other French possessions in North America were ceded to England. Pitt inveighed strongly—more strongly, perhaps, than was quite fair and candid—against the terms of this treaty ; but he took no active part to overthrow the existing administration. In August, 1763, the king made overtures to induce him to return to office ; and it is not very clearly known for what reason this negotiation failed. When Wilkes's case brought forward the question of general warrants, Pitt took a strong part in condemning the use of them. In January, 1765, he received a second remarkable testimony of respect for his public conduct, from Sir William Pynsent, an aged baronet of ancient family in Somersetshire, who, dying, bequeathed to him his property, to the amount of nearly £3000 a year.

To the scheme for raising a revenue in America Mr. Pitt was very strongly opposed. Illness prevented his attendance in the House of Commons when that scheme was first brought forward ; but in his speech on the meeting of parliament, January 14, 1766, after tidings of the disturbances in America had been received, he declared his opinion in the strongest terms. "It is a long time, Mr. Speaker, since I have attended in parliament. When the resolution was taken in the house to tax America, I was ill in bed.   If I could have endured to have been carried in my bed, so great was the agitation of my mind for the consequences, I would have solicited some kind friend to have laid me down on this floor, to have borne my testimony against it. . . . It is my opinion that this kingdom has no right to lay a tax upon the colonies.   At the same time, I assert the authority of this kingdom over the colonies to be sovereign and supreme in every circumstance of government and legislation whatsoever."   He recommended that the Stamp Act should be repealed absolutely and immediately; but that the repeal should be accompanied with an assertion of the sovereign power of the mother country over the colonies, couched in the strongest terms that could be devised, in every point whatsoever, except that of taking their money out of their pockets without their consent.   These declarations coincided with the policy of the Marquis of Rockingham, who had been summoned by the king to form an administration in July, 1765, and who, without any fault on his side, was involved in all the difficulties and dangers which had resulted from his predecessor's ill-judged scheme for taxing America.   Mr. Pitt had previously been applied to, but declined taking office upon the terms proposed; and he showed a coolness towards the Rockingham administration, which appears to have been uncalled for by any difference in their political opinions, and which, as far as we can conjecture from the course of events, was very prejudicial to the country. Disliked by the king; slighted by Mr. Pitt, whose influence in the nation was at this time at its height; harassed by a powerful opposition, which regarded it base to yield to the demands of America, the Rockingham government rather fell to pieces than was broken up, little more than a year after its formation; and Mr. Pitt reached the utmost limit of his ambition in being commissioned by the king to form a ministry, without the smallest limitation as to terms, in July, 1766.

Whatever gratification he may have felt at the moment, this high position added neither to his glory nor his happiness. It led, in the first place, to a violent quarrel with his most intimate friend and political associate, Lord Temple, who felt himself slighted by Mr. Pitt's arrangements. Many of the most important persons, whose support he desired, felt aggrieved by his past conduct, or were offended by the haughtiness of his demeanour; Lord Rockingham, in particular, refused even to grant him an interview. And when the government was formed at last, it was of that ill-assorted and motley character which led Burke, in an often-quoted passage of his speech on American taxation, to describe it as a "tesselated pavement without cement." The Duke of Grafton was placed at the Treasury, and for himself Pitt took a peerage and the Privy Seal. The astonishment of everybody at this was extreme.　　Lord Chesterfield says, " Mr. Pitt, who had a carte blanche given him, named every one of them (the new ministry); but what would you think he named himself for ?—Lord Privy Seal, and (what will astonish you as it does every mortal here) Earl of Chatham.　The joke here is, that he has had a fall up stairs, and has done himself so much hurt that he will never be able to stand upon his legs again.　Everybody is puzzled how to account for this step; though it would not be the first time that great abilities have been duped by low cunning.　But, be it what it will, he is now certainly only Earl of Chatham, and no longer Mr. Pitt in any respect whatever.　Such an event, I believe, was never heard nor read of. To withdraw in the fulness of his power, and in the utmost gratification of his ambition, from the House of Commons (which procured him his power, and which could alone ensure it to him), and to go into that hospital of incurables, the House of Lords, is a measure so unaccountable, that nothing but proof positive could have made me believe it ; but true it is."

At this time often recurring paroxysms of gout had greatly shattered Lord Chatham's constitution, and incapacitated him for that comprehensive superintendence over the affairs of government which he had exercised during his former glorious administration.　Surrounded by a disjointed set of men, fluctuating in opinion, attached neither to each other nor to their chief, it was more than ever necessary that the master-hand should retain its wonted dexterity and power.　But the case was very different.　During the whole session of parliament in

1767, Lord Chatham was prevented from attending to business by illness ; and after the rising of parliament he was compelled to inform the king, that " such was his ill state of health, that his majesty must not expect from him any farther advice or assistance in any arrangements whatever." This declaration may be considered as equivalent to a resignation ; but, unfortunately, he continued nominally in office until October 15, 1768, lending the sanction of his great name to a course of policy the reverse of that which he had advocated, especially in regard of the renewal of the attempt to tax America. On this subject Mr. Thackeray remarks, " A greater contrast in the feelings of the cabinet and of the nation upon the present resignation of Lord Chatham, to those which were evinced upon his dismission from office in 1757, and upon his retirement in 1761, can hardly be imagined. His dismission in 1757 excited one common cry of enthusiastic admiration towards himself, and of indignation against his political opponents. The attention not only of Great Britain, but of the whole of Europe, was attracted by his resignation in 1761 ; and, although the voices of his countrymen were not so universally united in his favour as upon the former occasion, the event was considered as affecting the interests of nations in the four corners of the globe. The resignation of Lord Chatham in 1768 was in fact nothing more than the official relinquishment of an appointment in which he had long ceased to exercise his authority or to exert his abilities. It was expected by the ministry, it was little regarded by the people of Great Britain, it was almost unknown on the Continent of Europe."

Repose soon wrought a favourable change in Lord Chatham's health, for in 1770 he led the opposition in the House of Lords. The proceedings in the House of Commons against Mr. Wilkes formed the principal topic of his first attack : but he warned the house against the fatal tendency of the attempts to raise a revenue in America ; and he took occasion, at an early period of the session, to express his belief of the necessity of introducing some reform into the representation of the people, and to proclaim his cordial reconciliation and union with the Rockingham party. At the end of January, to the general surprise of the nation, the Duke of Grafton resigned ; and Lord North succeeding him, formed the first durable administration which had existed since the death of Henry Pelham. During the years 1771, 1772, 1773, and 1774, Lord Chatham very seldom appeared in parliament. At the beginning of 1775 he made two vain attempts to induce the government to offer overtures of reconciliation to America : but during the greater part of that year, and the whole of 1776, the shattered state of his health prevented him from taking any part in public affairs. May 30, 1777, he came down to the house swathed in flannel, to move an address imploring the king to take the most speedy and effectual measures for putting a stop to hostilities in America, by removing the accumulated grievances of that country ; and predicted, with his usual energy and eloquence, the certain results of the conduct which the government was pursuing. " You may ravage, you cannot conquer ; it is impossible ; you cannot conquer the Americans. You talk of your numerous friends to annihilate the Congress, and of your powerful forces to disperse their army. I might as well talk of driving them before me with this crutch. What you have sent there are too many to make peace, too few to make war. If you conquer them, what then? You cannot make them respect you, you cannot make them wear your cloth : you will plant an invincible hatred in their breasts against you. Coming from the stock they do, they can never respect you." The events of that year, the capture of Philadelphia, and the surrender of Burgoyne, fully justified his predictions. These events had not been announced in England in November, when parliament again met; but in the debate on the address on the 18th, Lord Chatham again raised his warning voice to predict the certain failure of the contest in which the country was engaged. " I love and honour the English troops : I know their virtues and their valour : I know they can achieve anything except impossibilities ; and I know that the conquest of English America is an impossibility. You cannot, I venture to say it, you cannot conquer America." His speech on this occasion fortunately is very fully reported, and the records of Parliament contain none more eloquent.

In February, 1778, Lord North announced the resolution of government to yield every point in question to the Americans, except their nominal independence of the crown. To this, little opposition was offered in either house ; it probably was the line of conduct which Lord Chatham at this late hour would have advised. But the Americans had declared their independence, and were not now to be

L 2

satisfied with anything short of a formal acknowledgment of it ; and here the two great sections of opposition, the Rockingham and Shelburne parties, were divided.   The latter, with Lord Chatham at their head, regarded such an acknowledgment as the prelude to the certain ruin and degradation of the empire.   The former held that it was impossible to avoid it at last, and earnestly desired, since the colonists could not be retained as subjects, to secure their alliance to the mother country, and not to drive them into the arms of France.   The Duke of Richmond, on the 7th of April, moved an address imbodying these views : a day memorable for the most affecting scene ever witnessed within the walls of parliament.   We relate it as nearly as possible from the account communicated to Mr. Seward by an eyewitness, and published in his " Anecdotes of Distinguished Persons."

"Lord Chatham came into the House of Lords leaning on two friends, wrapped up in flannel, pale and emaciated.   Within his large wig little more was to be seen than his aquiline nose and his penetrating eye.   He looked like a dying man ; yet never was seen a figure of more dignity ; he appeared like a being of superior species.

"He rose from his seat with slowness and difficulty, leaning upon his crutches, and supported under each arm by his two friends.   He took one hand from his crutch, and raised it, casting his eyes towards Heaven, and said, 'I thank God that I have been enabled to come here this day, to perform my duty, and to speak on a subject which has so deeply impressed my mind.   I am old and infirm ; have one foot——more than one foot, in the grave. I am risen from my bed, to stand up in the cause of my country !—perhaps never again to speak in this house.'

" The reverence, the attention, the stillness of the house, was most affecting : if any one had dropped a handkerchief, the noise would have been heard. At first he spoke in a very low and feeble tone ; but, as he grew warm, his voice rose, and was as harmonious as ever ; oratorical and affecting, perhaps, more than at any former period, both from his own situation, and from the importance of the subject on which he spoke. He gave the whole history of the American war ; of all the measures to which he had objected ; and of all the evils which he had prophesied in consequence of them ; adding, at the end of each, ' And so it proved.' " He concluded with an energetic appeal against the " dismemberment of this ancient and most noble monarchy." To the Duke of Richmond's reply he listened with attention and composure : he then rose again, but his strength failed, and he fell back in convulsions in the arms of the peers who surrounded him. The House immediately adjourned. On the following day the Duke of Richmond's motion was negatived.

Lord Chatham was removed to Hayes, where he languished until May 12, 1778, on which day he expired. He was honoured with a public funeral, and a public monument in Westminster Abbey ; a sum of £20,000 was voted in discharge of his debts ; and a pension of £4000 a year was annexed to the Earldom of Chatham. He left five children by his wife, Lady Hester Grenville, sister of Earl Temple, whom he married November 6,

1754. He warmly loved and was beloved by his family, and in domestic life enjoyed all the happiness which unbroken confidence and harmony can bestow.

The character of this great man is thus drawn by Lord Chesterfield : " His constitution refused him the usual pleasures, and his genius forbade him the idle dissipations of youth ; for, so early as the age of sixteen, he was the martyr of an hereditary gout. He therefore employed the leisure which that tedious and painful distemper either procured or allowed him, in acquiring a great fund of premature and useful knowledge. Thus, by the unaccountable relation of causes and effects, what seemed the greatest misfortune of his life was perhaps the principal cause of its splendour. His private life was stained by no vice nor sullied by any meanness. All his sentiments were liberal and elevated. His ruling passion was an unbounded ambition, which, where supported by great abilities and crowned with great success, makes what the world calls a great man. He was haughty, imperious, impatient of contradiction, and overbearing ; qualities which too often accompany, but always clog great ones. He had manners and address, but one might discover through them too great a consciousness of his own superior talents. He was a most agreeable and lively companion in social life, and had such a versatility of wit that he could adapt it to all sorts of conversation. He had also a happy turn for poetry, but he seldom indulged, and seldom avowed it. He came young into Parliament, and upon that theatre he soon equalled the oldest and the ablest actors. His eloquence was of every kind, and he excelled in the argumentative as well as in the declamatory-way. But his invectives were terrible, and uttered with such energy of diction, and such dignity of action and countenance, that he intimidated those who were the most willing and best able to encounter him. Their arms fell out of their hands, and they shrunk under the ascendant which his genius gained over theirs."

Mr. Thackeray's "History of the Right Hon. W. Pitt, earl of Chatham," in addition to the fullest account of his public and private life, contains copious extracts from the reports of his speeches and his correspondence. The letters to his nephew, afterward Lord Camelford, deserve notice, as exhibiting his private character in a very amiable light. The same may be said of the letters to his son, William Pitt, printed by Dr. Tomline in his life of that statesman.

LINNÆUS.

CARL VON LINNE, commonly called Linnæus, was born at Rashult, in the province of Smaland, in Sweden, May 14, 1707. His father, the Protestant minister of the parish of Stenbrohult, was a collector of curious plants ; and Carl soon became acquainted with the plants in his father's garden, as well as with the indigenous species in the neighbourhood. Being intended for the church he was placed, first at the Latin school, and then at the Gymnasium of the neighbouring town of Wexio; but he neglected his professional studies to devote himself almost exclusively to the physical sciences. Botany, which was then little cultivated in Sweden, more particularly engrossed his attention; he formed a small library of botanical works, and, although unable to comprehend some of the authors he possessed, yet he continued to read them day and night. He even learned some of them by heart, and acquired, among his teachers and fellow-scholars, the name of the Little Botanist. His father, whose object was to fit his son for gaining a livelihood in his own sacred calling, and who was ill able to defray the expenses of a learned education, was greatly mortified by this (as he considered it) misapplication of time. He determined, therefore, without wasting any more money, to employ Carl in some manual occupation. His design, however, was changed by the interference of Dr. Rothman, a physician of Wexio, who advised him, instead of forcing his son into a profession for which he had no taste, to let him follow the study of medicine and natural history. Rothman rendered this scheme practicable by taking Carl into his own house for a twelvemonth; during which he instructed the young person in physiology, and likewise upon the right method of studying his favourite science of botany, according to the system of Tournefort.

Linnæus was equally fortunate in gaining admission into the family of Dr. Stobæus, professor of physic and botany at the University of Lund, whither he repaired in 1727. Here he pursued his botanical studies with zeal, and acquired the esteem

and affection of his host.   He went to the University of Upsal in 1728, by advice of his early friend
Dr. Rothman, hoping to obtain some situation in it.
But he was disappointed ; and, his scanty means
being soon exhausted, he found reason to repent of
having quitted the friendly roof of Stobæus, who was
much offended that a pupil, whom he had treated
so kindly, should have left the University without
consulting him.   A fortunate incident relieved him
from this state of anxious suspense.   One day, in
the autumn of 1729, while examining some plants
in the University Garden, he was accosted by an
aged clergyman, Dr. Olaf Celsius ; who, after some
inquiry into the nature and extent of his botanical
studies, received him into his own house, and employed him to assist him in a work on the plants
mentioned in Scripture, and to collect botanical
specimens around Upsal.

Linnæus enjoyed great advantages in his new
situation.   He had the full use of an extensive library, rich in botanical works ; he lived on most
familiar terms with his patron, by whom he was introduced to Dr. Rudbeck, the professor of botany ;
and Rudbeck, obliged by age to execute the duties
of his office by deputy, obtained that office for Linnæus in 1730.   The young man's reputation as a
naturalist was now established in the University ;
and in 1731 the Royal Academy of Sciences at
Upsal deputed him to make a tour through Lapland, with the sole view of examining the natural
productions of that desolate region.   He set out
on horseback, May 12, 1732 (Old Style), without
encumbrances of any kind, and bearing all his lug-
gage at his back.   In the flower of youth, bold, en-

terprising, and in robust health, he was well adapted to traverse the wild countries of northern Sweden and Lapland, in which he met with some romantic and dangerous adventures.   When in the districts of Pithea and Lulea, on the Gulf of Bothnia,
he was near perishing from a danger of which he
has given the following animated account :

" Several days ago the forests had been set on
fire by lightning, and the flames raged at this time
with great violence, owing to the drought of the
season.   I traversed a space three quarters of a
mile in extent, which was entirely burned, so that the
place, instead of appearing in its gay and verdant
attire, was in deep sable : a spectacle more abhor-
rent to my feelings than to see it clad in the white
livery of winter.   The fire was nearly extinguished
in most of the spots we visited, except in ant-hills
and dry trunks of trees.   After we had travelled
about half a quarter of a mile across one of these
scenes of desolation, the wind began to blow with
rather more force, upon which a sudden noise arose
in the half-burned forest, such as I can only compare
to what may be imagined among a large army attacked by an enemy ; we knew not whither to turn
our steps.   The smoke would not suffer us to remain where we stood, nor durst we turn back.   It
seemed best to hasten forward, in hopes of speedily reaching the outskirts of the wood ; but in this
we were disappointed.   We ran as fast as we could,
in order to avoid being crushed by the falling trees,
some of which threatened us every minute.   Sometimes the fall of a huge trunk was so sudden that
we stood aghast, not knowing whither to turn to
escape destruction, and throwing ourselves entirely

on the protection of Providence.   In one instance a large tree fell exactly between me and my guide, who walked not more than a fathom from me ; but, thanks to God! we both escaped in safety.   We were not a little rejoiced when this perilous adventure ended, for we had felt all the time like a couple of outlaws in momentary fear of surprise."

In the space of five months Linnæus performed, mostly on foot, a journey of 3798 English miles, and with the approach of winter he returned to Upsal.   On that occasion he was admitted a member of the Academy, and received about ten pounds for his expenses.   The " Flora Lapponica" was the result of this journey.   Scarce recovered from the fatigues of this tour through Lapland, he again felt the pressure of poverty.   He commenced a course of lectures on the assaying of metals, but his success excited the jealousy of Dr. Rosen, the successor of Dr. Rudbeck, who insisted that, in conformity with the statutes, Linnæus should no longer be allowed to lecture.   The Senate had no choice but to enforce the statutes, and this severe blow deprived Linnæus of all present means of advancement.   He quitted Upsal and took up his residence at Fahlun, the capital of Dalecarlia, where he gave lectures on assaying to the copper miners of that district.   In 1735, having saved a small sum of money, he resolved to travel, and take a medical degree at some foreign university.   He bent his course through Hamburgh to Holland, and obtained the degree of M.D. at the little university of Harderwych.   He gained the friendship of Gronovius and Boërhaave, by whom he was strongly urged to settle in Holland, then in the height of its commercial prosperity. But Linnæus' mind was set upon returning to Sweden, where he had formed an attachment to the eldest daughter of Dr. Moræus, a physician at Fahlun. Intending to pass homeward through Amsterdam, he obtained from Boërhaave an introduction to an eminent botanist, Dr. Burman, with whom he resided for a short time. During this visit he became acquainted with Mr. Clifford, a rich burgomaster of Amsterdam, who had a magnificent country-seat and garden at Hartecamp near Haarlem. This gentleman wished for the assistance of a man who could arrange his collections of natural history, and put his garden in order. Linnæus entered into his employment in this capacity, and the connexion proved equally satisfactory to both parties.

In 1736 Linnæus made a tour to England at the expense of Mr. Clifford, who wished him to inspect the gardens of that country, and to communicate with the eminent botanists then alive. The English professors were warmly attached to the system of Ray ; but Dillenius, the botanical professor at Oxford, was so impressed with the talents of Linnæus, that he urged him to take up his residence there, offering to share the profits of his professorship with him. Professor Martyn, of Cambridge, Miller, Collinson, &c., held friendly intercourse with him, and he returned to Holland with the most favourable impressions of the scientific men in England. Contrary to the wishes of Mr. Clifford, he left Hartecamp towards the close of 1737, with the intention of returning to Sweden. No stronger proof can be given of the estimation in which Linnæus was held in Holland, than the regard expressed for him by Boërhaave, even on his death-bed. Before the time of Linnæus's intended departure from Leyden, Boërhaave became too ill to admit visiters. Linnæus was the only person in whose favour an exception was made, that the dying physician might bid him an affectionate farewell. " I have lived," he said, " my time out, and my days are at an end ; I have done everything that was in my power : May God protect thee ! What the world required of me it has got ; but from thee it expects much more. Farewell, my dear Linnæus !"

When upon the point of leaving Leyden, Linnæus was attacked by illness ; and upon his recovery he determined to visit Paris before his return to Sweden. At Paris he experienced great kindness from the Jussieus ; and he received the high compliment of being elected a corresponding member of the Academy of Sciences. '

In the summer of 1738 he embarked at Rouen for Helsingburg. Soon after his arrival in Sweden he married the lady to whom he had been so long attached.

Dr. Pulteney, in his " View of the Writings of Linnæus," gives a full account of the numerous publications put forth by him during his residence in Holland; and adds : " It is scarcely to be conceived how this great man found time to finish so many works, any one of which would have been sufficient for establishing his character as a botanist." The most important of these were the " Systema Naturæ," in 1735, and the " Genera Plantarum," in 1737, in which the sexual system of plants is fully developed.

In 1738 Linnæus settled as a physician at Stockholm, where he met with so much opposition, that
he almost resolved to quit his native country.   But
by perseverance he worked his way into practice ;
and he was fortunate enough to be employed by
the Queen of Sweden.   In 1739 he contributed,
with some other spirited persons, to form an Academy at Stockholm, of which he was elected president.

His professional success did not lead him aside
from his favourite studies ; and he kept his eye
steadily on the great object of his ambition, the
botanical chair at Upsal.   In 1741 he was appointed medical professor.   He soon entered into an
agreement with Professor Rosen to allow him to
perform the duties of the botanical chair, while
his colleague lectured on physiology and other subjects.   Before entering on the duties of his professorship, he pronounced a Latin oration before
the University, " On the Necessity of Travelling in
our own Country."

Linnæus was now placed in the situation which
of all things he had most coveted.   The academical
garden was soon laid out on a new plan.   When he
was appointed professor, it did not contain above
fifty exotic plants.   In 1748, six years afterward,
he published a catalogue, from which it appears
that he had introduced eleven hundred, besides the
vegetable productions of Sweden itself.

He now applied to all his correspondents for
plants ; and, writing to Albert Haller, he says,
" Formerly I had plants, but no money ; and now,
of what use is my money without plants ?"   His
exertions so much extended the fame of the Uni-

versity, that the number of students considerably increased, particularly during the time he held the office of rector. They came from Russia, Norway, Denmark, Great Britain, Holland, Germany, Switzerland, and even from America. He made summer excursions, attended by his pupils, often to the number of two hundred. When some rare or remarkable plant, or other natural curiosity was found, a signal was given by a horn, at which the whole party assembled round their leader.

Linnæus published his " Amœnitates Academicæ," " Philosophia Botanica," and " Species Plantarum," respectively in 1749, 1751, and 1753. Of these, the first is a collection of treatises on various subjects ; the second is the foundation of the Linnæan system of botany, and from it most of our popular introductions have been compiled ; the third is termed by Haller, " Maximum opus, et æternum!" (*a great and immortal work.*) In this work he first employed trivial words as specific names : thus, the species of every genus is designated by a single epithet, expressive of some obvious character, and the tiresome plan of quoting an entire description to distinguish the species is abandoned. His fame had now rapidly increased, and his scientific connexions and correspondence with foreign countries had become very extensive.

In 1753 he was elected a Fellow of the Royal Society of London ; and in the same year his sovereign, Gustavus III., bestowed on him a most flattering mark of his regard, by creating him a knight of the Polar Star. This order had never before been conferred on any literary character ; nor had any person below the rank of a nobleman been honoured with it. Foreign countries were not backward in testifying their sense of his merits: he was a member of the Royal Academy of Sciences of Paris, of St. Petersburgh, and of Berlin; and there was hardly a learned body in Europe but was anxious to enrol his name among their numbers. The most flattering compliment which he received was from the King of Spain, who invited him to settle at Madrid, with an offer of an annual pension for life of 2000 pistoles, letters of nobility, and the free exercise of his own religion. He, however, did not accept of this offer, but answered, that if he had any merit, his services were due to his own country.

The University of Upsal had now become an object of curiosity: strangers were attracted there, and prolonged their stay, solely with the view of becoming acquainted with Linnæus. Among other visiters, the Earl of Macartney, when he was English minister at St. Petersburgh, went from that city on purpose to visit him. His writings were soon appreciated in foreign countries, and his system was first publicly taught in England by Professor Martyn, in the University of Cambridge. His pupils spread themselves over the globe; they carried everywhere with them the spirit of their master, and diffused the love of natural history. When Captain Cook's first voyage was undertaken, one of Linnæus's most celebrated pupils, Dr. Solander, accompanied Mr. Banks in the capacity of naturalist. It was not, however, from his pupils alone that Linnæus received information; in every part of the world persons were found anxious to forward specimens to him, and his collections thus became unrivalled.

The introduction of the Linnæan system was attended with such great change, especially of nomenclature, that it experienced considerable opposition from the older naturalists; and the biographers of Linnæus have recorded several literary feuds with distinguished contemporaries, and especially with Albert Haller, a genius of equal merit with himself.

The latter years of Linnæus were spent in a state of ease, affluence, and honour, very different from the poverty and obscurity of his early life. He was one of those great men who have shown by example how much the genius and activity of an individual are capable of accomplishing. He was the reformer of botany, and perhaps the greatest promoter of natural history that ever lived; and so much has never been done for that science, in so short a space of time, as at the period he flourished and immediately after.

In 1773 the reigning king of Sweden appointed him, in conjunction with others, to make a new translation of the Bible into the Swedish language. In the month of May, 1774, while lecturing in the Botanical Garden, he was attacked by apoplexy, the debilitating effects of which obliged him to relinquish the more active parts of his professional duties, and to close his literary career. In 1776 a second apoplectic fit paralyzed his right side and impaired his mental powers. Even in this painful and miserable state the study of nature remained his greatest pleasure, and he was constantly carried into his museum to survey the treasures there accumulated. He died January 10, 1778, in the seventy-first year of his age.

On his death a general mourning took place at Upsal. A medal was struck upon the occasion, and a monument erected to his memory in the cathedral church of Upsal. The King of Sweden himself pronounced a panegyric on his distinguished subject before the Royal Academy of Sweden.

Nature was eminently liberal in the endowments of Linnæus's mind. He had a lively imagination; a correct judgment, guided by the strict laws of system; a most retentive memory, and unremitting industry. He laboured to inspire the great and opulent with a taste for natural history, and he wished particularly that ecclesiastics should have some knowledge of it. He thought such knowledge would sweeten retirement, and that pastors had great opportunities for observing nature. He was decidedly religious himself, and not one of his greater works begins or ends without some passage expressive of admiration for the Supreme Creator.

His strength and weakness alike consisted in a rigid adherence to system. He arranged, according to a system of his own invention, all natural objects, from man down to the simple crystals. The Linnæan school is more fitted to arrange and describe the materials of science than to extend its boundaries. Its pupils have too rigidly adhered to a system which is ill adapted to our increased sphere of knowledge.

In botany the merits of Linnæus were transcendent. He found it a chaos, and reduced it to a system, which enabled the student to study it with ease. The great objection to his arrangement, founded on the sexual parts of plants, is, that it is artificial, and has rather retarded the knowledge of a system more philosophical, and in stricter accordance with the rules of nature. The labours of the Jussieus and De Candolle have done much to introduce a better system, but much still is wanting to complete it.

After the death of Linnæus's only son, in November, 1783, the late eminent botanist, Sir James Smith, purchased his museum of natural history, books, and manuscripts, for £1029. This collection consisted of nearly everything possessed by the great Linnæus and his son. Sir James Smith directed in his will that these treasures should be offered, after his own death, to the Linnæan Society of London. They were accordingly purchased by that body for 3000 guineas, and are now placed in the society's rooms in London.

This memoir is compiled almost entirely from a Life of Linnæus written for the Society for the Diffusion of Useful Knowledge, and from the article "Linnæus," in the "Biographie Universelle," by the late Baron Cuvier.

EULER.

LEONARD EULER* was born at Basle, April 15, 1707. His father was the clergyman of Reichen, near Basle, and had himself been a pupil of James

---

* We have followed the *éloge* of Condorcet as to facts and dates. We should have preferred that of M. Fuss, but have not had the opportunity of seeing it. The mere biographical details of Euler's life are, however, of the simplest character.

Bernouilli. He intended his son for his own pro
fession, and, after having been himself his first in
structor in mathematics, sent him to the university
of Basle. John Bernouilli was at this time professor, and his sons, Nicolas and Daniel, two more of
the *eight* Bernouillis known to the history of science, were under him. With the sons Euler contracted an intimate friendship, and obtained such
a degree of favour even with their father, that the
latter gave him a private lesson weekly, upon points
more advanced than those treated in the public
course. This was a strong mark of favour from
John Bernouilli, who was of an unamiable disposition, jealous of his brother, of his son, and finally
of almost every one who displayed a superior talent for mathematics. Euler at first turned his attention to theology, in accordance with the wishes
of his father, but this was not of long continuance.
At the age of nineteen, besides obtaining a degree
from his University, he had merited the notice of
the Academy of Sciences for a memoir on some
points of naval architecture. In the same year he
was an unsuccessful candidate for a professorship
at Basle : an unlucky event, M. Condorcet observes,
for his country, inasmuch as, a few days afterward,
he left it for Russia, and never returned. His
friends the Bernouillis (Nicolas and Daniel) had,
two years before, accepted invitations from the Empress Catharine ; and he followed them, in hopes of
obtaining employment and subsistence at St. Petersburgh. But, by the time he arrived, both Nicolas Bernouilli and the empress were dead, the
Academy of St. Petersburgh was left without a patron, and Euler, a nameless stranger, could not for

a long time obtain any settled avocation. How he maintained himself we are not told; but he was upon the point of entering the Russian service as a sailor when his prospects brightened, and he obtained the place of Professor of Natural Philosophy. In 1733 he succeeded Daniel Bernouilli, who returned to his own country, as Professor of Mathematics. In the same year he married a young lady named Gsell, the daughter of an artist of Basle, who had emigrated to Russia in the reign of Peter the Great.

The despotism of the Russian government could not please the republican born; but circumstances obliged him to endure it till 1741, when he quitted Petersburgh for Berlin, on the invitation of Frederic the Great. To the continual reserve and government of the tongue which was necessary in the Russian capital, has been attributed his love of silence and study, which exceeded all that is related of any of his contemporaries. The mother of Frederic, who was as much attached to the conversation of distinguished men as the king himself, could never obtain more than a few syllables from Euler at any one time. On her asking the reason why he would not speak, he is said to have replied, "Madam, I have lived in a country where men who speak are hanged."*

* Although things have changed greatly for the better in Russia since the time here referred to, the same system of espionage essentially exists; and the free expression of opinions exposes one not to the hazard, perhaps, of being hanged, but still to no little trouble and danger. In addition to the public police intrusted with the open execution of the laws, there is a secret and invisible department of the same, controlling the whole, and whose particular province it is to discover and punish all offences of a political nature; among which, speaking freely of the government and its measures is considered by no means the least venial.—*Am. Ed.*

Euler remained at Berlin till 1766. In 1761 he lost his mother, who had resided with him for eleven years. During this time he was not considered as having abandoned his Russian engagements, and a part of his salary was regularly paid. When the Russians invaded Brandenburgh in 1760, a farm belonging to him was destroyed, but he was immediately more than reimbursed by order of the Empress Elizabeth. On the invitation of that princess, he consented to return to Petersburgh in 1766. He had for some years suffered from weakness in the eyes ; and, not long after his return to Russia, he became so nearly blind that he could distinguish nothing except very large letters marked with chalk on a slate.* In this state he continued for the remainder of his life ; and by constant exercise he acquired a power of recollection, whether of mathematical formulæ or figures, which would be totally incredible were it not supported by strong evidence. He formed in his head, and retained in his memory, a table of the first six powers of all numbers up to 100, containing about 3000 figures. Two of his pupils had summed seventeen terms of a converging series, and differed by a unit in the fiftieth decimal of the result ; Euler decided between them correctly by a mental calculation.†

---

* Euler was in his fifty-ninth year when overtaken with this calamity. See Pursuit of Knowledge under Difficulties, i., 163, Harpers' Family Library.—*Am. Ed.*

† We suspect some mistake in this account, though it is constantly given. A very surprising story ought to be consistent ; now it is difficult to believe that any series which was actually employed in practice (and people do not sum series to fifty places for amusement) would converge so quickly as to give fifty places in seventeen terms. The well-known series for the base of Napier's logarithms is called a rapidly converging series, and gives

His chief amusement during this deprivation was the formation of artificial magnets, and the instruction of one of his grandchildren in mathematics. His studies were in no degree relaxed by it.[*] In 1771 Euler's house was destroyed by fire, together with a considerable part of the city. He was himself saved by a fellow-countryman named Grimm, and his manuscripts were also rescued. In 1776 he married the aunt of his first wife. No other event worthy of special notice occurred before his death, which took place suddenly, September 7, 1763. He had been employed in calculating the laws of the ascent of balloons, which were then newly introduced; he afterward dined with his family and M. Lexell, his pupil, conversed with them on the newly-discovered planet of Herschel, and was amusing himself with one of his grandchildren; suddenly the pipe which he held in his hand dropped on the ground, and it was found that "life and calculation were at an end."[†] He had thirteen children, of whom only three survived him; one of them, John Albert Euler, was known as a mathematician.

Of the scientific character of Euler it is impossible to speak in detail, since even the *résumé* of M. Condorcet, which is much longer than any account we can here insert, is meager in the extreme; and we imagine that the reader would form no idea

about fifteen places in seventeen terms. We cannot help thinking, either that Euler settled one disputed term only, or that there is some mistake about the number of figures.

[*] Some of his most profound and valuable works were composed after he had lost his sight: his Elements of Algebra, for example, and New Theory of the Moon's Motions.—*Am. Ed.*

[†] Il cessa de calculer et de vivre.—CONDORCET.

whatsoever of the man we are describing from any brief enumeration of discoveries for which we should be able to allow room. In more than fifty years of incessant thought, Euler wrote thirty separate works and more than seven hundred memoirs, which could not altogether be contained in forty large quarto volumes. These writings embrace every existing branch of mathematics, and almost every conceiveable application of them, to such an extent, that there is no one among mathematicians, past or present, who can be placed near to Euler in the enormous variety of the subjects which he treated. And the contents of these volumes are without exception the original fruit of his own brain, seeing that he left no subject as he found it. He is not a diffuse writer, except in giving a large number of examples, and this renders him in some respects the most instructive of all writers. His works are full of the most original thoughts developed in the most original manner; so that they have been a mine of information for his successors, which is even now far from being exhausted. Let a student be employed upon any subject connected with mathematics, however remotely, and he has discovered but little if he has not found out that Euler was there before him.

Of all mathematical writers, Euler is one of the most simple, and this in a manner which renders his writings not by any means a sound preparation for future investigations. Difficulties seem to have disappeared in the progress, or never to have been encountered; and the student is rather made to feel that Euler could take him anywhere, than furnished with the means of providing for himself when his guide shall have left him. Hence the writings of others, in every way inferior to Euler in elegance and simplicity, are to be preferred, and have been preferred, for the formation of mathematical power.

Euler is to be measured by the assistance which he gave to his immediate successors; and here it is well known that he paved the way for the research of others in a more effectual manner than any of his contemporaries. The incessant repetition of his name in later authors is sufficient authority for this assertion. His writings are the first in which the modern analysis is uniformly the instrument of investigation. His predecessors, James and John Bernouilli, had perhaps the largest share in bringing the infinitesimal analysis of Newton and Leibnitz to the state of power required for extensive application. To Euler (besides important extensions) belongs the distinct merit of showing how to apply it to physical investigations, in conjunction with D'Alembert, who ran a splendid and contemporary career of a similar character in this respect. But though it would be perhaps admitted that there are individual results of the latter which exceed anything done by the former, in generality of application there is no comparison whatever between the extent of the labours of the two.

Euler was a man of a simple, reserved, and benevolent mind; with a strong sense of devotion, and a decided religious habit, according to the Calvinism of the established church of his country. At the court of Frederic he himself conducted the devotions of his family every evening; a practice which then and there implies much moral courage and insensibility to ridicule. But he also possessed humour; for when he was asked to calculate the horoscope of one of the Russian princes, he quietly suggested that it was within the official province of the astronomer, and imposed the duty upon a colleague, who doubtless did not feel very much flattered by the compliment.

There are few men whom the usual biographical formulæ as to moral character and habits would better fit than Euler, according to every account which has appeared of him. But such praises are no distinction; and it will be more to the purpose to state, that the only occasion in which he was betrayed into printing a word which his eulogists have regretted, was in the dispute between Maupertuis and himself against others on the principle known by the name of *least action*, one of the warmest and most angry discussions which ever took place.

Perhaps it is to the quiet abstraction of his life that he owed the perpetuity of his power of investigation. Many eminent mathematical discoverers have run the brilliant part of their career while comparatively young. Euler "ceased to calculate and to live" at once. But it may be that this was a part of his natural constitution, and a distinct feature of his mind. The nature of his writings, indeed, rather confirm the latter supposition. There is the same difference between them and those of others that there is between conversation and oratory. He seems to be moving in his natural element, where others are swimming for their lives.

The best works of Euler for a young mathematician to read, in order to get an idea of his style and methods, are the "*Analysis Infinitorum*," and the "*Treatise on the Integral Calculus*."*

* For a catalogue of Euler's principal works, see his Letters on Natural Philosophy, i., 26, Harpers' Family Library.— *Am. Ed.*

BUFFON.

BUFFON is reported to have said—and the vanity which was his predominant foible may give some colour to the assertion—"I know but five great geniuses, Newton, Bacon, Leibnitz, Montesquieu, and myself." Probably no author ever received from his contemporaries so many excitements to such an exhibition of presumption and self-consequence. Louis XV. conferred upon him a title of nobility; the Empress of Russia was his correspondent; Prince Henry of Prussia addressed him in language of the most exaggerated compliment; and his statue was set up during his lifetime in the cabinet of Louis XVI., with such an inscription as is rarely bestowed even upon the most illustrious of past ages.* After the lapse of half a century, we may examine the personal character and the literary merits of this celebrated man with a more sober judgment.

The history of Buffon is singularly barren of incident. At an early age he devoted himself to those studies of natural history which have rendered his name so famous; and when eighty years old he was still labouring at the completion of the great plan to which he had dedicated his life.

George Louis le Clerc Buffon was born at Montbar, in Burgundy, on the 7th of September, 1707.

* Majestati naturæ per ingenium—*To the majesty* (sovereign) *of nature, through genius.*

His father, Benjamin le Clerc, was a man of fortune, who could afford to bestow the most careful education upon his children, and leave them unfettered in the choice of an occupation. The young Buffon had formed an acquaintance at Dijon with an Englishman of his own age, the Duke of Kingston. The tutor of this nobleman was, fortunately, an accomplished student of the physical sciences; and he gave a powerful impulse to the talents of Buffon, by leading them forward in their natural direction. Without the assistance of this judicious friend, the inclination of his mind towards honourable and useful exertion might have been suppressed by the temptations which too easily beset those who have an ample command of the goods of fortune. It was not so with Buffon. Although he succeeded, at the age of twenty-one, to the estate of his mother, which produced him an annual income of £12,000 (\$58,000), he devoted himself with unremitting assiduity to the acquisition of knowledge. Having travelled in Italy and resided some little time in England, he returned to his own country, to dedicate himself to the constant labours of a man of letters. His first productions were translations of two English works of very different character—"Hale's Vegetable Statics," and "Newton's Fluxions;" and, following up the pursuits for which he exhibited his love by these labours, he carried on a series of experiments on the strength of timber, and constructed a burning mirror in imitation of that of Archimedes.

The devotion to science which Buffon had thus manifested, marked him out for an appointment which determined the course of his future life.

His friend Du Fay, who was the Intendant of the "*Jardin du Roi*" (now called the "*Jardin des Plantes*"), on his death-bed recommended Buffon as the person best calculated to give a right direction to this establishment for the cultivation of natural history. Buffon seized upon the opportunities which this appointment afforded him of prosecuting his favourite studies, with that energetic perseverance for which he was remarkable. He saw that natural history was yet to be written in a manner that might render it the most attractive department of knowledge; and that philosophical views and eloquent descriptions might be made to supersede the dry nomenclatures, and the loose, contradictory, and too often fabulous narratives which resulted from the crude labours of ill-informed compilers. To carry forward his favourite object, it was necessary that the museum, over which he now had the control, should be put in order, and rendered more complete. He obtained from the government considerable funds for the erection of proper buildings; and the galleries of the "*Jardin des Plantes*," which now contain the fine collections of mammals and birds, were raised under his superintendence. Possessing, therefore, the most complete means which Europe afforded, he applied himself to the great task of describing the animal, vegetable, and mineral kingdoms of nature. A large portion of this immense undertaking was left unperformed, although, to use his own words, he laboured fifty years at his desk; and much of what he accomplished was greatly diminished in value by his determination to see natural objects only through the clouded medium of his own theories.

Nevertheless, he nas produced a work which, with all its faults, is an extraordinary monument of genius and industry, and which will long entitle him to the gratitude of mankind. "We read Buffon," says Condorcet, "to be interested as well as instructed. He will continue to excite a useful enthusiasm for the natural sciences ; and the world will long be indebted to him for the pleasure with which a young mind for the first time looks into nature, and the consolations with which a soul weary of the storms of life reposes upon the sight of the immensity of beings peaceably submitted to uniform and perpetual laws."

Buffon was in some particulars unqualified for the laborious duty he had undertaken. He delighted to indulge in broad and general views, and to permit his imagination to luxuriate in striking descriptions. But he had neither the patience nor the love of accuracy which would have carried him into those minute details which give to natural history its highest value. He had, however, the merit and the good fortune, in the early stages of his undertaking, to associate himself with a fellow-labourer possessing those qualities in which he was deficient. The first fifteen volumes of " *L'Histoire Naturelle*," which treat of the theory of the earth, the nature of animals, and the history of man and viviparous quadrupeds, were published between 1749 and 1767, as the joint work of Buffon and Daubenton. The general theories, the descriptions of the phenomena of nature, and the pictures of the habits of animals, were by Buffon. Daubenton confined himself to the precise delineation of their physical character, both in their external

forms and their anatomy. But Daubenton refused
to continue his assistance in the " History of Birds ;"
for Buffon, unwilling that the fame which he had acquired should be partaken by one whom he considered only as an humble and subordinate labourer,
allowed an edition of the History of Quadrupeds to
be published, of which the descriptive and anatomical parts had been greatly abridged. In the History of Birds, therefore, Buffon had to seek for
other associates ; and the form of the work was
greatly changed from that of the previous volumes.
The particular descriptions are here very meager,
and anatomical details are almost entirely excluded.
In some of the volumes, Buffon was assisted by
Guéneau de Montbeillard, who, instead of endeavouring to attain the accuracy of Daubenton, affected to imitate the style of his employer. To the
last three volumes of the Birds the Abbé Bexon
lent his aid. The nine volumes of Birds appeared
between 1770 and 1783. Buffon published alone
his " History of Minerals," which appeared in five
volumes between 1783 and 1788. Seven volumes
of Supplements complete the Natural History.
The first appeared in 1773, and the last was not
published till the year after its author's death, in
1789. The fifth volume of these Supplements is a
distinct work, the Epochs of Nature.*

The study of natural history, and the composition of his great work, occupied the mind of Buffon
from his first appointment as Intendant of the
Jardin du Roi" to within a few days of his
death. In the prosecution of the plan he had laid

* The best edition of the works of Buffon is the first, of 36
vols. 4to.

down, he never permitted the slightest interruption. Pleasure and indolence had their attractions, but they never held him for many hours from his favourite pursuits. Buffon spent the greater part of his time at Montbar, where, during some years, his friend Daubenton also resided. It was here that he composed nearly the whole of his works. Many interesting details have been preserved of his habits of life and his mode of composition. He was, like all men who have accomplished great literary undertakings, a severe economist of his time. The employment of every day was fixed with the greatest exactness. He used almost invariably to rise at five o'clock, compelling his man-servant to drag him out of bed whenever he was unwilling to get up. " I owe to poor Joseph," he used to say, " ten or twelve volumes of my works." At the end of his garden was a pavilion which served him as a study. Here he was seated for many hours of every day, in an old leathern chair, before a table of black birch, with his papers arranged in a large walnut-tree escrutoire. Before he began to write he was accustomed to meditate for a long time upon his subject. Composition was to him a real delight; and he used to declare that he had spent twelve or fourteen hours successively at his desk, continuing to the last in a state of pleasure. His endeavours to obtain the utmost correctness of expression furnished a remarkable proof of the persevering character of his mind. He composed, and copied, and read his works to friends, and recopied, till he was entirely satisfied. It is said that he made eleven transcripts of the Epochs of Nature. In his domestic habits there was little to admire in the character of Buffon. His conversation was trifling and licentious, and the grossness which too often discloses itself in his writings was ill concealed in his own conduct. He paid the most minute attention to dress, and delighted in walking to church to exhibit his finery to his wondering neighbours. Although he was entirely devoid of religious principle, and constantly endeavoured in his writings to throw discredit upon the belief of a great First Cause, he regularly attended high mass, received the communion, and distributed alms to beggars. In his whole character there appears a total absence of that simplicity which is the distinguishing attribute of men of the very highest genius.

The literary glory of Buffon, although surpassed, or even equalled, during his life by none of his contemporaries, with the exception, perhaps, of Voltaire and Rousseau, has not increased, and is, perhaps, materially diminished, after having been tried by the opinions of half a century. In literature as well as in politics, we have learned to attach a greater value to accurate facts, and, consequently, have become less captivated by the force of eloquence alone. Buffon gave an extraordinary impulse to the love of natural history by surrounding its details with splendid images, and escaping from its rigid investigations by bold and dazzling theories. He rejected classification, and took no pains to distinguish by precise names the objects which he described, because such accuracy would have impeded the progress of his magnificent generalizations. Without classification and an accurate nomenclature, natural history is a mere chaos.

Buffon saw the productions of nature only in masses. He made no endeavour to delineate with perfect accuracy any individual of that immense body, nor trace the relations of an individual to all the various forms of being by which it is surrounded. Although he was a profound admirer of Newton, and classed Bacon among the most illustrious of men, he constantly deviated from the principle of that philosophy upon which all modern discovery has been founded. He carried onward his hypotheses with little calculation and less experiment. And yet, although they are often misapplied, he has collected an astonishing number of facts : and even many of his boldest generalities have been based upon a sufficient foundation of truth to furnish important assistance to the investigations of more accurate inquirers. The persevering obliquity with which he turns away from the evidence of design in the creation, to rest upon some vague notions of a self-creative power, both in animate and inanimate existence, is one of the most unpleasant features of his writings. How much higher services might Buffon have rendered to natural history had he been imbued not only with a spirit of accurate and comprehensive classification, but with a perception of the constant agency of a Creator, of both of which merits he had so admirable an example in Ray.

The style of Buffon, viewed as an elaborate work of art, and without regard to the great object of style, that of conveying thoughts in the clearest and simplest manner, is captivating from its sustained harmony and occasional grandeur. But it is the style of a past age. Even in his own day it was a theme for ridicule with those who knew the real force of conciseness and simplicity. Voltaire described it as "*empoulé;*" and when some one talked to him of "*L'Histoire Naturelle*" (Natural History), he dryly replied, "*Pas si naturelle*" (Not so natural). But Buffon was not carried away by the mere love of fine writing. He knew his own power; and, looking at the state of science in his day, he seized upon the instrument which was best calculated to elevate him among his contemporaries. The very exaggerations of his style were perhaps necessary to render natural history at once attractive to all descriptions of people. Up to his time it had been a dry and repulsive study. He first clothed it with the picturesque and poetical; threw a moral sentiment around its commonest details; exhibited animals in connexion with man, in his mightiest and most useful works; and described the great phenomena of nature with a pomp of language which had never before been called to the service of philosophical investigation. The publication of his works carried the study of natural history out of the closets of the few, to become a source of delight and instruction to all men.

Buffon died at Paris on the 16th of April, 1788, aged 81. He was married in 1762 to Mademoiselle de St. Bélin; and he left an only son, who succeeded to his title. This unfortunate young man perished on the scaffold in 1795, almost one of the last victims of the fury of the revolution. When he ascended to the guillotine, he exclaimed, with great composure, "My name is Buffon."

A succinct and clear memoir of Buffon, by Cuvier, in the *Biographie Universelle*, may be advantageously consulted. Nearly all the details of his private life are derived from a curious work by Rénault de Séchelles, entitled *Voyage à Montbar*, which, like many other domestic histories of eminent men, has the disgrace of being founded upon a violation of the laws of hospitality.

DE L'EPÉE.

AMONG those persons who possess the highest claim to the gratitude of mankind, that of having devoted their lives, without a single selfish motive, to the alleviation of human misery, the Abbé de l'Epée claims a high and honourable place. Time. as is usual in cases of real excellence, has estab lished on a sure basis merits which were at first slowly acknowledged. Unknown and unappreciated, this good man lived for many years in obscurity; and, worse than this, he had to endure intolerance and persecution during the greater part of his beneficent career. There exists no memoir worthy of his exalted character. The brilliant genius of Bouilly has glanced upon his virtues and his talents; the eulogy of Bébian (himself a living and a worthy successor in the art of teaching the deaf and dumb) has shed additional lustre on a fame already bright; but still we have much to desire. Our glimpses of the good abbé in his public capacity, and in the retirement which he loved and courted, only present us with a faint outline of his character ; an outline, however, which is sufficiently distinct to show that the finished picture would have been surpassingly beautiful.

Charles Michel de l'Epée was born at Versailles in November, 1712. His father was the king's architect, a man of distinguished talents and enlightened piety. He devoted himself to the instruction of his children, and taught them from their earliest years to moderate their desires, to fear God, and to love their neighbour. Under such a guide, the docile heart of young De l'Epée imbibed its first feelings of virtue. The thought of evil was as displeasing as evil itself to his pure mind, so strictly had he been trained in the love of things "honest, just, pure, lovely, and of good report." It is said that when, at an advanced age, he looked back upon his long career, he did not remember to have had more than one trial to sustain ; and the humility which adorned his life led him to consider virtue which had been thus acquired without effort as possessing no merit. The piety which directed all his actions, and the obedience to the precepts of the Gospel which regulated his will, seemed peculiarly to fit him for the service of the altar. To this service his early wishes tended ; and his parents, who at first resisted, at length complied with his requests.

He received an education to fit him for the church, but at the commencement of his career he had to encounter difficulties and opposition. When he presented himself for admission into the priesthood, probably as a deacon, according to the established practice of the diocese of Paris he was

required to sign a formulary of faith.   As he was
a Jansenist, and as the form prescribed was contrary to his principles, he refused to avow by his
hand what his conscience disapproved.   Notwithstanding this, he was admitted to the rank of deacon, but was at the same time told never to pretend
to holy orders.   This humble station in the ministry was too humiliating for even this lowly-minded
man.   His breast glowed with ardent charity towards mankind, which he longed to put into practice,
but which could find no enlarged sphere for action
in his humble office at the foot of the altar.   The
intolerance of those ecclesiastics who stood in the
way of his preferment in the church at length
obliged him to direct his attention to the bar, to
which his parents had first destined him ; he passed, accordingly, through the course of prescribed
studies, and took the customary oath.   In the practice of the law, however, De l'Epée could find no
pleasure.   Its scenes of violence, cunning, and chi-
canery too deeply affected his mild and tranquil
spirit.   All his wishes were directed to the service
of the altar : his only desire was to be a minister of
the Gospel of peace, and at last he was successful.

A nephew of the learned and liberal Bossuet,
who seems to have emulated his uncle in piety and
liberality, was at this period the bishop of Troyes.
This good man loved to call around him ecclesiastics
of strict piety.   Through his means M. de l'Epée
was regained to the church ; he was ordained to
the sacred office, and received a canonry in the
cathedral of Troyes.   He now devoted himself to
the preaching of the gospel ; and he knew how to
render pleasing by his example those precepts

which penetrated the hearts of his hearers. Love towards our neighbour was his predominant theme, and his efforts produced abundant fruits. His happiness, however, was not of long duration. M. de Bossuet died, and Providence had decreed new trials for M. de l'Epée. About this time M. de Soanen was persecuted for holding the religious principles of the Jansenists; and his friend, M. de l'Epée, who held the same opinions as this virtuous prelate, was included in the same interdiction. Never was there a devotion less offensive, or a creed more tolerant than that professed by this worthy man. His eulogist says of him : " He spoke rarely to persons of a different opinion of the objects of their faith. When he was led into such subjects, his discussions never degenerated into disputes; he had the talent of keeping them within the boundary of those agreeable conversations where confidence reigns."

Circumstances apparently accidental, which will be related, led M. de l'Epée to devote himself to the wants of the deaf and dumb. In earlier times a few learned individuals had bestowed some attention upon the means of educating this unfortunate class of mankind, but they had done this philosophically rather than practically. One of the first of these experimenters was Pedro de Ponce, a Benedictine monk of Leon, who lived between the years 1520 and 1584. Paul Bonet, also a Spaniard, taught several deaf and dumb persons, and published the first known work on the subject in 1620. A relation of his success has been left us from the pen of Sir Kenelm Digby. Bonet's work was accompanied by a manual alphabet, from which

O 2

the one now used on the Continents of Europe and America was derived. In England, John Bulwer published his "Philocophus, or the Deaf and Dumb Man's Friend," in the year 1648. In 1653, Dr. Wallis appeared as an author on the same subject; he was succeeded by Dr. Holder, George Sibscota, and George Dalgarno. The latter published his "Didascalocophus, or Deaf and Dumb Man's Tutor," in 1680. During the same period the attention of several individuals in various parts of Europe was directed to a similar object; the most distinguished of whom was John Conrad Amman, a Swiss physician, who resided at Leyden.

It is not our province here to describe the various methods pointed out by these scientific philanthropists; we have mentioned their labours merely with the view of showing that the art was not altogether unknown to the learned of various countries previous to the time of the Abbé de l'Epée. France was the last to commence this labour of science and charity. It has, however, good cause to be proud of its successful efforts in the great work. It has produced a De l'Epée, a Sicard, a Bébian, and a De Gerando, all energetic labourers in the same vineyard; and its disinterested beneficence in our own days has done enough to perpetuate its name above all nations, in the hearts of those for whom its exertions have been called forth.

The following incident first directed M. de l'Epée's attention to the great work which became afterward the leading object of his life. It is said by M. Bébian, that, up to this period, he possessed no knowledge of the attempts previously made for

the instruction of the deaf; and we shall presently
give the abbé's own account of the first works on
the art which came under his notice. Business
took him one day to a house where he found only
two young women: they were occupied in needle-
work, which seemed to engross all their attention.
He addressed himself to them, but they did not answer, and their eyes continued fixed upon their
work. He questioned them again, but still obtained no reply. At this he was much surprised, being
ignorant that the two sisters were deaf and dumb.
The mother arrived soon after, and explained
to him, with tears, the nature of their infirmity and
of her sorrow. An ecclesiastic, named Vanin, had
commenced the education of these young perso us
by means of pictures. Death having taken away
from them this charitable man, they remained without farther assistance, no person being willing to
continue a task so difficult, and apparently so uncertain in its results. "Believing," says M. de
l'Epée, "that these two children would live and
die in ignorance of their religion if I did not attempt some means of instructing them, I was touched with compassion, and told the mother that she
might send them daily to my house, and that I
would do whatever I might find possible for them."
The pictures of Father Vanin he found to be a
feeble and unsatisfactory resource: the apparent
successes obtained by means of articulation had
not solidity enough to seduce his philosophical
mind. But he had not forgotten that, at the age
of sixteen, in a conversation with his tutor, who
was an excellent metaphysician, the latter had
proved to him this incontestable principle: that

there is no more natural connexion between metaphysical ideas and the inarticulated sounds which
strike the ear, than between these same ideas and
the written characters which strike the eye. He
also recollected that his tutor drew this immediate
conclusion from his premises—that it was as possible to instruct the deaf and dumb by writing, always accompanied by visible signs, as to teach
other men by words delivered orally, along with
gestures indicative of their signification. "How
little did I then think," says M. de l'Epée, "that
Providence was thus laying the foundation of the
work for which I was destined!" From that period he devoted himself exclusively to the work
which he had now commenced; and while some
people smiled at his endeavours, he found in this
new occupation his chief happiness. A respectable
minister, after being present at one of his lessons,
said to him, "I formerly pitied you, I now pity
you no longer; you are restoring to society and to
religion beings who have been strangers to both."
The sanguine temperament and zeal of M. de
l'Epée led him into some errors, particularly that
very pardonable one of supposing his pupils to understand more than they really did understand.
His report of their rapid advancement as compared with the actual practice of modern times, shows
this; but with a less active mind and with less
zeal, he would never have succeeded in awakening
the public feeling to the important object of his
life, nor ever have overcome the opposition of other
teachers, and of minds less generous than his own.

"One day," says M. de l'Epée, "a stranger came
to our public lesson, and, offering me a Spanish

book, he said that it would be a real service to the
owner if I would purchase it. I answered that, as
I did not understand the language, it would be totally useless to me ; but, opening it casually, what
should I see but the manual alphabet of the Span-
iards neatly executed in copper-plate ! I wanted
no farther inducement ; I paid the messenger his
demand, and kept the book. I then became impatient for the conclusion of the lesson ; and what
was my surprise when I found this title, *Arte para
enseñar á hablar los Mudos !* I had little difficulty
to guess that this signified *The Art of Teaching the
Dumb to Speak,* and I immediately resolved to acquire the Spanish language for the benefit of my
pupils."

Soon after meeting with this work of Bonet, he
heard of Amman's *Dissertatio de loquelâ Surdorum
et Mutorum,* in the library of a friend. Conducted
by the light of these two excellent guides, De l'Epée
continued his task with a success which quite satisfied himself.

It will be well, in the present Memoir, to touch
but lightly upon the disputes which agitated the
learned in France and Germany when the partial
success of the Abbé de l'Epée became generally
known. We cannot but give praise to the abbé
for the openness and candour with which he made
known his experience and his views ; and if his arguments to prove the superior excellence of his own
method appear unsatisfactory and inconclusive to
the enlarged experience of the present day, such
arguments ought to be viewed as those of a zeal-
ous-minded teacher of an art yet in the first stages
of its infancy. Had his antagonist M. Heinich,

the Leipsic teacher, been as communicative respecting his plans as his liberal opponent, good might have resulted from this learned warfare : as it was, to the satisfaction of almost-everybody, the Abbé de l'Epée was left master of the field, and received compliments from all quarters, among which should be especially noticed the "Decision" of the Academy of Zurich in his favour.

The chief fault in the system of the Abbé de l'Epée seems to have consisted in its being the philosophy of the master not sufficiently lowered to the comprehension of the pupil : a common error for master-minds to fall into. The pupil might mechanically translate methodical signs into language, without knowing the ideas intended to be conveyed by such signs and by such language. Has not this always been a fault among the instructers of youth ? and do not our school-books of the present day contain sufficient evidence of this failing ? Before the time of Pestalozzi it was scarcely dreamed of, that the teacher should exchange places with the learner ; that he should suffer himself to be led by his pupil to a certain point, in order that he may thus commence his superstructure on the foundation already formed ; that he should ascertain the manner in which infantine impressions are received, and become acquainted with the bent and genius of his pupil, to enable him to determine upon the best mode of rendering his lessons beneficial, so as to correct that which is erroneous, and develop that which is hidden. This is the "true method of instructing the deaf and dumb," and not less the true method of instructing children gifted with all their faculties. If the good abbé committed only that error which was common in his generation, and which is still too common in ours ; if he taught words instead of ideas, what did he more than others ? This is still the great fault in our seminaries of learning.

The number of children at different periods under the care of the Abbé de l'Epée was considerable. We read in one part of his writings of six hundred and eight pupils having been at various times under instruction, and this was written several years before he closed his career of usefulness. Again we are told of upward of sixty pupils being under his care at one time. All this was done *for the poor*, unaided by any pecuniary means except his own patrimony. It is stated that the income which the Abbé de l'Epée inherited from his father amounted to about £400 sterling ($1900) ; of this sum he allowed about £100 per annum for his own expenses ; and the remainder he considered as the inheritance of his adopted children——the indigent deaf and dumb—to whose use it was faithfully applied. " The rich," says he, " only come to my house by tolerance ; it is not to them that I devote myself——it is to the poor ; and but for these I should never have undertaken the education of the deaf and dumb." There was no kind of privation which he did not impose on himself for the sake of his pupils. In order to supply their wants, he limited his own. So strictly did he adhere to the appropriation which he had made of his income, that, in the rigorous winter of 1788, when suffering under the infirmities of age, he denied himself fuel, in order not to encroach upon the moderate sum to which he limited his annual expenditure. All the remonstrances of his friends on this point were fruitless. His housekeeper having observed his rigid restriction, and doubtless imputing it to its real motive, led into his apartment his forty pupils, who conjured him to preserve himself for their sakes. He yielded, not without difficulty, to their persuasions, but afterward reproached himself for this concession. Having exceeded his ordinary expenditure by about 300 livres (about $58), he would afterward exclaim in the midst of his pupils, "My poor children, I have wronged you of a hundred crowns!"

With that liberality which ever characterizes the true friend of mankind, the good abbé formed preceptors for many institutions. Germany, Switzerland, Italy, Spain, Holland, and many other countries participated in the benefits which were being conferred on the deaf-mutes of Paris.

It is worthy of remark, that two of the most distinguished sovereigns of that day encouraged the labours of the Abbé de l'Epée—Catharine II., empress of Russia, and Joseph II., emperor of Germany. In 1780 the ambassador of Catharine waited upon the abbé to congratulate him in her name, and to offer him rich presents from that sovereign, who knew how to appreciate whatever was truly great. "My lord," said the abbé, "I never receive gold; tell her majesty that, if my labours have appeared to her to claim her esteem, all that I ask is that she will send me a deaf and dumb person, or a master to be instructed in this art of teaching." The Emperor Joseph bestowed a still more flattering notice upon these labours. After witnessing the success of the Abbé de l'Epée, he re-

solved to found in his own dominions an institution
so necessary to the wants of his subjects. During
two hours and a half, the qualifications attainable
by the deaf and dumb, when their powers have been
properly developed, were attentively regarded by
the emperor, who had in his thoughts a young lady
of high birth at Vienna in this deplorable state,
whose parents wished to give her a Christian education. On being consulted as to the measures to
be taken for this end, the abbé offered either to ed-
ucate the young lady gratuitously if she were
brought to Paris, or to instruct any intelligent person who might be sent to him in the method to be
pursued. The emperor accepted the latter proposal, as it opened the prospect of permanent relief for others of his subjects who might be in the
same affecting circumstances. On his return to
Vienna he addressed a highly flattering letter to
M. de l'Epée by the Abbé Storch, the person whom
he selected for introducing the education of deaf-
mutes into his dominions. The Abbé Storch is
spoken of by the Abbé de l'Epée as " filled with the
purest sacerdotal spirit, and amply endowed with
every talent his mission could require." A royal
institution for deaf-mutes was accordingly founded
at Vienna, which was the first national establishment ever erected for the deaf and dumb.

A subject of painful and anxious interest occupied the thoughts of the Abbé de l'Epée during his
declining years. He had solicited from government an endowment to perpetuate his institution
after his own death, but he obtained only promises.
However, he knew that his art would exist in
Vienna if it should be forgotten at Paris, and this

gave him some consolation. When the Emperor
Joseph visited his institution, he expressed his astonishment, that a man so deserving had not obtained at least an abbey, whose revenues he might
apply to the wants of the deaf and dumb. He
offered to ask one for him, and even to give him
one in his own dominions. " I am already old,"
said M. de l'Epée : " if your majesty wishes well
to the deaf and dumb, it is not on *my* head, already
bending to the tomb, that the benefit must fall, it
is on the work itself."

M. de l'Epée found, however, some feeling hearts
in France. Many masters, taught by him, carried
the fruits of his instructions into different cities in
that kingdom, as well as into foreign countries.
At Bordeaux an establishment had been formed by
the archbishop, M. de Cicé, which owed its celebrity to its instructer, the Abbé Sicard, a young
priest who had been sent to learn the theory and
practice of the method employed by the illustrious
teacher at Paris. It is said by De Gerando that
" the pupil soon became acquainted with his master's views, and seized them with enthusiasm."
He was eminently calculated to appreciate their
value. Gifted with a vivid and fertile imagination,
he had a singular ability in clothing abstract notions in sensible forms ; he had a particular talent
for that pantomime which is the proper language
of the deaf-mute, and which the Abbé de l'Epée
had proposed to carry to a high degree of development in his system of methodic signs ; endowed
also with an enterprising and flexible mind, he
would search for and discover new and various
modes of expressing and explaining ideas and pre-

cepts. He appeared, indeed, to possess a kind of natural talent for communicating with deaf-mutes.

This was the man who was destined to succeed M. de l'Epée. His talents and his virtues proved him to be worthy of receiving that inheritance of glory and of beneficence. His successes filled his master with joy, who, in the overflowing of his hopes, said to him one day, " Mon ami, j'ai trouvé le verre, c'est à vous d'en faire les lunettes"—(*I have found the glass, my friend; it is for you to make the spectacles*). A testimony as honourable to the modesty of the one as to the talent of the other. Sicard was in full possession of his master's ideas; and amply has he developed and extended them by his own clear and analytical mind.

If the Abbé de l'Epée was not the first inventor of a system for teaching the deaf and dumb, he was the first who benefited society by any extensive application of the discovery. We hesitate not to assert that he was an inventor of great merit, particularly as regards those details which made the discovery of service to those for whose instruction it was designed. Previous to his time it had been discussed rather as a possible than as an extensively practicable art; and the few persons who had been before instructed must be considered rather as the results of experiments to test philosophical principles than as pupils regularly and systematically taught.

The Abbé de l'Epée died December 23, 1789, and the Abbé Fauchet, preacher to the king, pronounced his funeral oration. But, next to his mute eulogists in all countries, M. de Bébian and M. Bouilly have been the means of making his

fame and his merits most extensively known to the
world. From their writings much of the present
memoir is derived. M. de Seine, a deaf-mute pupil of the Abbé de l'Epée, wrote the following dis-
tich, to be placed under the bust of his benevolent
teacher :

"Il révèle à la fois secrets merveilleux,
De parler par les mains, d'entendre par les yeux"—
*He reveals at the same time these marvellous secrets—to speak with
the hands, and hear with the eyes.*

MOZART.

THAT most of those who are now by universal
consent numbered among the benefactors of the
human race, reaped little benefit from their genius,
however actively exerted, is a melancholy truth
not to be disputed, and seldom more strongly exemplified than in the instance of the great composer who is the subject of this memoir. He to
whom all the really civilized parts of the world are
so deeply indebted for the increase, to an almost
incalculable amount, of the stock of an intellectual
and innocent pleasure, scarcely ever enjoyed a moment's respite from ill-requited labour and corro-
ding anxieties: few, not in a state of actual want,
ever suffered more from the evils of poverty ; and
he who left so valuable a treasure to mankind had
not, in the hour of death, the consolation of feeling
that he had been able to secure against the mis-
eries of dependance an affectionate wife and her
helpless offspring.

JOHANN - CHRYSOSTOMUS - WOLFGANG - GOTTLIEB MOZART was born at Salzburg, January 20, 1756. His father, Leopold, was sub-chapelmaster, or organist, to the Prince-archbishop of Salzburg, and a skilful performer on the violin, a valuable treatise on which instrument he published in quarto, under the title of "Violinschule," in 1769. Whatever time the duties of his office left at his disposal, he devoted to the education of his two children, and he began to give his daughter, who was four years older than her brother, instructions on the harpsichord, when the latter had scarcely completed his third year. The boy's strong disposition for music then immediately developed itself; his delight was to seek out *thirds* on the instrument, and his joy was unbounded when he succeeded in discovering one of these harmonious concords.

When Wolfgang had attained his fourth year, says M. Schlichtegroll, his father began, though hardly in earnest, to teach him a few minuets and other short pieces of music. It took the child half an hour to learn a minuet, and proportionably more time to master compositions of greater length. In less than two years he had made such progress that he invented short pieces of music, which his father, to encourage such promising talent, committed to writing. It is to be regretted that not one of these curious manuscripts, if preserved, has ever been produced. Before he began to manifest a predilection for music, his amusements were like those of other children; and so ardent was he in the pursuit of them, that he would willingly have sacrificed his meals rather than be interrupted in his enjoyment. His great sensibility was observable as soon as he could make his feelings understood. Frequently he said to those about him, " Do you love me well ?" and when in sport he was answered in the negative, tears immediately began to flow. He pursued everything with extraordinary ardour. While learning the elements of arithmetic, the tables, chairs, even the walls, bore in chalk the marks of his calculations. And here it will not be irrelevant to state—what we believe has never yet appeared in print—that his talent for the science of numbers was only inferior to that for music ; had he not been distinguished by genius of a higher order, it is probable that his calculating powers would have been sufficiently remarkable to bring him into general notice.

When under six years of age Mozart surprised his father, though well accustomed to these premature manifestations of musical genius, by the production of a concerto for the harpsichord, written in every respect according to rule, the only objection to which was its difficulty of execution. This circumstance at once determined Leopold Mozart to let the youthful prodigy be seen at some of the courts of Germany. He therefore carried his whole family, as soon as Wolfgang had completed his sixth year, to Munich, where they were received by the Elector in so flattering a manner, that the party returned to Salzburg to prepare for other visits. In 1762 they proceeded to Vienna and performed at court. Here Mozart, when sitting down to play, said to the Emperor Francis I., " Is not M. Wagenseil here ? He ought to be present ; he understands such matters." The emperor sent for M. Wagenseil. "Sir," said the child to the composer, "I shall play one of your concertos—you must turn the leaves for me." About the same time a small violin was purchased for him, merely for his amusement; but, while it was supposed to be little more than a toy in his hands, he made himself so far a master of the instrument, that when Wenzl, the violinist, brought his newly-composed trios to Leopold Mozart for his opinion, Wolfgang supplicated to be allowed to take the second violin part, and accomplished the task as much to the satisfaction of the composer as to the wonder of all.

In 1763 the Mozart family commenced an extended tour, giving concerts in the principal cities through which they passed. In Paris they continued five months, and Wolfgang performed on the organ in the royal chapel in presence of the whole court. There he composed and published his first two works, which, compared with other productions of the day, are by no means trivial. In April, 1764, the party arrived in London, where they remained till the middle of the following year. Here, as in France, the boy exhibited his talents before the royal family, and underwent more severe trials than any to which he had before been exposed, through which he passed in a most triumphant manner. So much interest did he excite in London, that the Hon. Daines Barrington drew up an account of his extraordinary performances, which was read before the Royal Society, and declared by the council of that body to be sufficiently interesting and important to form a part of the Philosophical Transactions, in the seventieth volume of which it is published. But, some suspicions having been entertained by many persons that the declared was not the real age of the youthful prodigy, Mr. Barrington obtained, through Count Haslang, then Bavarian minister at the British court, a certificate of Wolfgang's birth, signed by the chaplain of the Archbishop of Salzburg, which at once dispelled all doubts on the subject.

In 1765 the family returned to the Continent. At the Hague, where Mozart published six sonatas, they remained some months; then paid a second long visit to Paris, and, passing through Switzerland, reached Salzburg in 1768. Some time after the children performed at Vienna before Joseph II., by whose desire Mozart composed an entire opera, *La finta Sposa.* Hasse and Metastasio both bestowed great commendations on the work, but it never was produced on the stage; and the probability is, that its merit was only of a relative kind.

In 1769 Mozart (in his fourteenth year!) was appointed director of the Archbishop of Salzburg's concerts. Shortly after, he proceeded with his father to Italy, where he was received with enthusiasm. At Rome he gave a proof of memory which is still a subject of conversation in that city. He heard the famous Miserere of Allegri in the pontifical chapel; and knowing that the pope's singers were forbidden, under pain of excommunication, to furnish a copy, or allow one, under any plea, to be taken, he gave his utmost attention to the composition during its performance, wrote it down when he returned home, and exultingly carried it with him to Germany. While in Italy the pope invested him with the order of the Golden Spur. At Bologna he was unanimously elected a member of the Philharmonic Academy. He reached Milan in October, 1770, and in the following December gave his second opera, Mitridate, which had a run of twenty nights. In 1773 he composed another serious opera, Lucio Silla; this was performed twenty-six nights successively. He produced many other works of various kinds between that year and 1779, when he fixed his residence permanently at Vienna.

In his twenty-fifth year he was captivated by Madlle. Constance Weber, an amiable, accomplished, and celebrated actress, to whom he soon made a proposal of marriage. This was courteously declined by her family, on the ground that his reputation was not then sufficiently established. Upon this he composed his Idomeneo, in order to prove what means were at his command; and, animated by the strongest passion that ever entered his heart, produced an opera which he always considered his highest effort: certainly it was the first that showed his positive strength. Parts of it are in his most original and grandest manner; but parts show that he had not quite emancipated himself from the thraldom of custom. Some of the airs, though far superior to those of his contemporaries, are too much in the opera style then prevailing, a style now become nearly obsolete; and when, a few years ago, it was wished to bring out Idomeneo at the King's Theatre, it became evident that, if performed as originally written, its success would be very doubtful. To Madlle. Weber, on whom the composer's affections were unalterably fixed, was assigned the principal character in the opera, and the high reputation which the author acquired by his work having immediately silenced the objections of Constance's family, her hand was shortly after the reward of his efforts.

In 1782 Mozart composed Die Entführung aus dem Serail (L'Enlévement du Sérail), and here it is evident that he had entirely broken the fetters which before he had only loosened. Here is exhibited that style which, in an improved state, afterward characterized all his dramatic works. It was on the first representation of this opera that Joseph II. remarked to the composer, "All this may be very fine, but there are too many notes for our ears." To which Mozart, with that independent spirit which always characterized him, replied, "There are, sire, just as many as there ought to be." Le Nozze di Figaro—second in merit only to Don Giovanni, if to that—was produced in 1786, by command of the emperor, and by whose authority alone an Italian conspiracy against it was suppressed.

In 1787 appeared, first at Prague, the *chef-d'œuvre* of Mozart, his Don Giovanni, which was received with enthusiasm by the Bohemians, but at that time, and, indeed, years after, was above the comprehension of the Viennese public, whose taste, unlike that which prevails in the north of Germany, still inclines them to prefer the nerveless, meager compositions of Italy. "This matchless work of its immortalized author" never found its way to the London stage till the year 1817, when it was performed in a manner that surpassed all former representations, and has never since been equalled. The production of Don Giovanni in London was so strenuously opposed by an Italian cabal, that, but for the courage and perseverance of the director of that season, it would have been put aside, even after all the expense of getting up and trouble of rehearsing had been incurred. The charming comic opera, Cosi fan tutti, was composed in 1790; Die Zauberflöte and La Clemenza di Tito, in 1791; the latter for the coronation of Leopold II.

The last, and, taken as the whole, the most sublime work of Mozart, his Requiem, was written on his death-bed; and, having been left in rather an unfinished state, his pupil, Süssmayer, filled up some of the accompaniments. This circumstance led, a few years ago, to a dispute concerning its authorship, some indiscreet friends of the latter having claimed as his composition the best parts of the mass. The assertions by which the claim was supported, and the arguments in its favour, proved unavailing against the internal evidence which the work afforded, and it is to be presumed that the controversy will never be renewed. A story, too, that an anonymous, mysterious stranger commissioned Mozart to compose the Requiem, raised many idle conjectures, some of them of the most grossly superstitious kind. The matter, however, has latterly been very satisfactorily explained.*

This illustrious composer, on whom nature bestowed so much vigour of imagination, but so little physical strength, never seemed destined to attain longevity. Slightly constructed, and feeble in constitution, he required more mental repose than his necessities would allow. His mind did not yield, but his body gave way; and on the 5th of December, 1792, prematurely worn out, he expired, thor-

* See Harmonicon, vol. iv., page 102.

oughly exhausted, without any appearance of organic disease.

It has been said of Mozart that his knowledge was bounded by his art, and that, detached from this, he was little better than a nonentity. That his thoughts were almost wholly bent on music was not a matter of choice, but of necessity. Had not his miserably-remunerated labours occupied nearly all his time, his means would have been still more limited than they were. But we have reason to think that his acquirements were far greater than is generally believed; in proof of which, we have the best authority for saying, that once, at a court masquerade given at Vienna, Mozart appeared as a physician, and wrote prescriptions in Latin, French, Italian, and German; in which not only an acquaintance with the several languages was shown, but great discernment of character, and considerable wit. Assuming this to be true, he could not have been a very ignorant man, nor always a dull one, out of his profession. But still stronger evidence in favour of his understanding may be extracted from his works. That he who, in his operas, adapted his music with such felicity to the different persons of the drama; who evinced such nicety of discrimination; who represented the passions so accurately; who coloured so faithfully; whose music is so expressive that, without the aid of words, it is almost sufficient to render the scene intelligible; that such a man should not have been endowed with a high order of intellect, is hard to be believed; but that his understanding should have been below mediocrity is incredible.

The compositions of Mozart are of every kind,

and so numerous that we cannot pretend to give even a bare list of them.   But it may be observed, generally, that from the sonata to the symphony, from the simplest romance to the most elaborate musical drama, he—whose career was stopped before he had completed his thirty-sixth year—composed in every imaginable style, and excelled in all. In each class he furnished models of the greatest attainable excellence : " exquisite melodies, profound harmonies, the playful, the tender, the pathetic, and the sublime," are to be found among his works.   It is the exclusive privilege of first-rate merit to be more admired as it is better known ; and, while inferior composers enjoy their day of fashion and are forgotten, Mozart's fame will continue to expand in proportion as mankind advances in taste and knowledge.

SIR W. JONES.

WILLIAM JONES, the most accomplished Oriental scholar of the last century, an upright magistrate, and eminent benefactor of the native subjects of the English empire in India, was born in London, on Michaelmas Eve, 1746.   His father, a man esteemed by his contemporaries, a skilful mathematician, and the friend of Newton, died in July, 1749. His mother then devoted herself entirely to the education of this her only surviving son ; and to her careful and judicious culture of his infant years,

VOL. II.—Q

bestowed, indeed, upon a happy soil, is to be ascribed the early development of that thirst for learning and faculty for profitable application, which enabled Jones to accumulate, in a short and busy life,
a quantity and variety of abstruse knowledge, such
as the same age does not often see equalled.   To
the end of her life he acknowledged and repaid her
care and affection by ardent love and unchanging
filial respect.   When only seven years old he was
sent to Harrow.   His progress, slow at first, afterward became most rapid ; and the head master,
Dr. Thackeray, a man not given to praise, spoke
of him as "a boy of so active a mind, that, if he
were left naked and friendless on Salisbury Plain,
he would find the way to fame and riches."
   At the time of his quitting school, besides a much
deeper acquaintance with the classical languages
than usually falls to the lot of a schoolboy, Jones
had acquired the French and Italian languages,
had commenced the study of Hebrew, and (a thing
only worth mention as indicative of his tastes) had
made himself acquainted with the Arabic letters.
Botany, the collection of fossils, and composition
in English verse, were his favourite amusements at
this period.   March 16, 1764, he was entered as
a student of University College, Oxford.   He was
elected a scholar on the Bennet foundation, October 30, 1764 ; and fellow on the same foundation,
August 7, 1766, before he was of standing to proceed to the degree of B.A., which he took in 1768.
At an early period of his residence he applied in
earnest to the study of Arabic ; and his zeal was
such, that, though habitually self-denying, and anxious not to trespass on his mother's slender in-

come, he maintained at Oxford, at his own expense, a Syrian, with whom he had become acquainted in London, for the benefit to be derived from his instruction. From the Arabic he proceeded to learn the Persian language.

His residence was changed, though his favourite studies do not appear to have been interrupted, by an invitation to undertake the care of the late Lord Spencer, then a boy of seven years old. This was in 1765. The next five years he spent with his pupil chiefly at Harrow, and occasionally at Althorp, or in London, or on the Continent. It appears from the college books that he resided at Oxford very little in the years 1766, 1767, and 1768. But, wherever he was, his time was diligently employed, not only in severer studies, but in the pursuit of personal accomplishments and the cultivation of valuable acquaintances, especially with those who, like himself, were attached to the investigation of Eastern languages and science. In 1768 he received a high but an unprofitable compliment, in being selected to render into French a Persian Life of Nadir Shah, transmitted to the English government by the King of Denmark for the purpose of translation. To this performance, which was printed in 1770, Mr. Jones added a " Treatise on Oriental Poetry," in which several of the odes of Hafiz are translated into verse. This also was written in French ; and it has justly been observed by a French writer in the " Biographie Universelle," that the occurrence of some imperfections of style ought not to interfere with our forming a high estimate of the talents of a man who, at the age of twenty-two, possessed the varied qualifications and recondite acquirements displayed in this work. By the end of the same year, 1770, the author finished his "Coummentaries on Asiatic Poetry," a Latin treatise, which, for its style, is commended by the competent authority of Dr. Parr; and which has also obtained high praise for the taste and judgment displayed in selecting and translating the passages by which the text is illustrated. It was not printed till 1774.

Not the least striking part of Mr. Jones's character was an ardent love of liberty, and a high and honourable feeling of independence in his own person. The former was displayed in his open and fearless advocacy of opinions calculated to close the road to preferment, such as an entire disapprobation of the American war, and a strong feeling of the necessity of reform in parliament. It should also be noticed, that at an early period he denounced in energetic language the abomination of the slave trade. His personal love of independence was at that time manifested in his resolution to quit the certain road to ease and competence which his connexion with the noble family of Spencer presented before him, to embark in the brilliant but uncertain course of legal adventure. Ambition was a prominent feature in Jones's character; and it was his hope and his earnest wish to distinguish himself in the House of Commons as well as at the bar. He was admitted of the Middle Temple November 19, 1770; and his Oriental studies, though not entirely abandoned, especially at first, was thenceforth much curtailed, until the prospect of being appointed to a judicial office in India furnished an adequate reason for the resumption of them. But he gave a proof that his devotion to Oriental had not destroyed his taste for Grecian learning, by publishing, in 1778, a translation of the "Orations of Isæus," relative to the laws of succession to property in Athens. The subject appears to have interested him; for in 1782, when his attention was again directed to the East, he published translations of two Arabian poems; one on the Mohammedan law of succession to the property of intestates, the other on the Mohammedan law of inheritance. About the same time he translated the seven ancient Arabian poems, called Moallakat, or "Suspended," because they had been hung up, in honour of their merit, in the Temple of Mecca; and to show, perhaps, that his attention had not been withdrawn from his immediate profession, he wrote an "Essay on the Law of Bailments."

Mr. Jones was called to the bar in 1774. Within two years' space he obtained a commissionership of bankrupts; by what influence does not appear, but it could not have been from any professional eminence. A letter, written to Lord Althorp so early as October, 1778, intimates a wish to obtain some judicial appointment in India, not only in consequence of the interest which he had felt from an early age in everything connected with the East, but from a motive which has sent other eminent men to the same unhealthy climate—a feeling that pecuniary independence was almost essential to success in political life, and the hope of returning in the prime of manhood with an honourable competence.

In 1780 Mr. Jones became a candidate to represent the University of Oxford. His political opinions were not calculated to win the favour of that learned body, and, though respectably supported, he did not find encouragement to warrant him in coming to a poll. From this time forward his mind was much occupied by the thought of going to India. His letters contain frequent allusions to the subject, and express doubt whether, notwithstanding the personal friendship of Lord North, his own views of politics, especially his often and strongly-declared reprobation of the American war, would not interfere with his obtaining the desired promotion. The event proved him to be right; for it was not until after the formation of the Shelburne ministry that he received information of his appointment to a seat in the Supreme Court of Judicature at Calcutta, March 3, 1783. For this he was indebted to the friendship of Lord Ashburton (Mr. Dunning). The state of uncertainty in which he was so long retained interfered considerably with his attention to his legal practice, which was rapidly increasing. He was the more anxious on this subject, inasmuch as he had been long attached to Miss Shipley, daughter of the Bishop of St. Asaph; and his union with her was only deferred until professional success should place him in a fit station to support a family. His marriage took place in April, and in the same month he embarked for India. It remains to be noticed, that in 1782 Mr. Jones had written an essay, entitled "The Principles of Government," in a dialogue between a farmer and country gentleman, intended to express, in a cheap and simple form, his own views on constitutional questions. This was first printed by the Society for Constitutional Information, of which the author was a member: it was reprinted by his brother-in-law, the Dean of St. Asaph, who was, in consequence, indicted for libel. In the prosecution which ensued, Mr. Erskine made one of his first and most remarkable efforts; and the series of speeches which he delivered in this case prepared the way for the Libel Bill of 1792.

Sir William Jones arrived in Calcutta in September, and entered on his judicial functions in December, 1783. One of his first employments was the organization of a scientific association, under the title of the Asiatic Society. The Governor-general, Warren Hastings, was requested to become president; and on his declining to accept, as an honorary distinction, an office, the real duties of which he was unable to fulfil, Sir William Jones was fitly placed at the head of that institution, which, but for him, would probably have never existed. The transactions of that society, under the name of "Asiatic Researches," were published under his superintendence, and owe a large portion of their interest to the labours of his pen. Another work, the "Asiatic Miscellany," was also indebted to him for several valuable contributions. But the perfect acquisition of the Sanscrit language was the chief employment of that time which could be spared from his judicial labours: a task, indeed, subsidiary to those labours, and performed with the benevolent design of ensuring to the Indian subjects of Britain a pure administration of justice, by rendering the knowledge of their laws accessible to British magistrates. Bound to adjudicate between the natives according to their own native laws, and ignorant, for the most part, of the very language in which those laws were written, the judges were obliged to have recourse to native lawyers, called Pundits, who were regularly attached to the courts as a species of assessors. Of these men Sir W. Jones, no harsh or hasty reprover, says, " It would be unjust and absurd to pass indiscriminate censure on so considerable a body of men ; but my experience justifies me in declaring that I could not, with an easy conscience, concur in a decision merely on the written opinion of native lawyers, in a case in which they could have the remotest interest in misleading the court." The obvious remedy was to obtain a trustworthy digest of the Hindoo laws, which should then be accurately translated into English. The scheme, indeed, had been already undertaken in part, at the desire of Mr. Hastings, by Mr. Halhed ; but as the code of Hindoo law compiled by that gentleman was merely a translation from a defective Persian version of the original Sanscrit, it did not possess the requisite correctness or authority. It appears from Sir W. Jones's correspondence, that at an early period he had contemplated supplying this great desideratum by his own labour and at his own expense. But prudence did not warrant such an uncalled-for act of liberality ; and he addressed a letter to Lord Cornwallis, dated March 19, 1788, in which the necessity for such a work, and the means by which it might be executed, are fully laid down. It was to be compiled by the Mohammedan or Hindoo lawyers, working under the superintendence of a director and translator, who should be qualified to check and correct intentional or careless error ; and a chief difficulty, in Sir W. Jones's own words, was " to find a person who, with a competent knowledge of the Sanscrit and Arabic, has a general acquaintance with the principles of jurisprudence, and a sufficient share even of legislative spirit, to arrange the plan of a digest, superintend the compilation of it, and render the whole, as it proceeds, into perspicuous English. Now," he continues, " though I am truly conscious of possessing a very moderate portion of those talents which I should require in the superintendent of such a work, yet I may, without vanity, profess myself equal to the labour of it ; and I cannot but know that the qualifications required, even in the low degree in which I possess them, are not often found united in the same person." The proposal, of course, was eagerly accepted. That he should have acquired the necessary acquaintance, first with the language, then with the law, in the space of four years and a half, is sufficiently remarkable ; and the method in which he proposed to execute it will startle those who know the enervating influence of a tropical climate. " I should be able," he says, " if my health continued firm, to translate every morning, before any other business is begun, as much as the lawyers could compile, and the writers copy, in the preceding day." The quantity of work which Jones did in India was, indeed, astonishing ; but he was a severe economist of time, and even his hours of recreation were rendered serviceable to the increase of knowledge. Botany especially was a favourite pursuit of his more leisure hours ; and his correspondence with Banks and others shows at once the zeal with which, when duty would permit, he followed that fascinating science, and the readiness with which he communicated his own discoveries to his friends, and laboured to answer their inquiries. Nor did he neglect poetry. Several odes to Hindoo deities, originally published in the Asiatic Miscellany, will be found in his works; and these, with an elegant and cultivated fancy, display considerable power of composition. He projected a still more serious undertaking, an epic poem, of which a Phœnician colonist of Britain was to be the hero, and the Hindoo mythology was to furnish the machinery; the whole being an allegorical panegyric on the British constitution, and furnishing the character of a perfect King of England. But the extravagant fictions of the Hindoo religion have never proved permanently popular in an English dress; and there is no reason to regret that this scheme never advanced beyond its first sketch. The author made a more acceptable present to European literature in translating "Sacontala, or the Fatal Ring," a very ancient Indian drama, which contains a lively, simple, and pleasing picture of the manners of Hindostan at a remote age. It is ascribed to the first century before Christ.

For a catalogue of Sir W. Jones's works, we must refer to the edition published by Lady Jones. We have only noticed a few of the most important: to which are to be added, the series of anniversary discourses addressed to the Asiatic Society, and the translation of the "Ordinances of Menu." The former, eleven in number, treat of the History, Antiquities, Arts, &c., of Asia, and more especially of the origin and connexion of the chief nations among whom that quarter of the globe is divided. His last work was the translation of the "Ordinances of Menu," "a system of duties" (we quote from the translator's preface), "religious and civil, and of law in all its branches, which the Hindoos firmly believe to have been promulged in the beginning of time by Menu, son or grandson of Brahma, or, in plain language, the first of created beings, and not the oldest only, but the holiest of legislators: a system so comprehensive and so minutely exact, that it may be considered as the Institutes of Hindoo law, preparatory to the copious Digest which has lately been compiled by Pundits of eminent learning." This was his last work. It was begun in 1786, though not completed and published till 1794, a short time before the author's death.

The private history of Sir William Jones, during the period of his life which he spent in India, affords very little scope for narration. During his first summer he nearly fell a victim to the climate; but an absence of seven months spent in travelling recruited his strength, and after his return to Calcutta in February, 1785, he seemed to be acclimated, and suffered little from serious illness till his last fatal attack. His domestic habits are thus described by his biographer, Lord Teignmouth. "The largest portion of each year was devoted to his professional duties and studies; and all the time that could be saved from these important avocations was dedicated to the cultivation of science and literature. While business required the daily attendance of Sir W. Jones in Calcutta, his usual resi-

dence was on the banks of the Ganges, at the distance of five miles from the court; to this spot he
returned every evening after sunset, and in the
morning rose so early as to reach his apartments
in town, by walking, at the first appearance of the
dawn. The intervening period of each morning,
until the opening of the court, was regularly allotted and applied to distinct studies. He passed the
months of vacation at his retirement at Crishnagur
(a villa about fifty miles from Calcutta) in his usual pursuits." Those portions of his correspondence which are preserved in Lord Teignmouth's
life may be read with pleasure; and, indeed, con-
stitute the chief interest of the latter part of the
work. Busy, tranquil, and cheerful, his life afforded little of material for the biographer; and, but
for the impaired health of his wife, his residence in
India would have been one of almost unmixed happiness. Lady Jones was compelled to embark for
England in December, 1793. The mere desire of
increasing a fortune, which he professed to find
already large enough for his moderate wishes,
would not have tempted Sir William Jones to remain alone in Bengal; but he felt an earnest desire to complete the great work on Hindoo Law
which he had originated; and no apprehension
was felt on his account, as his constitution seemed
to have become inured to the climate. But in the
following spring he was attacked by inflammation
of the liver, which ran its fatal course with unusual
rapidity. He died April 27, 1794. The "Digest,"
to which he had thus sacrificed his life, was completed by Mr. Colebrooke, and published in 1800.
    Blameless in his domestic relations, consistent

and enlightened in his political views, an honest
and indefatigable magistrate, few men have gone
through life with more credit, or, as far as it is
possible to form an opinion, with more happiness,
than Sir William Jones. As a scholar, the circumstances of his life being considered, his acquirements were extraordinary; and in this light
the most remarkable feature of his character was
his singular facility in learning languages. A list,
preserved in his own handwriting, thus classes
those with which he was in any degree acquainted; they are twenty-eight in number. " Eight languages studied critically—English, Latin, French,
Italian, Greek, Arabic, Persian, Sanscrit. Eight
studied less perfectly, but all intelligible with a dic-
tionary—Spanish, Portuguese, German, Runic, Hebrew, Bengalee, Hindoo, Turkish. Twelve studied
less perfectly, but all attainable—Thibetian, Páli,
Pahlair, Deri, Russian, Syriac, Ethiopic, Coptic,
Welsh, Swedish, Dutch, Chinese." Besides law,
which, as his profession, was his chief business
through life, his writings embrace a vast variety
of subjects in the several classes of philology, botany, zoology, poetry original and translated, political discussion, geography, mythology, astronomy,
as applied to chronology, and history, especially
that of the Asiatic nations. And the praise of
" adorning everything that he touched" is singularly
due to him for the elegance of his style, and his
power of throwing interest over the dry and uncertain inquiries in which he took such delight. As
far as England is concerned, he was her great
pioneer in Eastern learning; and if later scholars,
profiting in part by his labours, have found reason

to dissent from his opinions, it is to be recollected, as far as our estimate of his powers is concerned, that most men who have obtained eminence in this recondite department of literature, have done so by the devotion of their undivided powers : what Jones accomplished was performed, on the contrary, in the intervals of those official labours to which the best hours and energies of his life were, as his first point of duty, devoted. What he had meditated, if life and leisure had been granted, may be inferred from the list of "Desiderata," which his biographer (vol ii., p. 301, it is not said on what authority) regards as exhibiting his literary projects. The following emphatic panegyric, conceived in the warm language which affection naturally indulges in on such an occasion, has been pronounced on him by his friend and schoolfellow, Dr. Bennet, bishop of Cloyne : " I knew him from the early age of eight or nine, and he was always an uncommon boy. Great abilities, great particularity of thinking, fondness for writing verses and plays of various kinds, and a degree of integrity and manly courage, of which I remember many instances, distinguished him even at that period. I loved and revered him ; and, though one or two years older than he was, was always instructed by him from my earliest age. In a word, I can only say of this wonderful man, that he had more virtues and less faults than I ever yet saw in any human being ; and that the goodness of his head, admirable as it was, was exceeded by that of his heart. I have never ceased to admire him from the moment I first saw him ; and my esteem for his great qualities and regret for his loss will only end with my life."

Due honours were paid after death to this great man. The Court of Directors placed a statue of him in St. Paul's Cathedral; and Lady Jones erected a monument to him in the ante-chapel of University College, Oxford. In conformity with his own expressed opinion, that "the best monument that can be erected to a man of literary talent is a good edition of his works," she caused them to be collected and printed in 1799, in six quarto volumes. They have been reprinted in octavo. A life of Sir William Jones was afterward written by Lord Teignmouth, his intimate friend in India, at Lady Jones's request. There is a memoir in the Annual Obituary for 1817, which is chiefly devoted to set forth the political opinions of Sir William Jones in a stronger light than seemed fitting to his noble biographer.*

BURKE.

THE years which have elapsed since the death of Edmund Burke are not sufficient to secure a right and impartial sentence on his character. We are still within the heated temperature of the same political agitations in which he lived and struggled. We are not, perhaps our children will not be, qualified to judge him and his contemporaries with that calmness with which men weigh the

* For farther particulars of the labours and attainments of this extraordinary man, see Pursuit of Knowledge under Difficulties, vol. i., 88, Harpers' Family Library.—Am. Ed.

merits of things and persons who have exerted no perceptible influence over their own times. It is fortunate, therefore, that the limits of this brief Memoir prescribe rather a succinct statement of unquestioned facts, than a disputable adjudication between opposite opinions.

Edmund Burke, son of Richard Burke, an attorney in extensive practice in Dublin, was born in that city, January 1, 1730. Of his early life little is known with certainty. He appears to have distinguished himself at Trinity College, Dublin, by his acquirements and talents, especially by a decided taste and ability for the discussion of subjects relating to English history and politics. His first literary effort of any importance was made before he quitted that university, in some letters directed against a factious writer called Lucas, at that time the popular idol. These are not preserved. In 1750 he came to London, and was entered a student of the Middle Temple. It is singular that the idle rumour, expressly contradicted by himself, of his having completed his education at St. Omer's, should be still in some degree accredited by the author of the article "Burke," in the Biographie Universelle. Whether, in 1752 or 1753, he became a candidate for the chair of Logic at Glasgow, is a more doubtful question : the opinions of Dugald Stewart and Adam Smith, who took some pains to ascertain the truth, were in the negative. It is certain, however, that the extraordinary talents of Burke soon began to attract attention ; he wrote in many political and literary miscellanies, and formed an acquaintance with some distinguished characters of the time. Among these should be mentioned Lord Charlemont, Gerard Hamilton, Soame Jenyns, and, somewhat later, Goldsmith, Reynolds, Dr. Johnson, and Hume. His first avowed work, the "Vindication of Natural Society," was published in 1756, and excited very general admiration. The imitation of Bolingbroke's style in this essay was so perfect, that some admirers of the deceased philosopher are said to have overlooked the evident signs of irony, and to have believed it to be a genuine posthumous work. This may appear strange; but it is surely more strange, that forty years afterward this "Vindication" should have been republished by the French party, with a view of serving democratic interests. Before the close of 1756 appeared the "Philosophical Inquiry into the Origin of our Ideas of the Sublime and Beautiful," which added largely to Burke's reputation, and procured him the valuable friendship of Sir Joshua Reynolds. Shortly afterward, the public attention being at that time much directed to the American colonies, was published "An Account of the European Settlements in America," of which Burke was probably not the sole, though the principal author. It was much read, as well on the Continent as in England; and, indeed, no inconsiderable portion of it has been incorporated into the celebrated work of the Abbé Raynal. About this time Burke married the daughter of Dr. Nugent, an intelligent physician, who had invited him to his house while suffering under an illness, the result of laborious application. This union was a source of uninterrupted comfort to him through life. "Every care vanishes," he was in the habit of saying, "when I en-

R 2

ter my own home." ﹍ A confined income, however, rendered literary exertion still more indispensable to him than before; and in 1759 " The Annual Register," that most useful work, for many years entirely composed by Burke or under his immediate superintendence, was undertaken by him in conjunction with Dodsley. At length, in 1765, with the first Rockingham administration, he entered on a more extensive sphere of action, being appointed private secretary to the Marquis of Rockingham, through the recommendation of his friend Mr. Fitzherbert.

Coming now into Parliament as member for Wendover in Buckinghamshire, Burke became a distinguished supporter of the Whig party. The situation of affairs was critical. Mr. Grenville's stamp act, a fatal departure from the policy on which the colonies had been previously governed, had excited much discontent in America. A strong party, supported by the evident favour of the court and the general feeling of the country, urged the necessity of perseverance in this coercive policy. Lord Chatham and his adherents no less strenuously denied the right of the Imperial Legislature to impose taxes on America without her own consent. The Rockingham Whigs adopted a middle course between these extremes. They repealed the stamp act, declaring at the same time that the right of taxation resided inalienable in Parliament. Their administration was short-lived. Lord Chatham succeeded them in power, at the head of that " dove-tailed" cabinet which Burke has so admirably satirized in his " Speech on American Taxation." His influence was little more than nominal, and, in spite of it, schemes for raising a revenue in America were soon revived. From these measures the public attention was for a short time diverted by the domestic agitation caused by the proceedings against Wilkes, the disputed election in Middlesex, and the mysterious letters of Junius. The shadow of that name was at the time believed to rest on Burke ; a supposition long since rejected, and supported by scarce any evidence ; though his power as a writer, and his known facility in disguising his style, gave some degree of plausibility to the supposition. In his own name, and without any disguise, he came forward to attack the ministry of the Duke of Grafton, in a political treatise entitled " Thoughts on the Present Discontents." This has been termed the Whig Manual, and certainly contains the ablest exposition ever given of the principles held by that party for a long series of years. Shaken by this and other attacks, the duke retired, and left the state under the guidance of a minister whose merits have been overshadowed by the disastrous circumstances in which he was involved. From this time commenced that long and brilliant opposition, which, from a very low condition of numbers and influence, gradually worked its way through the most momentous parliamentary struggles ; and by a continued display of powers the most accomplished, and union the most effective, gained an ultimate victory, first over popular prepossessions, and then over royal obstinacy. The court party were so inferior in eloquence and genius, that their arguments are little remembered, while the speeches of the Whigs are in everybody's hands. They felt the importance of the

contest deeply, or they would not have been animated to their extraordinary exertions. But the
wisest of them could not foresee the prodigious extent of those consequences which, within the duration of their own lives, resulted from their endeavours. It was much for them to look forward to the
independence of America. What would it have
been to contemplate the spread of popular principles in Europe, and that mighty revolution which
has changed the balance of society? No member
of the opposition contributed so largely as Burke
to their final triumph. During the latter years of
the war, indeed, his fame as a debater was eclipsed
by the rising genius of Charles Fox, to whom he
willingly yielded the office of leader of the Whig
party. But the talents of Fox had been trained
and nourished by the wisdom of Burke; and in the
speeches published at different periods by the latter on American taxation [1774], and on conciliation with America [1775], and his "Letter to the
Sheriffs of Bristol" [1777] (written on the occasion of a temporary secession of the Rockingham
party in parliament), the friends of freedom found a
magazine of invaluable weapons. In 1774 Burke
was elected member of Parliament for Bristol; but
six years afterward he was unable to procure his
re-election for that borough, the people being displeased with his recent votes in favour of Irish
trade and of the Roman Catholics. His popularity was in a great measure restored by the famous
Bill of Economical Reform, brought forward by
him in 1782, when paymaster of the forces under
the second Rockingham ministry, after the overthrow of Lord North. The death of the Marquis

of Rockingham produced a schism among the Whigs : Lord Shelburne was appointed his successor, and the Rockingham division resigned their places. They soon returned to them, however, by means of that strange junction of force with Lord North, emphatically termed *The Coalition*, which raised a general cry of indignation throughout the country. Burke always vindicated this step, both at the time, and when the state of things which led to it had long passed away ; but it is generally supposed that he did not counsel it, and was only induced to give in his adhesion by the urgent entreaties of his political friends.

The celebrated East-India Bill, of which Burke is said to have been partly the author, and upon which he pronounced one of his most magnificent orations, was fatal to the Coalition. William Pitt, called at the age of twenty-four to occupy the first place in the counsels of his sovereign, fought an arduous but finally victorious fight against the Whig majority in the Commons. A dissolution followed : the new house supported the new ministers ; and a second long period of Whig opposition began, during which Fox was the acknowledged leader of the party, and was warmly supported in that capacity by Burke. The most important event of this second great division of Burke's parliamentary life is undoubtedly the impeachment of Warren Hastings. Throughout the long debates on the accusations brought against the Governor of India, and afterward throughout the trial itself, which began in 1788, and was not concluded until 1795, Burke was indefatigable. Never, perhaps, has greater oratorical genius been displayed than by that combination of great men who were appointed managers of the impeachment. Yet all their efforts failed to establish their case on a secure foundation. History still hesitates to decide with confidence on the guilt or innocence of Hastings. It is agreed, however, that the violence of Burke's proceedings on this trial was often unworthy of the situation he held and the cause he advocated. When, with harsh tones, and a look more expressive of personal than political hatred, he bade Mr. Hastings kneel before the court, it is said that Fox whispered to his friends, " In that moment I would rather have been Hastings than Burke."

At the latter end of 1788 arose the regency question, on which Burke, with all his party, maintained the opinion that any apparently irreparable incapacity in the sovereign caused a demise of the crown, because, the prerogatives of royalty being given for public benefit, it would be highly dangerous to suspend them for an indefinite period. Burke, however, did some injury to his party by the intemperate and imprudent language he adopted on this occasion, speaking of the king's situation in the tone of triumph rather than pity, and even using the expression, " God has hurled him from his throne." These constitutional questions, however important, were soon forgotten in a new absorbing interest, which began to occupy the minds of all men. The French revolution had taken place. That astonishing event was at first hailed with general sympathy and admiration in England. The supporters of Pitt either joined in the vehement delight of the Fox party, or took no pains to restrain it. Here and there some may have mur-

mured dislike ; but, in general, it was thought unworthy of Englishmen not to rejoice in the acquisition of liberty by a neighbouring people ; and not a few looked to this great change as the harbinger of political regeneration to Europe and the world. In this general acclamation one voice was wanting. Burke, from the very first meeting of the States-General, did not conceal his aversion to their proceedings and his apprehension of their results. Gradually, as the excesses of popular violence in Paris became more frequent, an Anti-Gallican party began to gather round him. On the 9th of February, 1790, during a debate on the army estimates, Burke took advantage of some expressions which Fox let fall in praise of the French revolution to open an attack against it, denying that there was any similarity between the English revolution of 1688 and the "strange thing" called by the same name in France. Fox, in his reply, spoke in memorable terms of his obligations to his friend, declaring that all he had ever learned from other sources was little in comparison with what he had gained from him. Sheridan attacked the speech just made by Burke in no measured terms, describing it as perfectly irreconcilable with the principles hitherto professed by that gentleman. On this Burke again rose, and in a few words declared that Sheridan and himself were thenceforth "separated in politics." Before the end of this year came out the celebrated "Reflections," which at once showed how irreparable was the schism between the author and his former associates. It roused an immediate war of opinion, which gave birth to a war of force throughout Europe. Innu-

merable pamphlets soon followed upon its publication, some denouncing the work as a specious apology for despotism, others advocating the opinions
contained in it with a vehemence which the authors
had not dared to show till they were encouraged
by the support of so eloquent and so distinguished
a partisan. The most remarkable attempts of the
former description were the "Rights of Man," by
Thomas Paine, which soon became the manual of
the democratic party; and the "Vindiciæ Galli-
cæ," by Mr., afterward Sir James Mackintosh, the
most illustrious, if not the only successor of Burke
himself in his peculiar line of philosophical politics.
Fox was loud in condemning the book; and although no formal breach of friendship had hitherto
taken place, such an event was obviously to be expected. On the 6th May, 1791, during a discussion on a plan for settling the constitution of Canada, this separation actually occurred, with a so-
lemnity worthy of the men and the event. From
that hour, during the six remaining years of his
life, one idea swayed with exclusive dominion the
mind of Burke. Utterly separated from Fox's
party, aloof from the ministry, retired, after a few
sessions, from parliament, he continued to wage
unceasing war, by speech and writing, against the
principles and practice of Jacobinism. Soon he
was pointed out as a prophet, and the verification
of his predictions in characters of blood was much
more powerful, because much more palpable, than
the vague anticipations of future advantage put forward by his opponents. In 1794, after his retirement from parliament, he received the grant of a
considerable pension for himself and his wife. The

democratic party did not scruple to stigmatize his
motives; and in answer to an accusation of this
sort was written the "Letter to a Noble Lord,"
perhaps the most astonishing specimen of his peculiar capacities of style.   In this year the death of
his son overwhelmed him with affliction.   Still he
continued his exertions.   His views of the war
differed widely from those of the ministry: he
ceased not to urge that it was a war, not against
France, but Jacobinism, and that it would be a degradation to Britain to treat with any of the Regi-
cides.   On this subject are written the two "Letters on a Regicide Peace," published in 1796, and
the others published since his death.   On the 8th
of July, 1797, this event took place, in the 68th
year of his age, at his own house at Beaconsfield,
whither, after seeking medical aid elsewhere in
vain, he had returned to die.

The mind of this great man may perhaps be
considered as a fair representative of the general
characteristics of English intellect.   Its groundwork was solid, practical, and conversant with the
details of business; but upon this, and secured by
this, arose a superstructure of imagination and moral sentiment.   He saw little, because it was painful to him to see anything beyond the limits of the
national character; with that and with the constitution, which he considered its appropriate expression,
all his sympathies were bound up.   But he loved
them with an intelligent and discriminating love,
making it his pains to comprehend thoroughly what
it was his delight to serve diligently.   His political
opinions, springing out of these dispositions, were
early fixed in favour of the Whig system of govern-

ing by great party connexions. These opinions, however, were swayed in their application by strong impulses of personal feeling. A temper impatient of control, an imagination prone to magnify those classes of facts which impressed him with alarm or hope, a command of language almost unlimited, and a copiousness of imagery misleading nearly as much as it illustrated or enforced; these were qualities which laid him open to many serious accusations. But his admirers have started a philosophic doubt, whether less of passion and prejudice would have been compatible with the peculiar station he was destined to occupy. In an age of revolution, it might be plausibly maintained, his genius was the counteracting force; alone he stood against the impulses communicated to European society by the philosophers of France : their enthusiasm could only be met by enthusiasm; their influence on the imaginations and hearts of men was capable of overbearing either a blind prejudice or a dispassionate logic. But Burke was an orator in all his thoughts, and a sage in all his eloquence; he held the principles of Conservation with the zeal of a Leveller, and tempered lofty ideas of improvement with the scrupulousness of official routine. As a debater in the House of Commons he was inferior to some otherwise inferior men. Pitt and Fox will be neglected, while the speeches of Burke shall still be read. It has been said of Fox by a philosophical panegyrist, that he was the most Demosthenean speaker since Demosthenes. Perhaps, of all great orators, Burke might be called the least Demosthenean. Probably a hearer of the great Athenian would have felt as extemporaneous and intuitive the slowly-wrought perfections of rhetorical art, while the listeners to Burke may have often set down to elaborate preparation what was really the inspiration of the moment. His conversation, however, seems to have been uniformly delightful. It is a true maxim in one sense, although in another it would often need reversal, that great men are always greater than their works. Much as we possess of Edmund Burke, very much is lost to us of that which formed the admiration of his contemporaries. "The mind of that man," said Dr. Johnson, " is a perennial stream ; no one grudges Burke the first place." He was acquainted with most subjects of literature, and possessed some knowledge of science. The philosophy of mind owes him one contribution of no inconsiderable value ; but the indirect results of his metaphysical studies, as seen in the tenour of his practical philosophy, are much more extensive. For in all things, while he deeply reverenced principles, he chose to deal with the concrete more than with abstractions : he studied men rather than man. In private life the character of Burke was unsullied even by reproach. A good father, a good husband, a good friend, he was sincerely attached to the Protestant religion of the English church, " not from indifference," as he said himself of the nation at large, " but from zeal." But his attachment was without bigotry ; the principles of toleration ever found in him a powerful advocate ; and he was ever zealous to remove imperfections and correct abuses in the establishment, as the best means of securing its permanent existence.

The works of Burke are collected in sixteen volumes octavo. His speeches are separately published in four volumes octavo. A small volume appeared in 1827, containing the correspondence, hitherto unpublished, between this great statesman and his friend Dr. Laurence. His life was written soon after his death by Mr. Bisset, and has been more recently by Mr. Prior. Several other biographical accounts were published about the time of his death, both in the periodical publications and as independent works : we are not aware that any of these are entitled to particular notice.

SCHWARTZ.

It is refreshing to turn from the scenes of war and bloodshed, and frequently of perfidy and oppression, by which the English empire in India was established and consolidated, to watch the progress of a benevolent and peaceful enterprise, the substitution of the Christian faith for the impure, and bloody, and oppressive superstitions of the Hindoos. We augur well of its success, though it is still far from its accomplishment ; for, since the first hand was put to it, it has advanced with slow, yet certain and unfaltering steps. Many able and good men have devoted themselves to the cause, and none with more distinguished success than he who has been called the Apostle of the East, CHRISTIAN SCHWARTZ. The saying of an eminent missionary, who preached to a far different people, the stern and high-minded Indians of North America, is exemplified in his life: "Prayer and pains, through faith, will do anything." For years Schwartz laboured in obscurity, with few scattered and broken rays of encouragement to cheer his way. But his patience, his integrity, his unwearied benevolence, his sincerity and unblemished purity of life, won a hearing for his words of doctrine; and he was rewarded at last by a more extended empire in the hearts of the Hindoos, both heathen and convert, than perhaps any other European has obtained.

Christian Frederic Schwartz was born at Sonnenburg, in the New Mark, Germany, October 26, 1726. His mother died while he was very young, and, in dying, devoted the child, in the presence of her husband and her spiritual guide, to the service of God, exacting from both of them a promise that they would use every means for the accomplishment of this her last and earnest wish. Schwartz received his education at the schools of Sonnenburg and Custrin. He grew up a serious and well-disposed boy, much under the influence of religious impressions; and a train of fortunate circumstances deepened those impressions, at a time when the vivacity of youth and the excitement of secular pursuits had nearly withdrawn him from the career to which he was dedicated. When about twenty years of age he entered the University of Halle, where he obtained the friendship of one of the professors, Herman Francke, a warm and generous supporter of the missionary cause. While resident at Halle, Schwartz, together with another student, was appointed to learn the Tamul or Malabar language, in order to superintend the printing of a Bible in that tongue. His labour was not thrown

VOL. II.—R

away, though the proposed edition was never completed; for it led Francke to propose to him that
he should go out to India as a missionary. The
suggestion suited his ardent and laborious character, and was at once accepted. The appointed
scene of his labours was Tranquebar, on the Coro-
mandel coast, the seat of a Danish mission; and,
after repairing to Copenhagen for ordination, he
embarked from London for India, January 21,
1750, and reached Tranquebar in July.

It is seldom that the life of one employed in advocating the faith of Christ presents much of adventure, except from the fiery trials of persecution;
or much of interest, except to those who will enter
into the missionary's chief joy or sorrow, the success or inefficiency of his preaching. From persecution Schwartz's whole life was free; his difficulties did not proceed from bigoted or interested
zeal, but from the apathetic subtlety of his Hindoo
hearers, ready to listen, slow to be convinced, enjoying the mental sword-play of hearing, and an-
swering, and being confuted, and renewing the
same or similar objections at the next meeting, as
if the preacher's former labours had not been.
The latter part of his life was possessed of active
interest; for he was no stranger to the court or
the camp, and his known probity and truthfulness
won for him the confidence of three most dissimilar
parties, a suspicious tyrant, an oppressed people,
and the martial and diplomatic directors of the
British empire in India. But the early years of
his abode in India possess interest neither from the
marked success of his preaching, nor from his
commerce with the busy scenes of conquest and

negotiation. For sixteen years he resided chiefly at Tranquebar, a member of the mission to which he was first attached; but at the end of that time, in 1766, he transferred his services to the Society for promoting Christian Knowledge, with which he acted until death, and to which the care of the Danish mission at Tranquebar was soon after transferred. He had already, in 1765, established a church and school at Tritchinopoly, and in that town he now took up his abode, holding the office of chaplain to the garrison, for which he received a salary of £100 yearly. This entire sum he devoted to the service of the mission.

For several years Schwartz resided principally at Tritchinopoly, visiting other places from time to time, especially Tanjore, where his labours ultimately had no small effect. He was heard with attention; he was everywhere received with respect; for the Hindoos could not but admire the beauty of his life, though it failed to win souls to his preaching. "The fruit," he said, "will perhaps appear when I am at rest." He had, however, the pleasure of seeing some portion of it ripen, for in more than one place a small congregation grew gradually up under his care. His toil was lightened and cheered in 1777, when another missionary was sent to his assistance from Tranquebar. Already he had derived help from some of his more advanced converts, who acted as catechists for the instruction of others. He was sedulous in preparing these men for their important duty. "The catechists," he says, "require to be daily admonished and stirred up, otherwise they fall into indolence and impurity." Accordingly, he daily assembled all those whose nearness permitted this frequency of intercourse ; he taught them to explain the doctrines of their religion ; he directed their labours for the day, and he received a report of those labours in the evening.

His visits to Tanjore became more frequent, and he obtained the confidence of the rajah or native prince, Tulia Maha, who ruled that city under the protection of the British.   In 1779 Schwartz procured permission from him to erect a church in his capital, and, with the sanction of the Madras government, set immediately to work on this task. His funds failing, he applied at Madras for farther aid ; but, in reply, he was summoned to the seat of government with all speed, and requested to act as an ambassador, to treat with Hyder Ali for the continuance of peace.   It has been said that Schwartz engaged more deeply than became his calling in the secular affairs of India.   The best apology for his interference, if apology be needful, is contained in his own account : " The novelty of the proposal surprised me at first ; I begged some time to consider of it.   At last I accepted of the offer, because, by so doing, I hoped to prevent evil and to promote the welfare of the country."   The reason for sending him is at least too honourable to him to be omitted ; it was the requisition of Hyder himself.   " Do not send to me," he said, " any of your agents, for I do not trust their words or treaties ; but if you wish me to listen to your proposals, send to me the missionary of whose character I hear so much from every one ; him I will receive and trust."

In his character of an envoy Schwartz succeeded

admirably. He conciliated the crafty, suspicious, and unfeeling despot, without compromising the dignity of those whom he represented, or forgetting the meekness of his calling. He would gladly have rendered his visit to Seringapatam available to higher than temporal interests; but here he met with little encouragement. Indifferent to all religion, Hyder suffered the preacher to speak to him of mercy and of judgment; but in these things his heart took no part. Some few converts Schwartz made during his abode of three months; but, on the whole, he met with little success. He parted with Hyder upon good terms, and returned with joy to Tanjore. The peace, however, was of no long continuance; and Schwartz complained that the British government were guilty of the infraction. Hyder invaded the Carnatic, wasting it with fire and sword; and the frightened inhabitants flocked for relief and protection to the towns. Tanjore and Tritchinopoly were filled with famishing multitudes. During the whole time from 1781 to 1783, this misery continued. At Tanjore especially, the scene was dreadful. Numbers perished in the streets from want and disease; corpses lay unburied, because the survivers had not resolution or strength to inter them; the bonds of affection were so broken that parents offered their children for sale; and the garrison, though less afflicted than the native population, were enfeebled and depressed by privation, and threatened by a powerful army without the walls. There were provisions in the country; but the cultivators, frightened and alienated by the customary exactions and ill usage, refused to bring it to the fort.

they would trust neither the British authorities nor the rajah, and all confidence, in short, was destroyed. "At last the rajah said to one of our principal gentlemen, 'We all, you and I, have lost our credit; let us try whether the inhabitants will trust Mr. Schwartz.' Accordingly, he sent me a blank paper, empowering me to make a proper agreement with the people. Here was no time for hesitation. The Sepoys fell down as dead people, being emaciated with hunger; our streets were lined with dead corpses every morning—our condition was deplorable. I sent, therefore, letters everywhere round about, promising to pay any one with my own hands, and to pay them for any bullock which might be taken by the enemy. In one or two days I got above a thousand bullocks, and sent one of our catechists and other Christians into the country. They went at the risk of their lives, made all possible haste, and brought into the fort, in a very short time, 80,000 kalams of grain. By this means the fort was saved. When all was over I paid the people, even with some money which belonged to others, made them a small present, and sent them home."

The letter from which this passage is extracted was written to the Society for promoting Christian Knowledge, in consequence of an attack made by a member of Parliament upon the character of the Hindoo converts, and his depreciation of the labours of the missionaries. To boast was not in Schwartz's nature; but he was not deterred by a false modesty from vindicating his own reputation when it was expedient for his master's service; and there has seldom been a more striking tribute paid

to virtue, unassisted by power, than in the conduct
of the Hindoos, as told in this simple statement.
His labours did not cease with this crisis, nor with
his personal exertions.　He bought a quantity of
rice at his own expense, and prevailed on some
European merchants to furnish him with a monthly supply, by means of which he preserved many
persons from perishing.　In 1784 he was again
employed by the Company on a mission to Tippoo
Saib ; but the son of Hyder refused to receive him.
About this period his health, hitherto robust, began
to fail ; and in a letter dated July, 1784, he speaks
of the approach of death, of his comfort in the prospect, and firm belief in the doctrines which he
preached.　In the same year the increase of his
congregation rendered it necessary to build a Malabar church in the suburbs of Tanjore, which was
done chiefly at his own expense.　In February,
1785, he engaged in a scheme for raising English
schools throughout the country, to facilitate the intercourse of the natives with Europeans.　Schools
were accordingly established at Tanjore and three
other places.　The pupils were chiefly children of
the upper classes—of Brahmins and merchants ;
and the good faith with which Schwartz conducted these establishments is no less entitled to praise
than his religious zeal.　" Their intention," he
says, " doubtless, is to learn the English language,
with a view to their temporal welfare ; but they
thereby become better acquainted with good principles.　No deceitful methods are used to bring
them over to the doctrines of Christ, though the
most earnest wishes are felt that they may attain
that knowledge which is life eternal."　In a tem-

poral view, these establishments proved very serviceable to many of the pupils; but, contrary to Schwartz's hopes and wishes, not one of the young men became a missionary.

In January, 1787, Schwartz's friend, the Rajah of Tanjore, lay at the point of death. Being childless, he had adopted a boy, yet in his minority, as his successor; a practice recognised by the Hindoo law. His brother, Ameer Sing, however, was supported by a strong British party, and it was not likely that he would submit quietly to his exclusion from the throne. In this strait Tulia Maha sent for Schwartz, as the only person to whom he could intrust his adopted son. "This," he said, "is not my, but your son: into your hands I deliver the child." Schwartz accepted the charge with reluctance: he represented his inability to protect the orphan, and suggested that Ameer Sing should be named regent and guardian. The advice, probably, was the best that could be given; but the regent proved false, or, at least, doubtful in his trust: and the charge proved a source of trouble and anxiety. But by Schwartz's care, and influence with the Company, the young prince was reared to manhood, and established in possession of his inheritance. Nor were Schwartz's pains unsuccessful in the cultivation of his young pupil's mind, who is characterized by Heber as an "extraordinary man." He repaid these fatherly cares with a filial affection, and long after the death of Schwartz testified, both by word and deed, his regard for his memory.

We find little to relate during the latter part of Schwartz's life. His efforts were unceasing to promote the good, temporal as well as spiritual, of the Indian population. On one occasion he was requested to inspect the water-courses by which the arid lands of the Carnatic are irrigated; and his labours were rewarded by a great increase in the annual produce. Once the inhabitants of the Tanjore country had been so grievously oppressed, that they abandoned their farms and fled the country. The cultivation which should have commenced in June was postponed even to the beginning of September, and all began to apprehend a famine. Schwartz says, in the letter which we have already quoted, "I entreated the rajah to remove that shameful oppression, and to recall the inhabitants. He sent them word that justice should be done them, but they disbelieved his promises. He then desired me to write to them, and to assure them that he, at my intercession, would show kindness to them. I did so. All immediately returned; and first of all the Collaries believed my word, so that 7000 men came back in one day. The rest of the inhabitants followed their example. When I exhorted them to exert themselves to the utmost because the time for cultivation was almost lost, they replied in the following manner: 'As you have showed kindness to us, you shall not have reason to repent of it; we intend to work night and day to show our regard for you.'"

His preaching was rewarded by a slow but not discouraging effect; and the number of missionaries having been increased by the society in England, the growth of the good seed which he had sown during a residence of forty years became more rapid and perceptible. In the country villages numerous congregations were formed, and preachers were established at Cuddalore, Vepery, Negapatam, and Palamcotta; as well as at the earlier stations of Tranquebar, Tritchinopoly, and Tanjore, whose chief recreation was the occasional intercourse with each other which their duty afforded them, and who lived in cordial harmony and union of mind and purpose. The last illness of Schwartz was cheered by the presence of almost all the missionaries in the south of India, who regarded him as a father, and called him by that endearing name. His labours did not diminish as his years increased. From the beginning of January to the middle of October, 1797, we are told by his pupil and assistant, Caspar Kolhoff, he preached every Sunday in the English and Tamul languages by turns; for several successive Wednesdays he gave lectures in their own languages to the Portuguese and German soldiers incorporated in the 51st regiment; during the week he explained the New Testament in his usual order at morning and evening prayer; and he dedicated an hour every day to the instruction of the Malabar school children. In October, though he had hitherto scarcely known disease, he received the warning of his mortality. He rallied for a while, and his friends hoped that he might yet be spared to them. But a relapse took place, and he expired February 13, 1798, having displayed, throughout a long and painful illness, a beautiful example of resignation and happiness, and an interest undiminished by pain in the welfare of all for and with whom he had laboured. His funeral, on the day after his death, presented a most affecting scene. It was delayed by the arrival of the rajah, who wished to behold once more his kind, and faithful, and vigilant friend and guardian. The coffin lid was removed: the prince gazed for the last time on the pale and composed features, and burst into tears. The funeral service was interrupted by the cries of a multitude, who loved the reliever of their distresses, and honoured the pure life of the preacher who for near fifty years had dwelt among them, careless alike of pleasure, interest, and ambition, pursuing a difficult and thankless task with unchanging ardour, the friend of princes, yet unsullied even by the suspicion of a bribe, devoting his whole income, beyond a scanty maintenance, to the service of the cause which his life was spent in advocating.

The rajah continued to cherish Schwartz's memory. He commissioned Flaxman to execute a monument, to be erected to him at Tanjore: he placed his picture among those of his own ancestors; he built more than one costly establishment for charitable purposes in honour of his name; and, though not professing Christianity, he secured to the Christians in his service not only liberty, but full convenience for the performance of their religious duties. Nor were the directors backward in testifying their gratitude for his services. They sent out a monument by Bacon to be erected in St. Mary's Church at Madras, with orders to pay every becoming honour to his memory, and especially to permit to the natives, by whom he was so revered, free access to view this memorial of his virtues.

It is to be regretted that no full memoir of the life and labours of this admirable man has been published. It is understood that his correspondence, preserved by the Society for promoting Christian Knowledge, would furnish ample materials for such a work. The facts of this account are taken from the only two memoirs of Schwartz which we know to be in print—a short one for cheap circulation, published by the Religious Tract Society ; and a more finished tribute to his memory, in Mr. Carne's " Lives of Eminent Missionaries," recently published. We conclude in the words of one whose praise carries with it authority, Bishop Heber: " Of Schwartz, and his fifty years' labour among the heathen, the extraordinary influence and popularity which he acquired, both with Mussulmans, Hindoos, and contending European governments, I need give you no account, except that my idea of him has been raised since I came into the south of India. I used to suspect that, with many admirable qualities, there was too great a mixture of intrigue in his character ; that he was too much of a political prophet ; and that the veneration which the heathen paid, and still pay him (and which, indeed, almost regards him as a superior being, putting crowns and burning lights before his statue), was purchased by some unwarrantable compromise with their prejudices. I find I was quite mistaken. He was really one of the most active and fearless, as he was one of the most successful missionaries who have appeared since the apostles. To say that he was disinterested in regard to money, is nothing ; he was perfectly careless of power, and renown never seemed to affect him, even so far as to induce an outward show of humility. His temper was perfectly simple, open, and cheerful ; and in his political negotiations (employments which he never sought, but which fell in his way) he never pretended to impartiality, but acted as the avowed, though certainly the successful and judicious, agent of the orphan prince committed to his care, and from attempting whose conversion to Christianity he seems to have abstained from a feeling of honour.* His other converts were between six and seven thousand, besides those which his companions and predecessors in the cause had brought over."

COWPER.

WILLIAM COWPER was born at the rectory of Berkhampstead, in Hertfordshire, Nov. 26, 1731. He was nearly related to the noble family of that name, his great-uncle having been chancellor and first Earl Cowper ; his grandfather, the brother of the chancellor, was a judge of the Common Pleas. Cowper's mother died before he was six years old. Soon afterward he was sent to a country school, from which, at the age of nine, he was removed to Westminster. It is probable that one cause among others of his future unhappiness was the early loss of that tender parent, whose " constant flow of love," beautifully acknowledged in his verses on receiving her picture, and in many parts of his cor-

* He probably acted on the same principle as in conducting the English schools above mentioned, using no " deceitful methods." That he was earnest in recommending the *means* of conversion, appears from a dying conversation with his pupil, Serfogee Rajah.

respondence, made a deep and lasting impression on his infant mind. Cowper was exactly the boy to require a mother's care. His constitution was delicate, his mind sensitive and timid ; and he discovered a tendency to dejection, which was aggravated by the tyranny then practiced at public schools. Quitting Westminster at eighteen, with a good character for talent and scholarship, he went at once into an attorney's office, where he spent three years, according to his own account, with very little profit. He then became a member of the Inner Temple, intending to practice at the bar. At this period of life he amused himself with composition, and showed a strong predilection for polite literature and agreeable society ; but he had no taste for the law, and took no pains to qualify himself for his profession. Long afterward he deeply lamented this loss of time during his early manhood, and earnestly warned his young friends against a similar error.

In 1763 Cowper was appointed to the lucrative office of reading clerk, and clerk of the private committees of the House of Lords. The fairest prospect of happiness now lay before him, for his union with one of his cousins, it is said, had only been deferred until he should obtain a satisfactoy establishment. But the idea of reading in public was intolerable to him ; and he gave up this office for the less valuable one of clerk of the journals, in which it was hoped that his personal appearance before the house would not be required. Unfortunately, it did prove necessary that he should appear at the bar to qualify himself for the post. "They whose spirits are formed like mine," he thus expressed himself in after-life, " to whom a public exhibition of themselves is mortal poison, may have some idea of the horrors of my situation : others can have none." He fought hard against this morbid feeling ; but, when the day arrived for entering upon his duties, such was his terror and distress, that even his friends acquiesced in his abandoning the attempt. But his mind had been disordered in the struggle, and he shortly after sank into deep religious despondency ; so that it was found necessary, in December, 1763, to place him in a lunatic asylum at St. Alban's, under the care of Dr. Cotton.

Cowper's insanity at this period, and the grievous dejection of the last twenty-seven years of his life, have been imputed to the so-called gloominess of his religious tenets. From that opinion we entirely dissent. No sense of religious abasement can be conceived sufficiently humiliating to drive a sane man to distraction at the thought of having to appear in a public capacity before Parliament ; and, besides, Cowper's struggles and mental distress upon that occasion were anterior to his receiving any serious religious impressions. It appears certain, also, that his recovery was due to more encouraging views of the doctrines of the Gospel, assisted by the kind and judicious mental, as well as bodily, treatment of Dr. Cotton. For eight years his religion was the source of unfailing cheerfulness and the most active benevolence ; and after he ceased to derive pleasure from it himself, he was still mild and charitable in his conduct towards others, and in his opinions concerning them. The extent of Cowper's mental wandering on subjects unconnected with his own spiritual state, is not, perhaps, gen-

erally known. A remarkable instance of it occurs
in a letter to his esteemed friend, Mr. Newton, dated October 2, 1787, from which it appears that, during thirteen years, Cowper had entertained doubts
of Mr. Newton's personal identity. At this latter
period, therefore, there was hallucination of mind
as well as religious gloom. Cowper's recovery
from his first illness is dated in July, 1764 ; but he
remained with his friendly and beloved physician
nearly a year more, after which he took lodgings
at Huntingdon, directed by the wish of being within easy reach of his brother, who was a resident
Fellow of Benet College, Cambridge.

He soon became acquainted with a family bearing the name of Unwin, consisting of a clergyman,
his wife and daughter, and one son, an under-graduate of Cambridge. Struck by Cowper's appearance, the latter threw himself into the stranger's
way ; and a feeling of mutual regard and esteem
led to Cowper's establishing himself as a permanent inmate in Mr. Unwin's family in November,
1765. After the lapse of nearly two years in tranquil happiness, the sudden death of Mr. Unwin led
to the family's departure from Huntingdom to Olney in Buckinghamshire, in October, 1767. But
the foundation had been laid of a friendship which
no misfortune or change of circumstances could destroy ; and Cowper and Mrs. Unwin united their
slender incomes, and continued to dwell under the
same roof. The first six years of their abode at
Olney were spent in domestic quiet and retirement
almost unbroken, except by the society of Mr. Newton, an eminent and examplary divine, who was then
curate on the living. The well-known collection

called the " Olney Hymns" were composed by Cowper and Newton, for the most part, during this period. But in 1773 Cowper's mental disease returned in the dreadful shape of religious despondency.
He conceived himself to be set apart for eternal
misery : yet, amid the deep gloom produced by the
loss of that spiritual happiness which he had enjoyed since his recovery from his first illness, he was
so entirely submissive, that he was accustomed to
say, " If holding up my finger would save me from
endless torments, I would not do it against the will
of God ;" and, in accordance with the belief that
his own fate was sealed, he ceased to pray, and ab-
sented himself entirely from divine worship. The
depth of his dejection was gradually cheered by the
affectionate, watchful, and judicious care of his
guardian friend, Mrs. Unwin. One of the first
signs of improvement was a desire to tame some
leverets. He was soon supplied with three, which
have obtained celebrity in prose and verse, such as
no other hares have enjoyed before or since. He
tried at different times gardening, drawing, and
a variety of trifling manual occupations, as methods of diverting his thoughts from his own miser-
ies. " Many arts I have exercised with this view,"
he says, in a letter to Mrs. King, dated October
11, 1788, " for which nature never designed me,
though among them were some in which I arrived
at considerable proficiency, by mere dint of the
most heroic perseverance. There is not a squire
in all this country who can boast of having made
better squirrel-houses, hutches for rabbits, or bird-
cages, than myself ; and in the article of cabbage-
nets I had no superior. But gardening was, of all

employments, that in which I succeeded best, though even in this I did not suddenly attain perfection." At last he devoted himself to writing ; "a whim," he says elsewhere, " that has served me longest and best, and will probably be my latest." His first volume of poems, containing " Table Talk," &c., was published in the summer of 1781, having been written chiefly in the preceding winter. It was undertaken at the instance of Mrs. Unwin, who, on his recovery from a long fit of unusual dejection, urged him to devote his attention to a work of some extent, and such as should require a considerable share of application and attention. At the same time she suggested as a subject the " Progress of Error," which is the second piece in the volume. Cowper had already written many of his lighter pieces, and that at the times when he was labouring under the severest depression. He accounts for this singular phenomenon with his usual playful humour : " The mind, long wearied with the sameness of a dull, dreary prospect, will gladly fix its eyes on anything that may make a little variety in its contemplations, though it were but a kitten playing with its tail."

Early in 1780 Cowper lost a valued friend, and almost his only associate, by the removal of Mr. Newton to London. In the following year he became acquainted with Lady Austen, who for a short time fills a prominent place in the poet's history. We must refer to fuller memoirs for the tale of her introduction, and the gradual growth of that strict intimacy which ensued between herself, Mrs. Unwin, and Cowper. For some time the three friends spent a considerable portion of every day in each other's society ; and Cowper was indebted to Lady Austen's liveliness in conversation and varied accomplishments for a great alleviation of his mental sufferings. The famous history of John Gilpin owes its birth to a story told by her one evening to rouse the poet out of a fit of despondency ; and it engaged his fancy so strongly, that in the course of the night, during which he was kept awake by fits of laughter, he turned it into verse. The ballad soon got abroad, and obtained uncommon popularity ; but it was long before the author was known. "The Task" was composed at Lady Austen's request. She saw the benefit which Cowper derived from earnest literary employment, and often urged him to try his strength in blank verse. After some pressing, he promised to comply, if she would furnish him with a subject. "Oh, you can write on anything," she said ; "write on this sofa." The lively answer chimed in with his peculiar humour, and he adopted it literally : his sofa forms the subject of the poem ; the first book of which is entitled "The Sofa," and opens with a history of the invention and merits of that piece of furniture, which is unsurpassed in its peculiar vein of humour. But the author soon rises into a higher strain, and in his discursive range paints the beauty of the country with that fidelity and exquisite sense of natural beauty which constitutes his chief poetic merit ; describes the peculiar appearances and occupations of the winter season ; weighs the evils and advantages attendant on a high state of civilization ; exhibits, in reproving the faults of the age, his power both in the lighter skirmishing of satire and in the stern outpourings of an honest indignation ; inculcates the doctrines of that religion of peace and love from which it was his own singular and melancholy lot to derive no peace; and all with a beauty and felicity of versification and power of illustration sufficient to attract many whom the grave nature of the subjects discussed would rather repel. The scope and conduct of the work is well described in the following lines at the conclusion, in which, anticipating death, he says:

> " It shall not grieve me then, that once, when called
> To dress a sofa with the flowers of verse,
> I play'd a while, obedient to the fair,
> With that light task : but soon, to please her more,
> Whom flowers alone I knew would little please,
> Let fall the unfinish'd wreath, and roved for fruit;
> Roved far and gather'd much : some harsh, 'tis true,
> Pick'd from the thorns and briers of reproof,
> But wholesome, well digested ; grateful some
> To palates that can taste immortal truth ;
> Insipid else, and sure to be despised."

"The Task" was accompanied by a shorter poem, entitled "Tirocinium," written expressly in dispraise of the existing system of public schools in England, and prompted by Cowper's bitter recollection of his sufferings at Westminster. The volume was published in 1785.

As soon as this was completed, Cowper engaged in another more laborious undertaking, the translation of Homer. This also was suggested by Lady Austen; and it had a most beneficial effect in furnishing the poet with constant employment from this time forward to the end of his life, with the exception of those periods in which the pressure of disease was too severe to admit of any exertion. He spared no pains in the execution of this great work; and, after his version was made, subjected it to a most careful revision, amounting nearly to a retranslation. It was published in 1791, and was preceded by a list of subscribers, whose number and individual eminence bear testimony to the high esteem in which Cowper was then held. His translation, however, has never been popular; he has avoided Pope's errors, but he has failed in giving life and interest, and in catching the vital spirit of his author.

During the long period which the literary labours above mentioned occupied, Cowper's domestic history is characterized by the same general depression and the same seclusion that we have above described. In 1784 his friendship with Lady Austen was interrupted by a disagreement between her and Mrs. Unwin, who seems to have feared that the former might obtain an influence over the poet paramount to her own; and to have been justly hurt at the prospect of becoming second in the affections of him, to whom, for so many years, she had devoted herself with a zeal which merited the utmost return. Cowper felt this, and he himself broke off his intercourse with Lady Austen in a way which was admitted by herself to do credit to his delicacy and judgment no less than to his generosity. In about a year after the termination of this valuable friendship, he received the best amends that could be made, in the renewal of intercourse, after it had been interrupted for twenty-three years, with his cousin Lady Hesketh, to whom from childhood he had been strongly attached. She visited Olney in June, 1786; and from that time forward her purse and her personal exertions were unsparingly bestowed to promote the comfort of her be

loved cousin.   At her instance his confined and
ruinous abode at Olney was exchanged, in November, 1786, for a commodious house in the pretty
neighbouring village· of Weston, which was especially recommended to Cowper as being the residence of his esteemed friends Mr. and Mrs. Throckmorton.   Here Lady Hesketh commonly spent
part of the year.   The state of Cowper's spirits during his residence at Weston was variable ; but he
made a few new acquaintance, and among them his
correspondent, Mr. Rose, and his biographer, Mr.
Hayley.   He also enjoyed a vivid pleasure in the
renewal of intercourse with his maternal relations,
among whom his young cousin Johnson, who afterward became his tender and devoted guardian,
obtained an especial place in his affections.   Still,
however, his mental malady continued unabated ;
and a new cause of uneasiness beset him in the
growing infirmities of Mrs. Unwin.   In March,
1792, the disease which had been for some time
sapping her strength manifested itself in a paralyt-
ic attack, from which she never entirely recovered.
From thenceforward Cowper's time and attention
were devoted, as his primary object, to contributing
to her comfort and amusement.   In her company he
quitted his home, the first time for twenty-seven
years, to visit Mr. Hayley's seat at Eartham, in
Sussex.   Two important works had engaged his
attention : one a poem on the four ages of man's
life, the other an edition of Milton.   These, however, were successively laid aside ; and such time
as his weak spirits and melancholy occupation allowed him, he employed in revising his Homer for
a second edition.   But Mrs. Unwin became more

and more enfeebled in mind and body; and in the beginning of 1794, Cowper relapsed into a gloom as deep as that which he had endured at the commencement of his malady. To watch over him in his melancholy, Lady Hesketh made Weston her constant instead of her occasional abode, until the middle of the following year, when her health gave way under the constant pressure of anxiety. Mr. Johnson, who had taken orders, and resided at East Dereham, in Norfolk, then took charge of his unhappy relation; removed him and Mrs. Unwin into his own neighbourhood, and watched over their decline with the most unwearied and judicious tenderness. But little could now be done to give Cowper pleasure. The pathetic poem, " To Mary," is supposed by Mr. Hayley to have been the last thing written by him before quitting Weston; and the only original verses which he composed afterward were some Latin lines, which he translated into English, on the appearance of some ice islands in the German Sea, and the touching poem called the "Cast-away," founded on the loss of a man overboard in Anson's voyage, and alluding, in an affecting strain, to his own unfortunate condition. After his departure from Weston, he, who had been so diligent a correspondent, only wrote three or four letters; nor could he be excited to converse by the visits even of his most intimate friends, as Mr. Rose and Sir John Throckmorton. In January, 1800, his final illness, which was dropsy, commenced. He died April 25th in the same year; nor to the last did one gleam of hope break through the darkness which had surrounded him for twenty-seven years.

It was Cowper's especial merit, as a poet, to cultivate simplicity and nature. He set the example of throwing aside conventional affectations and unmeaning pomp of diction; and, in consideration of this great service, may well be pardoned for occasionally incurring the opposite fault of being tame and prosaic. His genius was truly original: all his writings, whether moral, satirical, or descriptive, bear the legible impress of his own peculiar constitution of mind and habits of thinking. His minor and occasional poems are very happy; for his imagination could extract a deep and beautiful moral from slight occurrences, which commonly pass unnoticed in the bustle of life. Many of his letters are published in Hayley's Life of Cowper; and these are imbodied with the Private Correspondence afterward given to the world by Mr. Johnson, in the edition of Cowper's works by Mr. Grimshawe. As a letter writer Cowper appears to us to be unequalled in the English language. His correspondence is the genuine intercourse of friend with friend; full of wit and humour, but a humour that never vents itself in the depreciation of others; and abounding in passages of graver beauty, expressed in the most easy, yet elegant and correct language. When once a man knows that his letters are admired, he is in great danger of writing for admiration. Cowper was aware of this, and occasionally alludes to the temptation in lively terms. " I love praise dearly, especially from the judicious, and those who have so much delicacy themselves as not to offend mine in giving it. But then I found this consequence attending, or likely to attend, the eulogium you bestowed. If

my friend thought me witty before, he shall think
me ten times more witty hereafter ; where I joked
once I will joke five times ; and for every sensible
remark I will send him a dozen.   Now this foolish
vanity would have spoiled me quite, and have made
me as disgusting a letter writer as Pope, who
seems to have thought that, unless a sentence was
well turned, and every sentence pointed with some
conceit, it was not worth the carriage.   I was willing, therefore, to wait until the impression that
your commendation had made on the foolish part
of me was worn off, that I might scribble away as
usual, and write my uppermost thoughts, and those
only."   (June 8, 1780.   To the Rev. W. Unwin.)
No one ever avoided this danger better.   It is
strange, nay, wonderful, that these compositions,
which bear the stamp of so much cheerfulness and
benevolence, should have been written, most of
them, in his deepest gloom, and avowedly for the
purpose of withdrawing his thoughts from his own
misery.

PITT.

THE observations made at the beginning of our
memoir of Mr. Burke apply with greater force to
Mr. Pitt, on account both of the more recent date
of his death, and of the more important influence
which he exercised over the national welfare.   We
shall therefore lay before the reader a very succinct account of this celebrated statesman, endeav-

ouring not to colour it by the introduction of our own opinions, and avoiding any statements that can reasonably be controverted.

William Pitt, the second son of the first Earl of Chatham, was born at Hayes in Kent, May 28, 1759. He suffered much and frequently from ill health until he had nearly reached the age of manhood ; and his delicacy of constitution prevented his reading for honours at Pembroke College, Cambridge, of which he became a resident member at the age of fourteen. He therefore took the honorary degree of M.A., to which his birth entitled him, in 1776. His private tutor and biographer, the late Bishop of Winchester, has borne testimony to Mr. Pitt's proficiency in scholarship at the time when he commenced his residence, and to his diligent study of the ancient languages, of mathematics, and of modern literature, during the long period of seven years which he spent at Cambridge. His illustrious father was not slow to perceive and appreciate this early promise ; and the few letters which are extant, addressed by Lord Chatham to his son, contain a most pleasing picture of parental affection, confidence, and esteem.

Mr. Pitt was called to the bar June 12, 1780, and went the western circuit in that year and the following. In January, 1781, he was brought into Parliament by Sir James Lowther for the borough of Appleby. He made his maiden speech in support of Mr. Burke's bill for the reform of the civil list, and this being in a great measure in reply to former speakers, and therefore evidently not premeditated, produced the greater effect, and amply satisfied public expectation, which had been highly raised by his hereditary fame and reputed talents. Young as he was, he took a leading part in denouncing the impolicy and injustice of the American war, then drawing to its close, and in effecting the downfall of Lord North's administration, which occurred in March, 1782. In the Rockingham administration which followed, he bore no office : not that his talents were held cheap, for he was offered several important places ; but he had already determined, as he declared soon afterward, never to accept any office without a seat in the cabinet. He gave his support, however, to the measures of government ; and, with a determination which he again manifested at a later period, of securing his independence, he continued, notwithstanding his brilliant prospects in public life, his professional attendance at Westminster Hall. During this session he distinguished himself as an advocate of parliamentary reform, by supporting three measures relating to that subject : a motion, made by himself, for a committee to examine into the state of representation of the Commons ; a bill for shortening the duration of parliaments ; and a bill for the prevention of bribery, and the diminution of expense at elections. These, not being supported by government, were all thrown out.

The death of the Marquis of Rockingham, July 1, 1782, led to the appointment of the Earl of Shelburne as prime-minister, and to Mr. Fox's retirement from office. Mr. Pitt, at the age of twenty-three, was made Chancellor of the Exchequer. As a strong opposition was expected in the next session of parliament, it became desirable to effect a junction, if possible, with one of the ad-

verse parties. Against acting in concert with
Lord North, Mr. Pitt had formed an unchangeable
determination; and the negotiation with Mr. Fox
was stopped in the outset by that gentleman's resolution not to act under Lord Shelburne. Thus
two of the three principal parties into which the
House of Commons was then divided, were shut
out of office during the continuance of the existing
administration; and a strong motive was given
them to unite, even against all probability, considering the virulent hostility which had long existed
between their leaders. Mr. Fox and Lord North,
however, did form their celebrated Coalition; and,
in spite of its unpopularity, it had strength enough
to turn out the Shelburne ministry in the spring of
1783. Mr. Pitt, while in office, introduced a bill
for promoting economy, and removing many gross
abuses in various departments of the public service. This, after passing the Commons, was
thrown out by the Lords.

The king, it is well known, was exceedingly
averse to the readmission of Mr. Fox into office.
He pressed the task of forming an administration
upon Mr. Pitt, who, being convinced that no effective support could be hoped for at that time, either
in parliament or from the expression of public
opinion, steadily refused the offer. The coalition
ministry therefore came into power. In the session of 1783, Mr. Pitt again introduced the question of parliamentary reform, in the shape of three
resolutions, which provided that one hundred members should be added to those returned by the
counties and the metropolis, and that all boroughs
should be disfranchised where a majority of voters

had been proved guilty of corruption. These resolutions were however rejected.

On the meeting of parliament in November, Mr. Fox brought forward his celebrated India Bill. It was quickly carried through the lower house, but was thrown out in the upper, partly through the personal influence exerted by the king; and on the next day, December 18, Mr. Fox and Lord North received their dismissal. Mr. Pitt did not now hesitate to take his place at the head of government. He felt himself in a much stronger position than at the close of the Shelburne administration. He foresaw that the India Bill would become unpopular, though, as yet, little outcry had been made against it; and he resolved, with a courage, ability, and penetration which those who condemn his conduct most strongly cannot deny, to assume office in the teeth of a majority of the House of Commons, and to hold it in spite of the majorities continually arrayed against him. Nor, though strongly urged, would he resort to a dissolution; knowing that such a measure would be fatal, unless the new parliament should prove much more favourable to him than the existing one, being aware that Mr. Fox's popularity, though shaken by the Coalition, was not overthrown, and trusting to the growing unpopularity of the India Bill to dispose the nation more favourably to his own administration. It was therefore resolved to continue the sitting parliament; and the house adjourned on the 26th of December to the 12th of January. During the recess Mr. Pitt gained the applause of all parties by his disinterestedness in giving the valuable sinecure of Clerk of the Pells to Colonel Barré, on condition of his resigning a pension of £3000 a year, thus effecting a saving to the country of that amount.

On the 12th the new ministry was twice left in a minority, once of thirty-nine, and the second time of fifty-four. This not inducing them to resign, a series of motions were made to compel them to do so. It was never ventured, however, to stop the supplies. Between the 12th of January and the 8th of March, fourteen motions, besides those which passed without a division, were carried against the ministers, with various, but, on the whole, decreasing majorities; the last only by a majority of one. This ended the struggle. The minister saw that the time had now arrived when a dissolution was likely to tell in his favour, and it took place accordingly on the 25th of March.

He was now returned for the University of Cambridge. In the ensuing session his attention was principally engaged by the Westminster scrutiny, the state of the revenue, and the affairs of India. In the first he took a part which widened the breach between Mr. Fox and himself; and he had the mortification of being exposed to the charge of cherishing personal animosity against his illustrious antagonist, and of being deserted by many of his usual adherents, and finally left in a minority, on the 3d of March, 1785, when the scrutiny was ended by a vote of the house. Lord Hood and Mr. Fox were then returned. In his financial measures Mr. Pitt had eminent success. By economy. by resolutely facing the difficulties of the question, and, no doubt, by the assistance of that general prosperity, agricultural as well as commercial, which was beginning to succeed the depression of the American war, the revenue, which, on his accession to office, was considerably below the expenditure, was improved so much as, by the spring of 1786, to afford the promise of a million surplus. This was devoted to the formation of an effective sinking-fund. Mr. Pitt prided himself on this more than any other of his measures, and resisted all temptation to encroach upon it, even during the pressing difficulties of the latter years of his administration. The merit of having devised the scheme was claimed by Dr. Price; be this as it may, the principal merit, that of having rigidly carried it into execution, was Pitt's. Later authorities have denied the advantage of the system altogether. The India Bill, the other leading measure of this session, differed from Mr. Fox's chiefly in these important points—that the members of the Board of Control, like other members of administration, were removable at pleasure, and that nearly all the patronage of India was left in the hands of the Board of Directors. In 1785, for the last time, Mr. Pitt again brought forward the subject of parliamentary reform. His plan was to transfer the members of thirty-six decayed boroughs to the metropolis and to various counties, and, as other boroughs decayed, to give their franchises to populous and increasing towns. But the boroughs being regarded, in the words of his biographer, as " a species of valuable property and private inheritance, the voluntary surrender of their rights was not to be expected without an adequate consideration." This, not being treated as a government measure, was rejected by a large majority.

The other passages of most importance in Mr. Pitt's political life before the French Revolution, were his decided support of the impeachment of Warren Hastings, though without going the whole length of Mr. Burke and other opposition members, in 1786, and the conclusion of a commercial treaty with France on a more liberal footing than had yet been contemplated by the countries ; the successful opposition which he made to the repeal of the Test and Corporation Acts in 1787, notwithstanding the support he had received from the Dissenters a few years before ; his conduct on the Regency Bill, in opposition to the ill-advised assertion of Mr. Fox, that the Prince of Wales was entitled, as a matter of right, to the full possession of the powers of royalty, as sole regent, in 1788–9 ; and his support of the Abolition of the Slave Trade, for which he spoke and voted, but without making it a ministerial question.   Indeed, in consequence of Mr. Wilberforce's illness, Pitt was the first to bring that national disgrace and crime under the notice of the house, and he exerted his best eloquence in favour of its immediate abolition, and against the temporizing course which had been adopted.

It does not appear that in the beginning of the French Revolution Mr. Pitt anticipated any bad consequences to Great Britain, or that he expected or wished to be led into that protracted war, which, though ultimately triumphant, involved his country in imminent danger, enormous expense, and a debt still pressing it to the ground.   At least, in opening his budget in 1792, he spoke with more than usual confidence of the favourable prospects of the revenue, and prognosticated many years of peace. At the same time, he was already impressed with suspicion and fear of those in England who regarded with complacency the dawning of the revolution; and in the same session he declared himself opposed to the introduction of Mr. Grey's motion for reform in parliament, on the express grounds that men's minds were in a state of fermentation, which rendered any innovation inexpedient and dangerous. But the events of the summer and autumn changed Mr. Pitt's views more widely. After the deposition of Louis XVI. on the 10th of August, the British minister at Paris was recalled; and, as soon as the news of that unhappy sovereign's death reached England, the French minister in London was ordered to quit the kingdom. War was declared by France, February 1, 1793. We shall not attempt to compress the history of that eventful period into these pages. The policy of the British government was to make the sea the scene of their chief exertions, and their fleets were victorious in every quarter of the globe. But by land the conduct of the war was most unsuccessful. England was cautious of risking her own troops on the Continent; but the national wealth was profusely spent in subsidizing other nations, in combining alliances against France, which, one after another, proved utterly unable to withstand the energy of the French government and the talent of the republican generals, and in trifling expeditions, injurious if they failed, and useless when successful. Meanwhile the enormous expenditure of the day caused a corresponding increase of the public burdens, and, as was foreboded, a ruinous accession to the public debt. A large party, who were far from joining with those that would willingly have made England the subject of an experiment similar to the one going on in France, denied both the necessity and the expediency of the contest in which they were engaged ; party spirit reached a frantic height ; and these men, as sincere friends to their country as those who most strenuously supported the arbitrary measures of goverment, were denounced, and confounded with the small minority really hostile to domestic order. And no doubt the oppressive conduct of the administration drove many persons to extremes, which, in cooler moments and under a more equitable policy, they would not have countenanced. Then came the trials of Muir and Palmer in Scotland in 1793, of Hardy and Horne Tooke in 1794, the Alien Bill, the suspension of the Habeas Corpus Act, and other measures calculated, in the language of the times, to " prevent the spread of revolutionary principles," for which the minister was hailed by one party as the saviour of his country from anarchy, and denounced by another as a pillar of despotism, an enemy to the free constitution of his country, a deserter from the principles of his youth, and a persecutor of those associates who still adhered to them. Increased discontent was met by increased severity ; and, after the insults offered to the king's person, as he proceeded to open the session of parliament in 1796, the famous bills for the prevention of seditious meetings and for the better security of his majesty's person and government, commonly called the Pitt and Grenville Acts, were introduced and carried, though not without the utmost indignation and the most determined opposition by all means short of forcible resistance, both within the walls of parliament and without.

Mr. Fox and the other chief members of opposition, finding their utmost efforts unsuccessful, seceded openly from the House of Commons when the Seditious Meetings Bill went into committee. Meanwhile the country was beset by the most serious difficulties. The drain of specie produced by subsidies to foreign powers, the large advances required from the bank by government, and the disposition to hoard money, produced by the fear of invasion and domestic anarchy, gave reason to apprehend that the bank would be unable to meet its engagements; and in 1797 it was relieved by the Restriction Act from the obligation of paying cash in exchange for its notes. In the same year the mutiny at the Nore broke out; and in 1798 the rebellion in Ireland made a most formidable addition to the dangers and distresses of the nation. Meanwhile, all exertions had been powerless to check the victorious arms of France on the Continent of Europe, and a strong desire for peace was felt by many who had been Mr. Pitt's stanch supporters and advocates of the revolutionary war. This led to his retirement from office in 1801; unless, indeed, that event is rather to be ascribed to the king's fixed determination not to grant the Irish Catholics that full relief which had been held out as one inducement to secure the consent of Ireland to the Act of Union. It is to Mr. Pitt that the merit of carrying through that important measure is due; a measure which would probably have been attended with much more beneficial results

if the policy of its author with regard to Catholic
Emancipation had been adopted.   But not even the
importance of the object is sufficient to justify, and
can only palliate, the corrupt means which were
used in gaining the assent of the Irish parliament
to the Union, which was exceedingly unpopular
with the Irish nation.

Mr. Pitt resigned his office in February, 1801,
and was succeeded by Mr. Addington, who concluded the peace of Amiens in 1802, the preliminaries
having been signed the autumn before.   Mr. Pitt
defended the conditions of this treaty when it was
attacked in parliament, therein taking a different
course from several of his late colleagues.   But his
retirement in the first instance was regarded as not
much more than nominal, and he was generally
thought to be the adviser of the ministry after he
ceased to belong to it.   This state of affairs, however, was short-lived.   His support gradually sub-
sided, first into coldness, then into avowed disapprobation, and finally into hostility not less decided
than that of the regular opposition.   In the early
part of 1804, after the lapse of twenty years of violent enmity, Pitt and Fox were again seen speaking and voting on the same side.   A fruitless attempt was made by the ministry to procure the accession of the former ; and as it became clear that
the existing government could not stand, and as the
lapse of time and change in affairs had removed
many of the most irreconcilable grounds of party
variance, a strong hope was felt that an administration, uniting the best talents and most powerful
interests of the country, might be formed by the
junction of the three parties represented by Mr.

Pitt, Mr. Fox, and Lord Grenville. This hope appears to have been defeated by the king's personal objections to admit Mr. Fox to office. It is asserted by Mr. Rose that Mr. Pitt used his utmost endeavours to overcome that prejudice, "conceiving a strong government as important to the public welfare, and as calculated to call forth the united talents as well as the utmost resources of the empire ; in which endeavour he persisted till within a few months of his death." Unfortunately for his own fame, and, probably, for the interests of the country, he did not think fit to make this union of parties a condition of his own return to office. Lord Grenville, his relation, friend, and coadjutor, refused to become a member of an exclusive ministry, and Mr. Pitt took his station at the head of a cabinet singularly deficient in men of commanding talent, and more than half composed of Mr. Addington's colleagues. The disappointment of the nation was great : but the late period of the session (he was gazetted First Lord of the Treasury on the 12th of May) was of material service in enabling him to face the difficulties of his position ; and he employed the autumn in seeking to gain strength by forming an alliance with some other party. Lord Grenville, however, proved firm in his resolution not to accept office while Mr. Fox was excluded ; and the minister, assuredly with deep mortification, was compelled to make overtures of reconciliation to Mr. Addington, who was created Viscount Sidmouth, and appointed President of the Council in January, 1805. This alliance, after all, proved inefficient to strengthen the government, while it was fruitful in jealousies, which led to Lord

Sidmouth's speedy retirement from office in July; and the dismissal, and ultimate impeachment of his old and valued friend and ablest coadjutator, Mr. Dundas, now created Viscount Melville, during the same session, added another and still more distressing embarrassment to those by which the minister was already beset.

. On his return to office Mr. Pitt had again recourse to his former policy of raising up Continental alliances against France ; and he succeeded in uniting Austria and Russia in the confederacy which was crushed by the decisive battle of Austerlitz, December 2, 1805. At this time his constitution was rapidly giving way, exhausted by a life of excessive labour, which he sought to relieve by the immoderate use of wine, a habit first induced by original constitutional defects. In December he was ordered by his physicians to Bath; but he received no benefit from change of place, and returned to his residence at Putney by slow stages. He expired on the 23d of January, 1805.

In addition to his other offices, Mr. Pitt held the sinecure of Warden of the Cinque Ports, worth about £3000 per annum, which, unsolicited, was bestowed on him by the king in 1792, as a mark of personal esteem. But the pressure of public business left no time for the regulation of his domestic affairs ; and, notwithstanding his large income, he expended his small patrimonial estate, and died deeply involved in debt. The parliament was not slow to acknowledge his long services. His remains were interred at the public expense ; a monument was erected to him in Westminster Abbey ; £40,000 were voted to discharge his debts ; and, in conformity to his dying request, a pension of £1500 was conferred on his nieces, daughters of the Earl of Stanhope.

We abstain, for reasons already assigned, from attempting to give a summary of Mr. Pitt's qualifications and merits as a statesman, but it is a debt of justice to bear testimony to his unimpeached integrity in all pecuniary affairs.   As a speaker he possessed extraordinary powers ; clear, fluent, and singularly correct in his diction, unimpassioned, and seldom rising into flights of eloquence, he was always ready to profit by the indiscretions of an opponent, and his sarcasm was of the most cutting and effective kind.   His argumentative powers were of a high order, and the clearness and precision of his mind fitted him admirably for those minute financial statements which formed an important part of his official duties.   His voice, though wanting in variety, was sonorous and impressive in an extraordinary degree ; and his action, though awkward and ungainly at first sight, was not unpleasing, nor unsuited to his discourse.   In the relations of private life his character was unexceptionable. " With a manner somewhat reserved and distant in what might be termed his public deportment, no man was ever better qualified to gain, or more successful in fixing, the attachment of his friends, than Mr. Pitt.   They saw all the powerful energies of his character softened into the most perfect complacency and sweetness of disposition in the circles of private life, the pleasures of which no one more enjoyed or more agreeably promoted, where the paramount duties he conceived himself to owe to the public admitted of his mixing in them : that indignant severity with which he met and subdued what he considered unfounded opposition, that keenness of sarcasm with which he repelled and withered (as it might be said) the powers of most of his assailants in debate, were exchanged, in the society of his intimate friends, for a kindness of heart, a gentleness of demeanour, and a playfulness of good-humour, which none ever witnessed without interest or participated without delight." Such is the testimony borne to Mr. Pitt's social qualities by his intimate and attached friend, the Hon. George Rose, in his " Brief Examination into the Increase of the Revenue, &c., of Great Britain, during Mr. Pitt's administration."

FOX.

THE Right Honourable Charles James Fox was third son of the Right Honourable Henry Fox, afterward Lord Holland, and of Lady Georgiana Caroline Fox, eldest daughter of Charles, second Duke of Richmond. He was born January 24th, 1749, New Style.

Mr. Fox received his education at Eton ; and the favourite studies of the place had more than ordinary influence over his tastes and literary pursuits in after-life. Before he left school, his father was so imprudent as to carry him to Paris and Spa. To his early associations at the latter place may be ascribed that propensity to gaming which was the bane of two thirds of his life. As the present article is not designed to be a mere panegyric, we abandon the indulgence of this fatal passion to the severest censure that can be bestowed upon it by the philosopher and the moralist: but justice demands it at our hands to say, that, after the adjustment of Mr. Fox's affairs by his friends, personal and political, he resolutely conquered what habit had almost raised into second nature, and abstained from play with scrupulous fidelity. It may further be remarked, that while the paroxysms of the fever were most violent, his mind was never withdrawn from more worthy objects of pursuit.

The following anecdote will show the divided empire which discordant passions alternately usurped over his heart. On a night when he had sustained some serious losses, his deportment assumed so much of the character of despair that his friends became uneasy: they followed him, at distance enough to elude his observation, from the club-house to his home in the neighbourhood. They knocked at his door in time, as they thought, to have prevented any rash act, and rushed into the library. There they found the object of their anxiety stretched on the floor without his coat, before the fire; his hands grasping neither a razor nor a pistol, but his eyes intently fixed on the pages of Herodotus. The old historian had engrossed him wholly from the moment when he took up the volume, and the ruins of his own airbuilt castles vanished from before him as soon as he got sight of the venerable remains of the ancient world.

At Oxford Mr. Fox distinguished himself by his powers of application as well as by the intuitive quickness of his parts. On quitting the University he accompanied his father and mother to the

south of Europe. Not finding a good Italian master at Naples, he taught himself that language during the winter, and contracted a strong partiality
for Italian literature. In a letter from Florence
to Mr. Fitzpatrick, he conjures that gentleman to
learn Italian as fast as he can, if it were only to
read Ariosto ; and adds, " There is more good poetry in Italian than in all other languages I understand put together." At a later period of life, if
we may judge from the tenour of his correspondence
with eminent scholars, he would have transferred
that praise from the Italian to the Greek tongue.
At this time he was very fond of acting plays, and
was in all respects the man of fashion. Those who
recollect the simplicity, bordering on negligence, of
his outward garb late in life, will smile at the idea
of Mr. Fox with a powdered toupee and red heels
to his shoes, the hero of private theatricals. During his absence in 1768, he was chosen to represent Midhurst, and made his first speech on the
15th April, 1769. According to Horace Walpole,
he spoke with violence, but with infinite superiority
of parts.

Circumscribed as we are to space, we shall not
follow Mr. Fox's subaltern career in the House of
Commons. It was his breach with Lord North
that raised him into a party leader. He had previously formed an intimate acquaintance with Mr.
Burke. He began by receiving the lessons of that
eminent person as a pupil ; but the master was soon
so convinced of his scholar's greatness of character and statesman-like turn of mind, that he resigned the lead to him, and became an efficient coadjutor
in the Rockingham party, of which, in the House of

Commons, he had almost been the dictator. The American war roused all the energies of Mr. Fox's mind. The discussions to which it gave rise involved all the first principles of free government. The vicissitudes of the contest tried the firmness of the parliamentary opposition. Its duration exercised their perseverance. Its magnitude and the dangers of the country called forth their powers. Gibbon says, " Mr. Fox discovered powers for regular debate which neither his friends hoped nor his enemies dreaded." The following passage, from a letter to Mr. Fitzpatrick, written in 1778, illustrates his honourable and independent character : " People flatter me that I continue to gain rather than lose estimation as an orator; and I am so convinced that this is all I shall gain (unless I choose to be one of the meanest of men), that I never think of any other object of ambition. I am certainly ambitious by nature, but I have, or think I have, totally subdued that passion. I have still as much vanity as ever, which is a happier passion by far, because great reputation, I think, I may acquire and keep ; great situations I never can acquire, nor, if acquired, keep, without making sacrifices that I will never make." In the summer of 1778 he rejected Lord Weymouth's overtures to join the ministry, and took his station as the leading commoner in the Rockingham party, to which he had become attached on principle long before he enlisted permanently in its ranks. The conspicuous features of that party, and of Mr. Fox's public character, were the love of peace with foreign powers, the spirit of conciliation in home management, and an ardent attachment to civil and religious liberty.

The day of triumph came at last, when a resolution against the farther prosecution of the American war was carried in the Commons. The king was compelled, reluctantly, to part with the supporters of his favourite principles, and had nothing left but to sow the seeds of disunion between the Rockingham and Chatham or Shelburne party, united on the subject of America, but disagreeing on many other points both of external and internal policy. In this he was but too successful. We have neither space nor inclination to unravel the web of court intrigue; but we may remark that Lord Rockingham's demands were too extensive to be palatable : they involved the independence of America, the pacification of Ireland, and bills for economical and parliamentary reform, to be brought into parliament as ministerial measures. But the untimely death of Lord Rockingham frustrated his enlightened and enlarged designs, by dissolving the ministry over which he had presided. Mr. Fox has been blamed for the precipitancy of his resignation. The tone of sentiment in a letter before quoted will both account and apologize for the rashness if it were such ; and it is obvious that the sacrifice of personal feeling, or even of political consistency, could not long have deferred it, amid the cabals and clashing interests of party. Mr. Fox's policy was to detach Holland and America from France, and to form a Continental balance against the house of Bourbon. Lord Shelburne's system was to conciliate France, and to treat her allies as dependant powers. Lord Shelburne had the ear of the king. He strengthened himself with some of the old supporters of the American war, to fill the vacant offices, and made Mr. Pitt, just rising into eminence, his Chancellor of the Exchequer. There were now three parties in the Commons; the ministerial, the Whig or Rockingham, and a third consisting of those members of the late war-ministry who had not been invited to join the present. A coalition of some two of these three parties was almost unavoidable: the public would have most approved of a reunion among the Whigs; but there had been too much of mutual recrimination and dispute to admit of reconciliation. Nothing therefore remained but a junction of the two parties in opposition. A judicious friend of Mr. Fox said, "That to undertake the government with Lord North was to risk their credit on very unsafe grounds. Unless a real good government is the consequence of this junction, nothing can justify it to the public." Popular feeling was strongly against this coalition, mainly or account of some personal acrimony vented by Mr. Fox in the boiling over of his wrath during the American contest, which seemed to bear upon the moral character of his opponent. It is to be considered, however, that the most amiable persons, if enthusiastic, are apt, in the heat of passion, to launch out into invective far more violent than their natural benevolence would justify in their cooler moments. The question on which Mr. Fox and Lord North had been so acrimoniously opposed had ceased to exist, and perhaps there existed no solid reason against the union of the two parties. But the measure was almost universally believed to arise from corrupt motives: it afforded a fine scope for satire and caricature; and these have no small influence upon the politics of the many. While the people were displeased, the king was decidedly unfriendly to the administration which had forced itself upon him. He considered the Rockingham party as enemies to his prerogative as well as friends to American independence. He was forced to take them in, but resolved to throw them out again. The unpopular India bill which Mr. Pitt afterward adopted with some modifications, furnished the opportunity. The offence taken by the people against the coalition made them lend a ready ear to the charge of ministerial oligarchy; while the king, disguising his sentiments till the last moment, procured the rejection of the bill in the Lords, and instantly dismissed his ministers.

The coalition was still in possession of the House of Commons; but the voice of the people supported the minister, a dissolution was resorted to, and the will of the king was accomplished.

From 1784 to 1792, Mr. Fox was leader of a powerful party in the House of Commons, in opposition to Mr. Pitt. The Westminster Scrutiny, the Regency, the abatement of Impeachments by a dissolution of parliament, the Libel Bill, the Russian Armament, and the Repeal of the Corporation and Test Acts, were the topics which called forth his most powerful exertions. His force as a professed orator was conspicuously displayed in Westminster Hall on the trial of Warren Hastings; but the triumph of his talents is to be found in those masterly replies to his antagonists, in which cutting sarcasm and close argument, logical acuteness and metaphysical subtlety, were so combined as to surpass all that modern experience had witnessed. The constitutional doctrines of Mr. Fox on the Regency Question were much canvassed, and, by many, severely censured. The fact was, that the case was new; provided for neither by law, precedent, nor analogy. Lord Loughborough first suggested the prince's claim of right; and it was hastily adopted by Mr. Fox, who had returned from Italy just as the discussion was pending. Mr. Fox's Libel Bill places him among the most constitutional of English legislators. He saved his country from an unnecessary, unjust, and expensive war by his exertions on occasion of the Russian Armament.

The controversy on the Test and Corporation Acts has lost its interest, from having since been satisfactorily set at rest. But as, in a sketch like the present, we have more to do with the character of Mr. Fox's mind than with his political history, we will here introduce an anecdote which the writer of this life heard related many years ago by Dr. Abraham Rees, well known both in the scientific world and as a leading divine in the dissenting interest. We have already spoken of the intuitive quickness of Mr. Fox's parts, and the following anecdote will set that peculiarity in a strong light:

When the dissenting ministers applied for relief on the subject of subscription, a committee, consisting of Dr. Stennett, Dr. Rees, and others, waited on the leading members of the House of Commons to enforce their claims. With Fox they were unable to obtain an interview till the day of the debate. He received them courteously; but, though

a friend to religious liberty, was evidently unacquainted with the strong points and principal bear-
ings of their peculiar case.   He listened attentively to their exposition, and, with an eye that looked
them *through and through*, put four or five search-
ing questions.   They withdrew after a short conference, and, as they walked up St. James's-street,
Mr. Fox passed them, booted, as going to take air
and exercise, to enable him to encounter the heat
of the house and the storm of debate.   From the
gallery they saw him enter the house with whip in
hand, as just dismounted.   When he rose to speak,
he displayed such mastery of his subject, his arguments and illustrations were so various, his views
so profound and statesman-like, that a stranger
must have imagined the question at issue between
the High Church party and the Dissenters to have
been the main subject of his study throughout life.
That his principles of civil and religious liberty
should have enabled him to declaim in splendid
generalities was to be expected; but he entered
as fully and deeply into the fundamental principles
and most subtle distinctions of the question, as did
those to whom it was of vital importance, and that
after a short conference of some twenty minutes.
    The French Revolution is a topic of such magni-
tude, that we can only touch upon Mr. Fox's opinions and conduct with respect to it.   After the
taking of the Bastile, he describes it as "the greatest, and much the best event that ever happened in
the world : all my prepossessions against French
connexions for this country will be at an end, and,
indeed, most part of my European system of politics will be altered, if this revolution have the con-

sequence that I expect." But it had not that consequence ; and his views were completely changed by the trial and execution of the king and queen of France. But, because he did not catch that contagious disease, made up of alarm and desperate violence, which involved his country in a disastrous war, he was represented as the blind apologist of injustice and massacre ; as the careless, if not Jacobinical, spectator of the downfall of monarchy. Mr. Burke was the first to quarrel with Mr. Fox, and this quarrel led to the temporary estrangement from him of many of his oldest and most valuable friends. But "time and the hour" restored the good understanding between the members of the party, with the exception of Mr. Burke, who died while the paroxysm of anti-Gallican mania was at its height.

Mr. Fox opposed to the utmost the war into which the minister was unwillingly forced. But, as his passions became heated and the difficulties of his situation increased, Mr. Pitt adopted all Mr. Burke's views, and the rash project of a *bellum internecinum.** Both the public principles and the personal character of Mr. Fox were the subject of daily calumnies ; and the warmth of his early testimony in favour of the French Revolution was continually thrown in his teeth after the 10th of August, the massacres of September, and the success of Dumourier. But his whole conduct during this struggle was clear and consistent. At the dawn of the revolution he felt and spoke as a citizen of the world ; but he was the last man alive to have

* A war of extermination.

merged patriotism in the vague generalities of universal benevolence. When his own country became implicated in the strife, he no longer felt and spoke as a citizen of the world, but as a British statesman ; and endeavoured to persuade his countrymen, not for French interests, but for their own, to stand aloof from Continental politics, relying for the maintenance of a proud independence and dignified neutrality on their insular situation and their wooden walls. His advice was not listened to, and his mind grew indisposed towards public business. He says in a letter, dated April, 1795, "I am perfectly happy in the country. I have quite resources enough to employ my mind, and the great resource of literature I am fonder of every day." After making a vigorous but unsuccessful opposition to the Treason and Sedition bills, he and his remaining friends seceded from Parliament. He passed the years from 1797 to 1802 principally in retirement at St. Ann's Hill ; and they were the happiest of his life. His mornings passed in gardening and farming, his evenings over books and in conversation with his family and friends. During this period his attention was much given to the Greek tragedies and to Homer, whom he read not only with the ardent mind of a poet, but with the microscopic eye of a critic. His correspondence with an eminent scholar of the time was full of sagacious remarks on the suggestions and explanations of the commentators, as well as on the text of the poem. At this time, also, he conceived the plan of that history, of which he left only a splendid fragment in a state fit for publication. He had been diligent in collecting ma-

terials and scrupulous in verifying them. His
partiality for the Greek classics followed him into
this pursuit, and probably retarded his progress.
He is considered to have taken for his model Thu-
cydides, a writer strictly impartial in his narrative,
and grave even to severity in his style. He went
to Paris with Mrs. Fox in the summer of 1802,
partly to satisfy their mutual curiosity after so
long an estrangement from the Continent, but principally for the purpose of examining the copious
materials for the reign of James II. deposited in
the Scotch college there. Everything was thrown
open to him in the most liberal manner; and, as
the unflinching friend of peace through good and
evil report, he was received with enthusiasm both
by the people and the government. He had several interviews with Bonaparte : the chief topics
of their conversation were the Concordat ; the trial
by jury ; the freedom, amounting, in the opinion of
the First Consul, to licentiousness, of the English
press ; and the difference between Asiatic and European society. On one occasion he indignantly
repelled the charge against Mr. Wyndham, of
being accessary to the plot of the *infernal ma-
chine,* alleging the utter impossibility of an English
gentleman descending to so disgraceful a device.
During his stay in France he visited Lafayette at
his country seat of La Grange.

Our limits will not allow us to enter, ever so
cursorily, into his political career after the renewal
of the war. His advice was wise, and consistent
with himself ; but it was not accepted. The
king's dislike of him was not to be overcome.
The death of Mr. Pitt, however, made the admis-

sion of Mr. Fox and the Whigs, in conjunction with Lord Grenville, a matter of necessity. Mr. Fox's desire of peace induced him to take the office of Secretary of State for Foreign Affairs ; and, before his fatal illness, he had begun a negotiation for that main object of his whole life with every apparent prospect of success. The hopes entertained from his accession to power were prematurely cut off; but his short career in office was honourably marked by the ministerial measure, determined on during his life, and carried after his decease, of the abolition of the Slave Trade.

The complaint of which he died was dropsy, occasioned probably by the duties of office and the fatigue of constant attendance in the House of Commons, after the comparative seclusion and learned ease in which he had lived for several years. He expired on the 13th of September, 1806, with his senses perfect and his understanding unclouded to the last.

We conclude this brief account of Mr. Fox with the character drawn of him by one who knew him well and was fully qualified to appreciate him—Sir James Macintosh.

"Mr. Fox united in a most remarkable degree the seemingly repugnant characters of the mildest of men and the most vehement of orators. In private life he was gentle, modest, placable, kind, of simple manners, and so averse from dogmatism as to be not only unostentatious, but even something inactive in conversation. His superiority was never felt but in the instruction which he imparted, or in the attention which his generous preference usually directed to the more obscure mem-

bers of the company. The simplicity of his manners was far from excluding that perfect urbanity
and amenity which flowed still more from the mild-
ness of his nature than from familiar intercourse
with the most polished society of Europe. The
pleasantry, perhaps, of no man of wit had so un-
laboured an appearance. It seemed rather to escape from his mind than to be produced by it.
He had lived on the most intimate terms with all
his contemporaries distinguished by wit, politeness,
or philosophy ; by learning, or the talents of public
life. In the course of thirty years he had known
almost every man in Europe whose intercourse
could strengthen, or enrich, or polish the mind.
His own literature was various and elegant. In
classical erudition, which, by the custom of England, is more peculiarly called learning, he was
inferior to few professed scholars. Like all men
of genius, he delighted to take refuge in poetry
from the vulgarity and irritation of business. His
own verses were easy and pleasant, and might have
claimed no low place among those which the
French call *vers de société.** The poetical character of his mind was displayed by his extraordinary partiality for the poetry of the two most poetical nations, or, at least, languages of the West,
those of the Greeks and of the Italians. He disliked political conversation, and never willingly
took any part in it.

" To speak of him justly as an orator would re
quire a long essay. Everywhere natural, he car
ried into public something of that simple and neg

* Social verses.

ligent exterior which belonged to him in private.
When he began to speak, a common observer might
have thought him awkward; and even a consum-
mate judge could only have been struck with the
exquisite justness of his ideas, and the transparent
simplicity of his manners. But, no sooner had he
spoken for some time, than he was changed into
another being. He forgot himself and everything
around him. He thought of nothing but the subject. His genius warmed and kindled as he went
on. He darted fire into his audience. Torrents
of impetuous and irresistible eloquence swept along
their feelings and conviction. He certainly possessed, above all moderns, that union of reason, simplicity, and vehemence, which formed the prince of
orators. He was the most Demosthenean speaker since the days of Demosthenes. 'I knew him,'
says Mr. Burke, in a pamphlet written after their
unhappy difference, 'when he was nineteen; since
which time he has risen, by slow degrees, to be the
most brilliant and accomplished debater the world
ever saw.'

"The quiet dignity of a mind roused only by
great objects, the absence of petty bustle, the contempt of show, the abhorrence of intrigue, the
plainness and downrightness, and the thorough
good-nature which distinguished Mr. Fox, seem
to render him no unfit representative of the old
English character, which, if it ever changed, we
should be sanguine indeed to expect to see it succeeded by a better. The simplicity of his character inspired confidence, the ardour of his eloquence
roused enthusiasm, and the gentleness of his manners invited friendship. 'I admired,' says Mr.

Gibbon, after describing a day passed with him at Lausanne, 'the powers of a superior man, as they are blended, in his attractive character, with all the softness and simplicity of a child; no human being was ever more free from any taint of malignity, vanity, or falsehood.'

"The measures which he supported or opposed may divide the opinion of posterity, as they have divided those of the present age. But he will most certainly command the unanimous reverence of future generations by his pure sentiments towards the commonwealth; by his zeal for the civil and religious rights of men; by his liberal principles, favourable to mild government, to the unfettered exercise of the human faculties, and the progressive civilization of mankind; by his ardent love for a country, of which the well-being and greatness were, indeed, inseparable from his own glory; and by his profound reverence for that free constitution which he was universally admitted to understand better than any other man of his age, both in an exactly legal and in a comprehensively philosophical sense."

KOSCIUSKO.

AMONG the remarkable men of modern times, there is perhaps none whose fame is purer from reproach than that of Thaddeus Kosciusko. His name is enshrined in the ruins of his unhappy country, which, with heroic bravery and devotion, he sought to defend against foreign oppression and foreign domination.   Kosciusko was born at Warsaw, about the year 1755.   He was educated at the school of Cadets in that city, where he distinguished himself so much in scientific studies as well as in drawing, that he was selected as one of four students of that institution, who were sent to travel at the expense of the state, with a view of perfecting their acquirements.   In this capacity he visited France, where he remained for several years, devoting himself to studies of various kinds. On his return to his own country he entered the army, and obtained the command of a company. But he was soon obliged to expatriate himself again, in order to fly from a violent but unrequited passion for the daughter of the Marshal of Lithuania, one of the first officers of state of the Polish court.

He bent his steps to that part of North America which was then waging its war of independence against England.   Here he entered the army, and served with distinction, as one of the adjutants of General Washington.   While thus employed, he became acquainted with Lafayette, Lameth, and other distinguished Frenchmen serving in the same cause, and was honoured by receiving the most flattering praises from Franklin, as well as the public thanks of the Congress of the United States.   He was also decorated with the new American order of Cincinnatus, being the only European, except Lafayette, to whom it was given.

At the termination of the war he returned to his own country, where he lived in retirement till the year 1789, at which period he was promoted by the Diet to the rank of major-general. That body was at this time endeavouring to place its military force upon a respectable footing, in the vain hope of restraining and diminishing the domineering influence of foreign powers in what still remained of Poland. It also occupied itself in reforming the vicious constitution of that unfortunate and ill-governed country—in rendering the monarchy hereditary—in declaring universal toleration—and in preserving the privileges of the nobility, while, at the same time, it ameliorated the condition of the lower orders. In all these improvements Stanislas Poniatowski, the reigning king, readily concurred, though the avowed intention of the Diet was to render the crown hereditary in the Saxon family. The King of Prussia (Frederic William II.), who, from the time of the treaty of Cherson in 1787 between Russia and Austria, had become hostile to the former power, also encouraged the Poles in their proceedings; and even gave them the most positive assurances of assisting them in case the changes they were effecting occasioned any attacks from other sovereigns.

Russia at length having made peace with the Turks, prepared to throw her sword into the scale. A formidable opposition to the measures of the Diet had arisen, even among the Poles themselves, occasioning what was called the confederation of Targowicz, to which the Empress of Russia promised her assistance. The feeble Stanislas, who had proclaimed the new constitution in 1791, bound himself in 1792 to sanction the Diet of Grodno, which restored the ancient constitution, with all its vices and abuses. In the mean time, Frederic William, King of Prussia, who had so much contributed to excite the Poles to these measures, basely deserted them, and refused to afford them any assistance. On the contrary, he stood aloof from the contest, waiting for that share of the spoil which the haughty Empress of the North might think proper to allot to him as a reward of his non-interference.

But, though thus betrayed on all sides, the Poles were not disposed to submit without a struggle. They flew to arms, and found in the nephew of their king, the prince Joseph Poniatowski, a general worthy to conduct so glorious a cause. Under his command Kosciusko first became known in European warfare. He distinguished himself in the battle of Zielenec, and still more in that of Dubienska, which took place on the 18th of June, 1792. Upon this latter occasion he defended for six hours, with only four thousand men against fifteen thousand Russians, a post which had been slightly fortified in twenty-four hours, and at last retired with inconsiderable loss.

But the contest was too unequal to last; the patriots were overwhelmed by enemies from without, and betrayed by traitors within, at the head of whom was their own sovereign. The Russians took possession of the country, and proceeded to appropriate those portions of Lithunia and Volhynia which suited their convenience; while Prussia, the friendly Prussia, invaded another part of the kingdom.

Under these circumstances, the most distinguished officers in the Polish army retired from the ser.

vice, and of this number was Kosciusko.　Miserable at the fate of his unhappy country, and, at the
same time, an object of suspicion to the ruling powers, he left his native land and retired to Leipsic,
where he received intelligence of the honour which
had been conferred upon him by the Legislative
Assembly of France, who had invested him with
the rights of a French citizen.

But his fellow-countrymen were still anxious to
make another struggle for independence, and they
unanimously selected Kosciusko as their chief and
generalissimo.　He obeyed the call, and found the
patriots eager to combat under his orders.　Even
the noble Joseph Poniatowski, who had previously
commanded in chief, returned from France, whither he had retired, and received from the hands of
Kosciusko the charge of a portion of his army.

The patriots had risen in the north of Poland,
to which part Kosciusko first directed his steps.
Anxious to begin his campaign with some bold action, he marched rapidly to Cracow, which town
he entered triumphantly on the 24th of March,
1794.　He forthwith published a manifesto against
the Russians ; and then, at the head of only five
thousand men, marched to meet their army.　On
the 4th of April he encountered ten thousand Russians at a place called Wraclawic, and entirely defeated them after a combat of four hours.　He returned in triumph to Cracow, and shortly afterward
marched along the left bank of the Vistula to Pola-
niec, where he established his headquarters.

Meanwhile, the inhabitants of Warsaw, animated
by the recital of the heroic deeds of their countrymen, had also raised the standard of independence,

and were successful in driving the Russians from
the city after a murderous conflict of three days.
In Lithuania and Samogitia an equally successful
revolution was effected before the end of April;
while the Polish troops stationed in Volhynia and
Podolia marched to the re-enforcement of Kosciusko.

Thus far fortune seemed to smile upon the cause
of Polish freedom; the scene was, however, about
to change. The undaunted Kosciusko, having first
organized a national council to conduct the affairs
of government, again advanced against the Russians. On his march he met a new enemy, in the
person of the faithless Frederic William of Prussia, who, without having even gone through the
preliminary of declaring war, had advanced into
Poland at the head of forty thousand men.

Kosciusko, with but thirteen thousand men, attacked the Prussian army on the 8th of June at
Szcekociny. The battle was long and bloody: at
length, overwhelmed by numbers, he was obliged
to retreat towards Warsaw. This he effected in
so able a manner, that his enemies did not dare to
harass him in his march; and he effectually cover-
ed the capital, and maintained his position for two
months against desperate and continued attacks.
Immediately after this reverse, the Polish general
Zaionczeck lost the battle of Chelm, and the Governor of Cracow had the baseness to deliver the
town to the Prussians without attempting a defence.

These disasters occasioned disturbances among
the disaffected at Warsaw, which, however, were
put down by the vigour and firmness of Kosciusko.
On the 13th of July, the combined forces of Prussia

and Russia, amounting to fifty thousand men, assembled under the walls of Warsaw, and commenced the siege of that city. After six weeks spent before the place, and a succession of bloody conflicts, the confederates were obliged to raise the siege ; but this respite to the Poles was but of short duration.

Their enemies increased fearfully in number, while their own resources diminished. Austria, now determined to assist in the annihilation of Poland, had caused a body of her troops to enter that kingdom. Nearly at the same moment the Russians ravaged Lithuania ; and the two corps of the Russian army, commanded by Suwarof and Fersen, effected their junction in spite of the battle of Krupezyce, which the Poles had ventured upon with doubtful issue, against the first of these commanders, on the 16th of September.

Upon receiving intelligence of these events, Kosciusko left Warsaw and placed himself at the head of the Polish army. He was attacked by the very superior forces of the confederates on the 10th of October, 1794, at a place called Macieiowice, and for many hours supported the combat against overwhelming odds. At length he was severely wounded, and as he fell he uttered the prophetic words, " *Finis Poloniæ.*"* It is asserted that he had exacted from his followers an oath not to suffer him to fall alive into the hands of the Russians, and that, in consequence, the Polish cavalry, being unable to carry him off, inflicted some severe sabre wounds on him, and left him for dead on the field :

* The end of Poland.

a savage fidelity, which we half admire even in condemning it. Be this as it may, he was recognised and delivered from the plunderers by some Cossack chiefs ; and thus was saved from death to meet a scarcely preferable fate—imprisonment in a Russian dungeon.

Thomas Wawrzecki became the successor of Kosciusko in the command of the army ; but, with the loss of their heroic leader, all hope had deserted the breasts of the Poles. They still, however, fought with all the obstinacy of despair, and defended the suburb of Warsaw, called Praga, with great gallantry. At length this post was wrested from them. Warsaw itself capitulated on the 9th of November, 1794 ; and this calamity was followed by the entire dissolution of the Polish army on the 18th of the same month.

During this time Kosciusko remained in prison at Petersburgh ; but, at the end of two years, the death of his persecutress, the Empress Catharine, released him. One of the first acts of the Emperor Paul was to restore him to liberty, and to load him with various marks of his favour. Among other gifts of the autocrat was a pension, by which, however, the high-spirited patriot would never consent to profit. No sooner was he beyond the reach of Russian influence, than he returned to the donor the instrument by which this humiliating favour was conferred. From this period the life of Kosciusko was passed in retirement. He went first to England, and then to the United States of America. He returned to the Old World in 1798, and took up his abode in France, where he divided his time between Paris and a country-house he had purchased near Fontainbleau.   While here he received the appropriate present of the sword of John Sobieski, which was sent to him by some of his countrymen serving in the French armies in Italy, who had found it in the Shrine at Loretto.

Napoleon, when about to invade Poland in 1807, wished to use the name of Kosciusko in order to rally the people of the country around his standard. The patriot, aware that no real freedom was to be hoped for under such auspices, at once refused to lend himself to his wishes.   Upon this the emperor forged Kosciusko's signature to an address to the Poles, which was distributed throughout the country ; nor would he permit the injured person to deny the authenticity of this act in any public manner.   The real state of the case was, however, made known to many through the private representations of Kosciusko ; but he was never able to publish a formal denial of the transaction till after the fall of Napoleon.

When the Russians, in 1814, had penetrated into Champagne and were advancing towards Paris, they were astonished to hear that their former adversary was living in retirement in that part of the country.   The circumstances of this discovery were striking.   The commune in which Kosciusko lived was subjected to plunder, and among the troops thus engaged he observed a Polish regiment.   Transported with anger, he rushed among them, and thus addressed the officers : " When I commanded brave soldiers, they never pillaged ; and I should have punished severely subalterns who allowed of disorders such as those which we see around.   Still more severely should I have

punished older officers, who authorized such conduct by their culpable neglect." " And who are
you," was the general cry, " that you dare to
speak with such boldness to us ?" " I am Kosciusko." The effect was electric : the soldiers
threw down their arms, prostrated themselves at
his feet, and cast dust upon their heads according
to a national usage, supplicating his forgiveness for
the fault which they had committed. For twenty
years the name of Kosciusko had not been heard
in Poland save as that of an exile ; yet it still retained its ancient power over Polish hearts ; a
power never used but for some good and generous
end.

The Emperor Alexander honoured him with a
long interview, and offered him an asylum in his
own country. But nothing could induce Kosciusko again to see his unfortunate native land. In
1815 he retired to Soleure in Switzerland, where
he died, October 16th, 1817, in consequence of an
injury received by a fall from his horse. Not long
before, he had abolished slavery upon his Polish
estate, and declared all his serfs entirely free, by a
deed registered and executed with every formality
that could ensure the full performance of his intention. The mortal remains of Kosciusko were removed to Poland at the expense of Alexander, and
have found a fitting place of rest in the cathedral
of Cracow, between those of his companions in
arms, Joseph Poniatowski, and the greatest of
Polish warriors, John Sobieski.

JENNER.

EDWARD, the third son of the Rev. Stephen Jenner, was born May 17, 1749, in the vicarage-house of Berkeley, in Gloucestershire, of which parish his father, a man of independent fortune, and of a family long established and esteemed in that neighbourhood, was incumbent. At the death of that parent in 1754, the care of Edward Jenner's education devolved upon his eldest brother Stephen, who succeeded to the living of Berkeley, and faithfully and affectionately discharged the duties of a father towards him.

He began at a very early age to give tokens of that fondness and aptitude for the study of natural history which first directed the choice of his profession, and afterward led him, by steps which may be easily traced, to the discovery of a method of securing the constitution against the smallpox by a remedy so mild as to be scarcely an inconvenience, yet so effectual as almost to have extinguished that disease in some countries where it has been energetically used.

Having finished his school education and fixed upon a profession, Jenner was apprenticed at the usual age to Mr. Ludlow, a surgeon practising at Sodbury, near Bristol; and in 1770, when nearly twenty-one, he came to London, and put himself under the tuition of John Hunter, in whose house he lived for two years, as much in the capacity of a friend as in that of a pupil, with great advantage to his professional studies. The intimacy between these two eminent men was very close and cordial, and subsisted till Hunter's sudden death in 1793, as is attested by numerous letters from Mr. Hunter which Jenner carefully preserved : his own were probably destroyed, with the rest of Hunter's papers, by the late Sir Everard Home. Their correspondence relates chiefly to facts and experiments in natural history.

The success with which Jenner had already pursued his studies, and the respect entertained for his talents by his illustrious instructer at a period when their intercourse was yet in its infancy, may be gathered from his being selected in 1771, on the recommendation of Mr. Hunter, to arrange the collections in natural history which had been made by Sir Joseph Banks in his voyage round the world with Captain Cook, then just completed. Jenner acquitted himself so well of this charge, that he was offered, though little more than twenty-two years of age, the situation of naturalist to the second expedition under the command of Cook, which sailed in 1772. This was a flattering proposal to so young a man, and consonant to Jenner's ruling tastes ; nevertheless, he declined it. It is fortunate for mankind that he chose the laborious seclusion of a country practice in preference to aiming at distinction and wealth ; for in no other sphere could he have found opportunities for pursuing his discovery of vaccination through all the perplexities into which his early researches into that subject involved him. Indeed, it is probable that considerations of this kind, independently of his fondness for a country life, had their weight with him in the choice ; for the idea had already taken strong hold of his naturally sanguine feelings and quick apprehension, that he was furnished with a clew which might lead him to a result of the highest importance to mankind.

It may be added here, that a few years after this time he declined a very lucrative situation in India, as well as a much more tempting proposal from Mr. Hunter in 1775, to join him in a project for establishing in London a school of natural history, including medicine, of which Jenner was to undertake the anatomical department.

Having determined to settle in the country, and being amply provided with the requisite knowledge, Jenner established himself as a general practitioner at Berkeley. Here he speedily acquired a profitable and extensive practice ; so much so, indeed, that, finding his health giving way, he was obliged to limit himself to the practice of medicine alone ; for which purpose he purchased, as was then customary, the degree of doctor at St. Andrew's in 1792.

He not only attained at an early age to a high degree of professional reputation, but won the affectionate esteem of all with whom he associated. It is related of him that his friends were in the habit of joining in his daily professional rides, often of considerable extent, for the sake of his agreeable and instructive conversation ; and that, when any of them were ill, he would sometimes make their houses the headquarters of his practice for the time being, and remain in close attendance upon them till their recovery.

Music, the lighter kinds of literature, both as a reader and occasionally as an author, and the innocent recreations of society, which no one enjoyed more keenly than himself, were the means by which Jenner lightened the burden of his professional labours ; but his chief amusement was natural history, including geology, a science then in its infancy, for the study of which his position in the vale of Gloucester afforded ample opportunity, the neighbourhood abounding with fossil remains, and exhibiting a great variety of terrestrial structure. Towards subjects of this nature he was led, not only by his original bias, but by his correspondence with Hunter, Banks, and Parry.

In 1778 he formed a medical society, which held its periodical meetings at Rodborough, for the purpose of communicating professional information, and promoting a friendly feeling among the members. In furtherance of these objects, Jenner contributed several important and original papers, the substance of which is now imbodied in medical science, without his property in them being generally known. Among these were essays on the nature and causes of Angina Pectoris, on a peculiar disease of the heart occurring in acute rheumatism, and on several of the more severe affections of the eye. He also belonged to another medical society, meeting at Alveston near Bristol, to the members of which, who were men of congenial dispositions with his own, he was personally much attached. Upon one topic, however, they did not agree ; for it is said that he was in the habit of enlarging so frequently upon his favourite speculation of the cow-pox, that the subject was at length proscribed, and he was jestingly forbidden to renew it on pain of expulsion. This club was for many years a source of much enjoyment and advantage to him, and we may suppose that he was a very important contrib. utor to the entertainment of the other members ; for it ceased to exist in 1789, when other objects began to engross the time that he could spare from his practice. In March of the previous year, at the age of thirty-seven, he married Miss Catharine Kingscote, by whom he had several children. The choice appears to have been a very fortunate one for his domestic happiness.

In 1786 he had communicated to Mr. Hunter, in the form of an essay, the result of several years' careful observation of the singular habits of the cuckoo, till then a mystery to naturalists. It was presented by Mr. Hunter to the Royal Society, and was printed entire in their Transactions in 1789, having been returned to Jenner in the mean time, in order that he might record some additional facts which he had ascertained. This tract has been considered as a very masterly performance, and was the occasion of the author's being elected to the fellowship of the Royal Society. It is not a little remarkable, that Mr. Hunter, like Jenner's friends at Alveston, thought so doubtingly of his views on the subject of vaccination, that he cautioned him against publishing them, lest they should interfere with the fame he had acquired in the learned world by his " Essay on the Cuckoo." But the event proved that the caution, though well meant, was unnecessary. Jenner was not more disposed than his gifted master to admit any conclusion on merely collateral grounds that might be put to the test of experiment. This, however, was too new and important a matter to be lightly or prematurely hazarded; and Jenner waited long and patiently for an opportunity of thus testing his opinions, losing, in the mean time, no opportunity of collecting additional information. The idea, thus watchfully and laboriously improved, was first excited in his mind while he was an apprentice at Sodbury, by a remark accidentally dropped by a young countrywoman in his master's surgery, who, overhearing a conversation about the smallpox, observed that she had no fear of catching that disease, as she had taken the *cowpox.* Jenner, who was always alive to any subject connected with natural history, was induced to make more particular inquiries into this complaint, of which he had never heard before; and the answers he received were such as to suggest to him the probability of substituting it with advantage for the inoculated smallpox. Of this theory he never lost sight till he established it on the clearest evidence, and with it his unrivalled claim to the perpetual gratitude of mankind.

The cowpox is a disease of the eruptive kind, which is sometimes extensively prevalent among cattle in large dairy countries where they are herded together in numbers, but often disappears for a long time together. Though commonly mild, it is occasionally so severe as to terminate fatally; and it is believed, on strong grounds, to have been at different times even pestilential among them, and, as such, to have been mentioned by various writers on rural economy, ancient and modern, as well as in medical and other histories. It is generally, however, a very mild disorder, appearing on the udder of the cow, at first in the form of vesicles much resembling those of smallpox; and is sometimes, as in the instance which first attracted the attention of Jenner, communicated to the hands of milkers. In such cases, an eruption of similar vesicles takes place on the hands and arms, not without much swelling and inflammation, and occasionally with fever and disturbance of the health for some days. It has never been known to prove fatal when thus communicated, or to have left any unpleasant effects behind it, except indented marks in the situation occupied by the pustules. It is not communicable, like smallpox in the human subject, by the effluvia; but the matter, or lymph, as it is called, contained in the vesicles, must be actually inserted under the skin, or applied to a raw or an absorbing surface. But the most important of its peculiarities is the security which it affords against the infection of smallpox. This property was well known among the agricultural classes in the grazing districts before the time of Jenner, and it has been stated that individuals among them had turned their knowledge of it to account for the protection of their families, by inoculating them with the vaccine disease. But this circumstance, alleged on very scanty evidence by those who were opposed to Jenner's claims, cannot lessen the merit of his independent discovery, of which each step was communicated in succession to a numerous circle of medical friends, and is recorded in the most authentic form. His reputation is, on the other hand, enhanced by the fact that, although the immunity conferred by the casual disease in milkers had frequently come under the notice of medical men, from

their failing in such persons to produce the smallpox by inoculation, yet the idea of introducing the
disease of an animal into the human frame was so
little in consonance with any former practice, that
Jenner was the first among his brethren to conjecture that cowpox, as the milder disease, might advantageously supersede the inoculated smallpox;
and that, as the latter is rendered less virulent by
inoculation, so the former, introduced in the same
way, might be milder than the casual complaint,
and yet retain its protecting power. He had even
communicated this conjecture to Hunter, himself
no mean innovator in medicine, so early as the year
1770; and Mr. Hunter was for many years in the
habit of mentioning it in his public lectures, coupled
with Jenner's name : but the proposed substitution
was so distasteful, or appeared of such questionable
propriety, that it obtained no favourable notice till
it was forced by the inventor on the public attention, thirty years after it had first attracted his own.

It would be interesting to enter into a detail of
the progress of Jenner's discovery, and of its introduction into general use, as well as to show its
inestimable value to society by a reference to sta-
tistical facts. This, however, can only be done
here in a very cursory manner.

The way in which the idea was first suggested
to him has been already mentioned. After his
return to Berkeley from London, he pursued the
subject with great patience and sagacity for many
years. In the course of these preliminary inquiries, he found reason to believe, that of several kinds
of vesicular disease in the cow, but one had the
property of protecting from the smallpox, and that

one exclusively, or, at least, with the greatest cer
tainty, in its first stage. He also ascertained that
the horse is subject to an eruption of similar vesicles, apparently arising without infection, and pop-
ularly known by the name of the *grease.* The
matter issuing from these is sometimes conveyed
to the cow by milkers engaged in farriery; and
Jenner conceived it to be the original and only
source of cowpox among the herds. This opinion,
however, is not generally held at present to its full
extent; but experiments by himself and others
since the publication of his "Inquiry," have proved
a fact, much disputed at the time, that he was right
in believing the diseases to be identical, whatever
may be their origin.

After a laborious investigation of the subject
during twenty-six years, Dr. Jenner at length arrived at a rational conviction of the safety of the
experiment which he meditated, from observing
the invariable harmlessness of the disease when
casually taken: he determined, therefore, to put his
long-cherished idea to the trial the first opportunity. This occurred on the 14th of May, 1796,
the anniversary of which is still kept as a festival
at Berlin. On that day he inoculated a boy of the
name of Phipps in the arm, from a pustule on the
hand of a young woman who was infected by her
master's cows. The boy went favourably through
the disease. On the 1st of July he was inoculated
for the smallpox, and, as Jenner had predicted,
without effect.

The feelings of the sanguine philanthropist may
readily be conceived. They cannot be better described than they have been by himself in the fol.

lowing terms : " While the vaccine discovery was progressive, the joy I felt at the prospect before me, of being the instrument destined to take away from the world one of its greatest calamities, blended with the fond hope of enjoying independence and domestic peace and happiness, was often so excessive, that, in pursuing my favourite subject among the meadows, I have sometimes found myself in a revery. It is pleasant to me to recollect that these reflections always ended in devout acknowledgments to that Being from whom this and all other mercies flow."

During the next two years many other equally successful trials were made ; and at length the discovery was published to the world in June, 1798, in a quarto pamphlet of seventy pages, which had been previously subjected to the most rigorous criticism and revision by a few chosen friends, who met for that purpose at the house of Thomas Westfaling, Esq., at Rudhall, near Ross. It is entitled, " An Inquiry into the Causes and Effects of the Variolæ Vaccinæ ; a disease discovered in some of the Western Counties of England, particularly Gloucestershire, and known by the name of the Cowpox." The pamphlet is enriched with the detail of sixteen cases of the casual, and seven of the inoculated disease, the latter including the case of one of the author's sons ; and with coloured drawings of the appearances in both.

The style of this pamphlet (as well as of others which succeeded it from Jenner's pen in the course of a few years) is remarkably modest, and admirable in all respects, which probably contributed much to the early favour it received. The facts were such as to defy contradiction, and the conclusions so just and mature that the experience of nearly forty years has been able to add little more than its seal of confirmation to them. The few errors that have been detected relate chiefly to the degree of protection afforded by the cowpox, which Jenner affirmed to be perfect: it is now, however, believed to be incomplete, perhaps in three instances out of every hundred; that small proportionate number passing, in general after the lapse of some years, through a very mild and modified smallpox, in which the per centage of fatal cases is certainly not more, and probably much less, than five, being not more than three in 2000 of all vaccinated persons; while the rate of mortality even in inoculated smallpox is one in fifty, or forty in 2000. It should likewise be borne in mind, that smallpox itself sometimes occurs a second time, even in a severe and fatal form, as in the case of Louis XV. Some constitutional peculiarity is probably the occasion of both these anomalies; and this supposition will also account for the often-observed fact, that smallpox after vaccination commonly affects several members of the same family almost simultaneously, thus giving an appearance of failure in a proportion much greater than the truth.

Another position advanced by Jenner in this pamphlet is too remarkable to be passed over. After stating his belief that the cowpox originates from the horse in the way already mentioned, he proceeds to suggest that the smallpox may have been itself originally morbid matter of the same kind, aggravated into a malignant and contagious form by accidental circumstances. But this opin.ion, though plausible, is not considered by any means as established.

Favourably as his work was received, the author, who had come to London partly to superin.tend the publication, was unable to obtain an opportunity of displaying the disease in that city, which had been the chief object of his visit ; and returned, much disappointed, to Cheltenham, where he now frequently resided, in the middle of July. He left, however, some vaccine lymph with Mr. Cline, who was the first surgeon in London that ventured to make a trial of it. The complete success of the experiment, which was publicly performed, so strongly interested the profession, that the new practice became quickly popular, in spite of a warm though partial opposition, which was put down in the summer of 1799 by a manifesto expressive of confidence in its efficacy and safety, signed by seventy-three of the most eminent medical men in the metropolis. In the same year some unfortunate occurrences took place, in consequence of Dr. Woodville, the physician of the Smallpox Hospital, having incautiously used and distributed matter from persons whom he had inoculated with smallpox a few days after vaccination, and before the vaccine matter had taken a sufficient hold. The mongrel lymph thus produced sometimes occasioned one, sometimes the other disease ; their effects were confounded ; and some deaths which ensued, as well as a general eruption of the skin, which took place in many instances, were attributed to the cowpox. This and other mistakes would probably have much retarded the general adoption of vaccination but for the promptitude of Jenner to discover and expose the source of the error.

In 1802 a parliamentary inquiry into the value of the new method of preventing smallpox, including Jenner's claim to the discovery of it, was instituted, and a grant was voted to him of £10,000. In 1807 he received an additional vote of £20,000, which, considering that he had been the instrument of saving in England alone at least 45,000 lives annually, will seem by no means an extravagant mark of national gratitude and respect.

In 1803, the Royal Jennerian Society for the encouragement of vaccination was established in London under the superintendence of Dr. Jenner. In 1808 this society was merged, by his advice, in the National Vaccine Establishment, which still continues to dispense the blessings of the antidote without charge.

The growing interest in the public mind in favour of vaccination was of course everywhere extended to its author, who, in spite of several unworthy cabals, and attempts to deprive him of the credit of a discovery peculiarly his own, was received among all ranks with the highest distinction at home, and also gratified with various Continental honours. If he had thought fit to settle in London, he might undoubtedly have secured wealth in proportion to his reputation; but he preferred the quiet enjoyment of rural life and domestic happiness. His death took place at Berkeley, from a sudden attack of apoplexy, in February, 1823, in the seventy-fourth year of his age. The latter years of his life were spent between Berkeley and

Cheltenham, and in occasional visits to London, in the zealous prosecution of his favourite subjects of research, and in successful endeavours to diffuse the blessings of his discovery more widely in his own and other lands.

In England, however, these have not been so extensively felt as in some other countries, where the form of government has given facilities for the enforcement of vaccination. The smallpox consequently prevails to a considerable extent in that country, and especially in London. Yet the annual number of deaths from smallpox in that city, within the bills of mortality, is at present under 700; the largest number in any one year since the general practice of vaccination having been 1299, in 1825. A century ago, when the population certainly did not reach half its present amount, the yearly average was 2000, the maximum being in 1796, when the mortality swelled to 3549. That this decrease is wholly due to vaccination cannot be doubted; the advantage, however, is partly indirect, and has arisen from the discontinuance of the practice of inoculating for the smallpox, which afforded security to individuals, but increased the general mortality by keeping alive a constant source of infection. But the most striking examples of the advantage derived from vaccination are to be found on the Continent. Thus, at Berlin, where the average annual amount of deaths from smallpox was 472 for the twenty years previous to 1802, and where, in 1801, 1646 died of this disease, the mortality so speedily diminished after the enforcement of vaccination by law, that in 1821 and 1822 there was only one death in each year.

These, and similar instances which might be adduced from other countries, seem almost to warrant us in adopting the sanguine expectation of Jenner, that by means of his discovery this disgusting and dreadful malady, from which not four in a hundred of the human race formerly escaped, and which destroyed a tenth part of all that were born, and disfigured where it did not destroy, may yet be swept from the face of the earth.

The best books of reference on the subjects of this memoir are Baron's " Life of Jenner," Moore's " History of the Cowpox," Dr. Gregory's admirable articles in the " Encyclopædia of Medicine," and the reports of various parliamentary committees, especially those of 1802 and 1833.

CUVIER.

GEORGE LEOPOLD CHRISTIAN FREDERIC DAGOBERT CUVIER was born August 23, 1769, at Montbeliard, a small town in Alsace, which then formed part of the territory of the Duke of Wurtemberg. His father was a retired officer, living upon his pension, who had formerly held a commission in a Swiss regiment in the service of France. He had the inestimable advantage of possessing a very sensible mother, who even in infancy attended with sedulous care to the formation of his character and the development of his mind. He gave early indications that Nature had endowed him with her choicest intellectual gifts. A memory of extraordinary strength, joined to industry, and to the power of fixing his attention steadily upon whatever he was engaged in, enabled him to master all the ordinary studies of youth with facility ; and by the time he was fourteen years of age, he had acquired a fair knowledge of the ancient, and of several modern languages, and had made considerable progress in the mathematics, besides having enriched his mind by a wide range of historical reading. He very early gave evidences of a talent for drawing, which in after-life proved of material service in his researches into natural history. When he was but twelve years old he read the works of Buffon with avidity, and he no doubt received from the writings of that accomplished and elegant historian of nature an early bias towards the study of zoology. While he was at school he instituted a little academy of sciences among his companions, of which he was elected the president : his sleeping-room was their hall of meeting, and the foot of his bed the president's chair. They read extracts from books of history, travels, and natural philosophy, which they afterward discussed ; and the debate was usually followed by an opinion on the merits of the question, pronounced from the chair.

In 1783 the reigning Duke of Wurtemberg visited Montbeliard, and became acquainted with the unusual attainments of young Cuvier, who had then reached the fourteenth year of his age. Struck by such early promise of future eminence, he offered to take him under his own protection. The proposal was readily accepted, and the future philosopher went to Stutgard, to prosecute his studies in the university of that place. He continued there for four years, and did not fail to turn to good account the excellent opportunities which were afforded him of laying the foundation of that extensive acquaintance with every important department of human knowledge in which he was in after-life so eminently distinguished. The universality of his genius was no less remarkable than the depth and accuracy of his learning in the particular field of science with which his name is more especially associated. He not only gained the highest academical prizes, but was decorated by the duke with an order; a distinction ordinarily conferred only on five or six out of the four hundred students at the university.

He had now arrived at an age when it was necessary for him to choose a profession, and his inclination led him to seek employment in one of the public offices under the government of his patron. This he might probably have obtained; but, happily for science, the circumstances of his parents made it impossible for him to linger in expectation, and he changed his views. In July, 1788, being then in his nineteenth year, he accepted the office of tutor in a Protestant family in Normandy, having been himself brought up in that faith.

The family lived in a very retired situation near the sea; and Cuvier was not so constantly engaged with his pupils as to prevent him from cultivating those branches of science, for which he had imbibed a decided taste while listening to the lectures of Abel, the professor of natural history at Stutgard. He devoted himself especially to the study of the Mollusca, for which his vicinity to the sea afforded him good opportunities; and he continued his researches uninterruptedly for six years in this retirement. The reign of terror at Paris, which spared neither virtue nor talent, drove M. Tessier, a member of the Academy of Sciences, to seek refuge in Normandy. He became acquainted with the young naturalist, and soon learned to appreciate his talents ; and he introduced him to the correspondence of several of the more eminent men of science in Paris, among whom were Lametheric, Olivier, and Lacepède. The impression which Cuvier made upon his correspondents was so great, that, when tranquillity was restored, they invited him to come to the capital. He accepted the invitation, and in the spring of 1795 removed to Paris. He was soon afterward appointed professor of Natural History in the central school of the Pantheon.

Being very desirous of obtaining some official connexion with the Museum of Natural History at the Jardin des Plantes, with the view of gaining free access to the valuable collections there deposited, he solicited the aid of his scientific friends, and by their exertions, particularly those of De Jussieu, Geoffroy, and Lacepède, he was nominated assistant to Mertrud, the professor of comparative anatomy, a chair which had been recently instituted. Here he had free scope to indulge his passion for that branch of science, and, by his indefatigable exertions, he speedily brought together a very copious supply of illustrations for his lectures. He never ceased to make the museum a primary object of his care, and at last formed the most perfect and the most splendid collection of comparative anatomy which exists in the world. The excellence of his lectures, in which the interest of the subject was heightened by his eloquence and easy delivery, attracted a crowd of auditors; and while he thus excited and extended a taste for a department of science previously but little cultivated, those who listened to him spread the fame of the young professor.

At the establishment of the Institute in 1796, he was chosen one of the original members; and the papers which he read before that body, giving an account of his researches and discoveries in comparative anatomy, enriched their memoirs, and procured for him a high and widely-extended reputation at an early period of life. In 1800 he was appointed secretary to the Institute, and in the same year Bonaparte was appointed president. Cuvier thus, by virtue of his office, was brought into immediate and frequent communication with that extraordinary man; an event which had a material influence upon his future destiny, and opened new and wide fields of usefulness and distinction. Such were the powers of his mind, and so great was the versatility of his genius, that, in whatever situation he was placed, his superiority was soon acknowledged by his associates.

In the year 1802 the attention of the First Consul was directed to the subject of public instruction, and six inspectors-general were commissioned to organize lyceums or colleges in thirty towns of France. Cuvier was one of them; and he left Paris to execute the duties which had been assigned to him in the provinces. From this period his attention was always particularly directed to the subject of education; and his labours in that cause have had the most important influence upon every institution for public instruction in France, from the University of Paris down to the most humble village school. At the foundation of the Imperial University in 1808, Cuvier was named a member of its council for life. When Italy was annexed to the French empire, he was charged at three different times with missions to that country, for the purpose of reorganizing the old academies and colleges, and of establishing new ones ; and in the last of those missions, in 1813, although a Protestant, he was sent to organize the University at Rome. In 1811 he went into Belgium and Holland to perform similar duties ; and the reports which he drew up on that occasion, which were afterward published, possess great interest, especially those parts where he speaks of the schools in Holland for the lower classes. He felt how important it is to the welfare of a nation that good education should be within reach of the poor : and there is no country in Europe where that subject is attended to with more enlightened views than in Holland, where excellent primary schools have been in operation for nearly half a century. When the great measure for the general introduction of schools for the lower classes throughout France was brought forward in 1821, the duty of drawing up the plan upon which they were to be established was confided to Cuvier ; and his enlightened benevolence and practical good sense are equally conspicuous in the system which, on his recommendation, was adopted. It has proved admirably adapted to the ends in view. The direction of the Protestant schools was more particularly intrusted to him; and he introduced into all those which had previously existed many important improvements.

In February, 1815, the University was remodelled by the Bourbon government, and Cuvier was appointed a member of the Royal Council of Public Instruction. Shortly afterward came the events of the Hundred Days, and among them the restoration of the Imperial University. Cuvier was reappointed to his seat in the council, for they felt that they could not do there without him. In four months another revolution took place in the university, as in other public establishments; and as it was found that the system of the Royal University could not be resumed, a commission was appointed to execute the functions of the grand-master, the chancellor, and the treasurer. In this commission, the duties which had belonged to the chancellor were assigned to Cuvier; in which station he was eminently useful in maintaining the rights of the University under circumstances of no ordinary difficulty. He was twice President of the Commission, and each time for a year; but, on account of his being a Protestant, he could not retain that place permanently. But the bishop, who, as a member of the commission, had discharged the duties which belonged to the grand-master of the University, was appointed minister for ecclesiastical affairs, and Cuvier was nominated as his successor, so far as concerned the Protestant faculty of theology, and continued to act in this capacity during the rest of his life. As a member of the Council of State, and attached to the department of the Minister of the Interior, he had the direction of all matters relating to Protestant, and other religious congregations not Catholic.

During his mission to Rome in 1813, he was appointed by Napoleon a member of the Council of State; and on the restoration of the Bourbons his political opinions formed no obstacle to his continuing in that place. Although he was left undisturbed in his situation at the University, he was removed from the Council of State during the Hundred Days; but resumed his seat when the fate of his former patron and master was sealed. It is to be regretted that a mind so powerful as that of Cuvier should not have felt the paramount importance of having settled opinions on the great principles of government; and the facility with which he made himself acceptable to the despotic emperor, the weak and bigoted Bourbons, and the liberal government of Louis Philippe, showed a want of fixed public principle which casts a shade upon the memory of this great man.

As a member of the Council of State he took a distinguished lead, which, indeed, he never failed to do wherever he was placed, and he was eminently useful by his extraordinary talent for the despatch of business. He was a patient listener, and was never forward with his opinion; he allowed the useless talkers to have their course, and, while he appeared indifferent to what was going on, he was often drawing up a resolution, which his colleagues usually adopted without farther discussion, after he had given a short and luminous exposition of his views. For thirteen years previous to his death he was chairman of the Committee of the Council of State, to which the affairs of the interior belong; and the quantity of business which passed through his hands was wonderful. It was accomplished by his great skill in making those useful with whom he acted; by his talent in keeping his colleagues to the point in their discussions; and by his prodigious readiness of memory, which enabled him to go back at once to former decisions, where the principle of the question under deliberation had been already settled. His historical reading had been very extensive, and his attention was ever alive to what was passing around him, as well in other countries as in France; so that he brought to bear on the matter in debate, not speculative opinions merely, but maxims drawn from the experience of past and present times. In the Chamber of Deputies, of which he was a member for several years, he took an active part, and often originated measures. His manner as a speaker was very impressive, and the rich stores of his mind, and his ready and natural eloquence, commanded attention. At the end of 1831 he was created a peer; and, during the short time he sat in the Upper Chamber, he took a prominent part in its business, and drew up some important reports of committees to which he belonged.

But his reputation as a statesman was confined to France: his achievements in science have spread his fame over the civilized world. We can in this place do little more than mention the titles of the most important of Cuvier's works; even to name them all would carry us beyond our limits. His earliest production was a memoir read before the Natural History Society of Paris in 1795, and published in the Décade Philosophique. In this paper he objects to the divisions of certain of the lower animals adopted by Linnæus, and proposes a more scientific classification of the mollusca, crustacea, worms, insects, and other invertebrate animals. His attention had been long directed to that branch of natural history, and his subsequent researches in the same department, most of which have been communicated to the world through the medium of the " Annales du Museum," have thrown great light on that obscure and curious part of the creation. Three years afterward he published his Elementary View of the Natural History of Animals, which contains an outline of the lectures he delivered at the Pantheon. In this work he displayed the vast extent of his acquaintance with the works of his predecessors, and, at the same time, the originality of his own mind, by introducing a new arrangement of the animal kingdom, founded on more exact investigation and comparison of the varieties which exist in anatomical structure. With the assistance of his friends Dumeril and Duvernay, he published, in 1802, his " Leçons d'Anatomie Comparée" (*Lectures on Comparative Anatomy*), in two volumes, octavo, afterward extended to five. These are singularly lucid and exact, and form the most complete work on the subject which has yet appeared.

The next important publication we have to notice is one in which he imbodied the results of his extensive researches in a very interesting field of inquiry, concerning the remains of extinct species of animals which are found enveloped in solid rocks, or buried in the beds of gravel that cover the surface of the earth. We are disposed to think his " Recherches sur les Ossemens Fossiles" (*Inquiries concerning Fossil Bones*) the most important of his works, the most illustrious and imperishable monument of his fame. The quarries in the neighbourhood of Paris abound in fossil bones; and he had great facilities for collecting the valuable specimens which were almost daily discovered in the ordinary working of the quarry. When he went to Italy, he had an opportunity of seeing animal remains of the same sort procured by the naturalists of that country from their native soil, and preserved in their museums. His attention became now specially attracted to this subject; and, having accumulated materials from all parts of the world, he announced the important truths at which he had arrived in the work above mentioned, in four quarto volumes, in the year 1812. A new edition, enlarged to five volumes, appeared in 1817, and in 1824 it was extended to seven volumes, illustrated by two hundred engravings. No one who was not profoundly skilled in comparative anatomy could have entered upon the inquiry with any prospect of success; and Cuvier not only possessed that qualification, but was singularly constituted by nature for the task. His powerful memory was particularly susceptible of retaining impressions conveyed to it by the eye: he saw at a glance the most minute variations of form, and what he saw he not only never forgot, but he had the power of representing upon paper with the utmost accuracy and despatch. It is very seldom that the entire skeleton of an animal is found in a fossil state; in most instances the bones have been separated and scattered before they were entombed, and a tusk, a jaw, or a single joint of the backbone is very often all that is met with, and frequently, too, in a mutilated state. But an instructed mind like that of Cuvier was able to reconstruct the whole animal from the inspection of one fragment. He had discovered by his previous researches such a connexion between the several bones, that a particular curvature, or a small protuberance on a jaw, or a tooth, was sufficient to indicate a particular species of animal, and to prove that the fragment could not have belonged to any other. The "Recherches sur les Ossemens Fossiles" have made us acquainted with more than seventy species of animals before unknown.

The preliminary discourse in the first volume is a masterly exposition of the revolutions which the crust of the earth has undergone; revolutions to which the animal creation has been equally subject. It is written with great clearness and elegance, and is so much calculated to interest general readers as well as men of science, that it has been translated into most of the European languages. The English translation by Professor Jameson, published under the title of " Essay on the Theory of the Earth," has gone through several editions.

In his examination of the fossil bones found near Paris, Cuvier was led to inquire into the geological structure of the country around that capital. He took M. Alexander Brongniart to be his associate, and the result of their joint labours is contained in one of the volumes of the work now under consideration, in an Essay on the Mineralogy of the Environs of Paris. This essay formed a great epoch in geological science, for it was then that the grand division of the tertiary formations was first shown to form a distinct class. A new direction and a fresh impulse was thus given to geological investigations ; and many of the most important general truths at which we have since arrived in this science have been established by discoveries to which the essay of Cuvier and Brongniart led the way.

In 1817 appeared the first edition of the " Règne Animal" (*The Animal Kingdom*), in four octavo volumes, one of which was written by the celebrated naturalist Latreille. This work gives an account of the structure and history of all existing and extinct races of animals : it has subsequently been enlarged. Cuvier began, in conjunction with M. Valenciennes, an extensive general work on fishes, which it was calculated would extend to twenty volumes. Eight only have appeared ; for the embarrassments among the Parisian booksellers in 1830 suspended the publication, and it has thus been left incomplete ; but a great mass of materials was collected, and we may hope that they will yet be published. In addition to these great undertakings, he had been for years collecting materials for a stupendous work, a complete system of comparative anatomy, to be illustrated by drawings from nature, and chiefly from objects in the Museum at the Jardin des Plantes. Above a thousand drawings, many executed by his own hand, are said to have been made. Looking back to what he had already accomplished, and considering his health and age, for he was only in his sixty-third year, it was not unreasonable in him to hope to see the great edifice erected, of which he had laid the foundation and collected the materials. But, unfortunately for the cause of science, it was ordered otherwise, and there is something particularly touching in the last words he uttered to his friend the Baron Pasquier, and in sounds, too, scarcely articulate, from the malady which so suddenly cut short his career, " *Vous le voyez, il y a loin de l'homme du Mardi (nous nous étions rencontrés ce jour là) à l'homme du Dimanche : et tant de choses, cependant, qui me restaient à faire ! trois ouvrages importans à mettre au jour, les matériaux préparés, tout était disposé dans ma tête, il ne me restait plus qu'à écrire.*"—" You see how it is, how different the man of Tuesday (we had met on that day) from the man of Sunday ; and so many things, too, that remained for me to do ! three important works to bring out, the materials prepared, all disposed in order in my head, I had nothing left to do but to write." Only four hours afterward that wonderfully-organized head became a mere mass of insensible matter.

Besides the works above enumerated, and many memoirs in the transactions of the scientific bodies of Paris, he has given to the world, in four octavo volumes, a History of the Progress of the Physical Sciences from 1789 to 1827, which evinces his genius and extensive erudition. The first volume is a reprint of a report which he presented, as perpetual secretary of the Institute, to Napoleon, in 1808, on the Progress of the Physical Sciences from 1789 to 1807. In the same capacity, during thirty-two years, he pronounced the customary eloges upon deceased members of the Institute.

These are collected in three octavo volumes, and bear witness to the versatility of his genius and the extent of his attainments; for whether he is recording the merits of a mathematician, a chymist, a botanist, a geologist, or the cultivator of any other department of science, he shows himself equally conversant with his subject.

He lived at the Jardin des Plantes for nearly forty years, surrounded by the objects which engrossed so great a portion of his thoughts, and there received every Saturday the men of science of Paris, and all others who visited that capital from any part of the world. Professors and pupils met in his rooms to listen with edification and delight to his conversation, for he was accessible to all. Although compelled to be a very rigid economist of his time, he was so good-natured and considerate, that, if any person who had business to transact with him called at an unexpected hour, he never sent him away; saying, that to one who lived so far off he had no right to deny himself. Everything in his house was so arranged as to secure economy of time; his library consisted of several apartments, and each great subject he attended to had a separate room allotted to it; and he usually worked in the apartment belonging to the subject he was at the moment engaged with, so that he might be surrounded with his materials. His ordinary custom, when he returned from attending public business in Paris, was to go at once to his study, passing a few minutes by the way in the room where his family sat, which latterly consisted of Madame Cuvier and her daughter by a former marriage. He came back when dinner was announced, usual-

ly with a book in his hand, and returned soon after dinner to his study, where he remained till elev-
en. He then came to Madame Cuvier's room, and
had generally some of the lighter literature of the
day read aloud to him. Sometimes the book selected was of a graver cast ; it is said that during
the last year of his life he had the greater part of
Cicero read to him. His manner was courteous,
kind, and encouraging : every one who took an interest in any subject with which Cuvier was familiar felt assured that he might approach him without fear of meeting with a cold or discouraging reception.

He had four children, but lost them all. The
last taken from him was a daughter, who was suddenly carried off by consumption on the eve of her
marriage. He was tenderly attached to her, and
it required all the efforts of his powerful mind to
prevent his sinking under the blow. He found diversion by intense thought on other subjects, but
not consolation, for the wound never healed.

On Tuesday, the 8th of May, 1832, he opened
his usual course at the College of France with a
particularly eloquent introductory lecture, full of
enthusiasm in his subject, to the great delight of
his numerous audience. As he left the room he
was attacked with the first symptoms of the disease
which was so soon to prove fatal : it was a para-
lytic seizure. He was well enough, however, to
preside the next day at the Committee of the Council of State, but that was the last duty he performed. He died on the following Sunday, leaving
behind him an imperishable name, which will be
held in honour in the most advanced state of human learning.

SIR W. SCOTT.

WALTER SCOTT was born in the Old Town of Edinburgh, April 15, 1771, in a house at the head of the College Wynd, which has been pulled down to make way for the new buildings of the University. His father was a writer to the signet, his grandfather a farmer resident in Roxburghshire, who traced his descent to the ancient Border family of Scott of Harden. His infancy gave no promise of the robust manhood which he attained ; and, in addition to general weakness of constitution, his right foot received an early injury, which rendered him lame through life. This delicacy of health induced his parents to send him, when almost an infant, to his grandfather's farm at Sandyknow in Roxburghshire, adjoining the Border fortress called Smailholm Tower, in the heart of that romantic pastoral district whose scenery and legends he has rendered famous. *"His residence at this secluded spot, which, after early boyhood, was, we believe, occasionally renewed during the summer vacations of the High School and College, was undoubtedly fraught with many advantages, physical and mental. It was here that his feeble constitution was, by the aid of free air and exercise, gradually strengthened into robustness ; and, though he never got rid of his lameness, it was so far overcome as to be in after-life rather a deformity than

* This, and the other passages marked with inverted commas, except those taken from Scott's Autobiography, are derived from a memoir of Sir Walter Scott published in the Penny Magazine, No. 37, and written by Scott's countryman and acquaintance, the late Mr. Pringle.

an inconvenience.   It was here that his love of ballad lore and border story was fostered into a passion ; and it was here, doubtless, and at the house
of one of his uncles, Mr. Thomas Scott of Woolee,
also a Roxburghshire farmer, that he early acquired that intimate acquaintance with the manners,
character, and language of the Scottish peasantry
which he afterward turned to such admirable account in his novels."

In October, 1779, he entered the High School
of Edinburgh, which he attended during four
years.   He there acquired the character of being
"a remarkably active and dauntless boy, full of all
manner of fun, and ready for all manner of mischief;" and, so far from being timid or quiet on
account of his lameness, that very defect (as he
himself remarked to be usually the case in similar
circumstances with boys of enterprising disposition) prompted him to take the lead among all the
stirring boys in the street where he lived and in the
school which he attended.   In Greek and Latin he
made little progress, and obtained no great credit
for talent or industry from his masters ; but he has
invoked his surviving schoolfellows, in the Introduction to the last edition of the Waverley Novels,
" to bear witness that I had a distinguished character for talent as a tale-teller, at a time when the
applause of my companions was the recompense for
the disgraces and punishments which the future
romance-writer incurred for being idle himself
and keeping others idle during hours of the day
that should have been employed upon our tasks."

He entered the University of Edinburgh in October, 1783 ; but his attendance there was only

for two sessions. About the age of fifteen the rupture of a bloodvessel again reduced him to a very weak state, and during the space of two years bodily and mental exertion were forbidden. He had recourse for amusement to a circulating library, " rich," he says, " in works of fiction, from the romances of chivalry, and the ponderous folios of Cyrus and Cassandra, down to the most approved works of later times. I was plunged into this great ocean of reading without compass or pilot, and, unless when some one had the charity to play at chess with me, I was allowed to do nothing, save read, from morning to night. . . . I believe I read almost all the old romances, old plays, and epic poetry in that formidable collection, and no doubt was unconsciously amassing materials for the task in which it has been my lot to be so much employed. At the same time, I did not in all respects abuse the license permitted me. Familiar acquaintance with the specious miracles of fiction brought with it some degree of satiety, and I began, by degrees, to seek in histories, memoirs, voyages and travels, and the like, events nearly as wonderful as those which were the work of the imagination, with the additional advantage that they were, at least in a great measure, true. The lapse of two years, during which I was left to the service of my own free will, was followed by a temporary residence in the country, where I was again very lonely but for the amusement which I derived from a good though oldfashioned library. The vague and wild use which I made of this advantage, I cannot describe better than by referring my reader to the desultory studies of Waverley in a similar situation; the passages concerning whose reading were imitated from recollections of my own."

After recovering from this illness his constitution changed, and he became unusually robust, and capable of enduring great bodily and mental fatigue; even his lameness occasioning no serious inconvenience. He then applied himself in earnest to the study of law, and, to acquire a thorough knowledge of its technicalities, went through the duties of a clerk in his father's office. He completed the usual course of education, and was called to the bar in July, 1792. He seemed, however, little anxious for business; and, as usual, business unsought came slowly: in his legal capacity, therefore, he acquired neither wealth nor distinction. But, in amends for this, in those days of volunteer corps, he made an admirable quartermaster to the Edinburgh Light Dragoons; and his zeal and skill, and the popularity which his high powers of social entertainment procured, recommended him to the friendship of the Duke of Buccleugh, by whose interest he obtained, in December, 1799, the appointment of sheriff of Selkirkshire, with a salary of £300. In 1797 he had married Miss Carpenter, a lady of foreign birth but of English parentage, possessed of fortune sufficient, when added to the salary of his office and his own patrimonial inheritance, to release him from the necessity of labouring at the bar for a livelihood. This was a point on which his mind had been some time bent. "My profession and I," he says, "came to stand nearly on the footing which honest Slender consoled himself on having established with Mistress Anne Page—'There was no great love between us at the beginning, and it pleased Heaven to decrease it on farther acquaintance.' I became sensible that the time was come when I must either buckle myself resolutely to ' the toil by day, the lamp by night,' renouncing all the Dalilahs of my imagination, or bid adieu to the profession of the law and hold another course."

Scott was not a premature writer; he had reached his twenty-fifth year before he tried his strength in composition, excepting a few trivial attempts in childhood; and his name was still unknown to the public when he resolved to devote his powers to literature. His first essays were made about 1796, when his attention was caught by the Leonora, and other poems of Bürger, which he translated and published anonymously. " The adventure," he says, " proved a dead loss, and a great part of this edition was condemned to the service of the trunk-maker." His next performance was a translation of Goethe's drama, Goetz of Berlichingen, published in 1799. But he continued his devotion to ballad poetry, and, as his confidence rose, essayed his strength in Glenfinlas and the Eve of St. John, his first original compositions. At Lasswade, on the banks of the Esk, about five miles from Edinburgh, where he spent several summers after his marriage, he prosecuted with increased zeal and success his favourite inquiries into the antiquities and legendary song of his country, and commenced the work which first gave him a name in literature, the Minstrelsy of the Scottish Border. " The materials for this work were collected during various excursions, or *raids*, as Sir Walter was wont to call them, through the most remote recesses of the border glens, made by the poetical compiler in person, assisted by one

or two other enthusiasts in ballad lore.   Pre-emi-
nent among his coadjutors in this undertaking was
Dr. John Leyden, an enthusiastic borderer and
ballad-monger like himself, and to whom he has
gratefully acknowledged his obligations both in
verse and prose."

"Some amusing anecdotes have been printed,
and others are still extant in oral tradition among
the border hills, of the circumstances attending the
collection of these ballads.   The old women, who
were almost the only remaining depositories of ancient song and tradition, though proud of being solicited to recite them by ' so grand a man' as an
Edinburgh advocate, could not repress their astonishment that ' a man o' sense and lair' should spend
his time in writing into a book auld ballads and
stories of the bluidy Border wars and paipish
times.' . . . . The Minstrelsy was printed at Kel-
so in 1802, at first in two volumes, to which a third
was added in the second edition.   Two years subsequently Scott published the romance of Sir Tris-
tram, a Scottish metrical tale of the thirteenth century, which he showed, in a learned disquisition,
to have been composed by Thomas of Ercildown,
commonly called the Rymer."

"These works, especially the Border Minstrelsy, were favourably received by the public, and established Scott's reputation on a very respectable
footing as an excellent poetical antiquary, and as
a writer of considerable power and promise, both
in verse and prose.   As yet, however, he had produced no composition of originality and importance
sufficient to secure that high and permanent rank
in literature to which his secret ambition led him
to aspire.   But he had now a subject in hand

which was destined to attain for him a popularity far beyond what his most sanguine hopes could have ventured to anticipate."

" The Lay of the Last Minstrel appeared in 1805. The structure of the verse was suggested, as the author states, by the Christabel of Coleridge; a part of which had been repeated to him about the year 1800. The originality, wildness, poetical beauty, and descriptive powers of Scott's Border romance, produced an effect on the public mind only to be equalled perhaps by some of the earlier works of Byron."

" In the spring of 1806. Sir Walter obtained an appointment, which, he says, completely met his moderate wishes as to preferment. This was the office of a principal clerk of session, of which the duties are by no means heavy, though personal attendance during the sitting of the courts is required. Mr. Pitt, under whose administration the appointment had been granted, having died before it was officially completed, the succeeding Whig ministry had the satisfaction of confirming it. The emoluments of this office were about £1200 a year; but Scott received no part of the salary till 1812, the appointment being a reversionary one."

His reputation and his fortune seemed now to be completely established. Marmion, published in 1808, and the Lady of the Lake, in 1810, were received each with greater favour than its predecessor. Don Roderick, however, in 1811, was not successful; and Rokeby, in 1813, and The Lord of the Isles, in 1814, were generally thought inferior in merit to his earlier works. This might arise, in part, from the extraordinary rapidity of their composition; for Rokeby was commenced

September 15th, and finished December 31st, 1812;
and the Lord of the Isles was written in the follow.
ing autumn, with equal rapidity, but under cir.
cumstances which rendered the task a burden, and
damped the fire of his muse.   Still these, like their
predecessors, commanded very large sales, and
brought in large sums to the author, and large prof.
its to the publishers.   Still his popularity was on
the ebb, and it was the general impression that
Scott had nearly written himself out.   At the time
when this was said, he had already published one
anonymous poem, the Bridal of Triermain, in 1810,
as if ashamed of his prolific pen.   Afterward, in
1817, he published Harold the Dauntless in the
same way.   The censure, however, was not unfounded; and the last two acknowledged poems
of Scott were inferior both in interest and execution to his earlier productions.   Another reason
for the decrease of Scott's popularity he has himself assigned, in the rapid growth of Lord Byron's.
   It was about the end of 1813 that accident threw
in his way the mislaid manuscript of the beginning
of Waverley, seven chapters of which he had composed in 1805, and had thrown aside in deference
to the unfavourable opinion of a critical friend.
At different times he had been inclined to resume
this work, but had been prevented by the loss of
the manuscript, which he now applied himself in
earnest to complete.   Waverley was published in
the summer of 1814, and obtained success beyond
the author's fondest expectations.   The history of
this wonderful series of works of fiction, and the
author's reasons for adopting and retaining his in-
cognito, are familiar to the public, through his own
account in the Introduction to the Waverley Nov-

els. The manner in which the secret was kept is a remarkable circumstance in literary history : for, whatever conclusions might be drawn from internal evidence by Scott's intimate friends, and from putting things together by the public, not a particle of external evidence was produced to fasten it upon him, until the failure of Constable's house in 1826 led to Scott's public avowal of the authorship in 1827. Perhaps this mystery tended to keep alive the public interest : perhaps, also, Scott had a keener relish of the homage paid to the Great Unknown than if it had been offered to him in his own person.

Scott's metrical romances, as they were composed with unexampled rapidity, commanded also unexampled prices from the booksellers. And, at the same time, he found leisure for a variety of laborious works in criticism, biography, and miscellaneous literature, which added considerably both to his funds and his reputation. Among these were new editions of the works of Dryden and Swift, with biographical accounts ; Sadler's State Papers ; Somers's Tracts ; Lives of the Novelists ; besides numerous contributions to encyclopædias, reviews, and other periodical publications. His scheme of devoting himself to literature had borne fruit of fame and profit beyond his brightest anticipations. His certain income (we presume after the year 1812) is said by Mr. Pringle to have exceeded £2000 ; and he was supposed to double that sum by the exuberant harvest of his brain.

" Amid all this labour, Scott found abundant leisure, not only for his official avocations, but for social enjoyment and rural recreation. While the Court of Session was sitting, he lived in Edinburgh, in a good substantial house in North Castle-street. During the vacations he resided in the country, and appeared to enter with ardour into the ordinary occupations and amusements of country gentlemen. After he was appointed sheriff of Selkirk he hired for his summer residence the house and farm of Ashiesteil, on the banks of the Tweed; and here many of his poetical works were written. But with the increase of his resources grew the desire to possess landed property of his own, where he might indulge his tastes for building, planting, and gardening. Commencing with moderation, he purchased a small farm of about one hundred acres, lying on the south bank of the Tweed, three miles above Melrose, and in the very centre of that romantic and legendary country which his first great poem has made familiar to every reader. This spot, then called Cartly Hole, had a northern exposure, and at that time a somewhat bleak and uninviting aspect: the only habitable house upon it was a small and inconvenient farmhouse. Such was the nucleus of the mansion and estate of Abbotsford. By degrees, as his resources increased, he added farm after farm to his domain, and reared his chateau, turret after turret, till he had completed what a French tourist not ineptly terms 'a romance of stone and lime,' clothing, meanwhile, the hills behind, and embowering the lawns before with flourishing woods of his own planting. The embellishment of his house and grounds, and the enlargement of his landed property, became, after the establishment of his literary reputation, the objects, apparently, of Scott's most engrossing interest; and whatever may be the intrinsic value of the estate, as a heritage to his posterity, he has at least succeeded in erecting a scene altogether of no ordinary attractions, and worthy of being asso-ciated with his distinguished name."

" During the greater part of the summer and au-tumn he kept house at Abbotsford like a wealthy country gentleman, receiving with a cordial yet courtly hospitality the many distinguished persons, both from England and the Continent, who found means to obtain an introduction to his enchanted castle. Anything more delightful than a visit to Abbotsford, when Sir Walter was in the full enjoy-ment of his health and spirits, can scarcely be im-agined. After his morning labours, which, even when busiest, were seldom protracted beyond mid-day (his time for composition being usually from seven to eleven or twelve o'clock), he devoted him-self to the entertainment of his guests with so much unaffected cordiality, such hilarity of spirits, and such homely kindliness of manner, and, above all, with such an entire absence of literary pretension, that the shyest stranger found himself at once on terms of the easiest familiarity with the most illus-trious man in Europe."

In the spring of 1820 Scott was created a baro-net by George IV., as a testimony of personal re-gard; and on the king's visit to Scotland in 1822, he was appointed to superintend the arrangements for his majesty's reception; an office gratifying to his national feelings and antiquarian tastes, as well as to his aristocratical predilections.

The profuseness of his expenditure no doubt had considerable effect in strengthening the general be-lief that Scott was the author of the Waverley Novels; inasmuch as he possessed no ostensible means from which the expenses incurred in the

purchase and improvement of Abbotsford, as well
as the liberal hospitality which he there exercised,
could be defrayed.   His urbanity, his innate kindliness of nature, his unassuming demeanour, and
readiness to foster humble merit, had almost dis-
armed ill-will, besides softening the asperity of party feelings; and men looked without envy on a
fortune which, to be the produce of one man's literary labours in the short space of twenty years,
seemed almost beyond belief, as well as example,
while they acknowledged it to be deserved, without
a doubt of its continuance or reality.   In this latter persuasion (for otherwise he would have acted
differently, being naturally a prudent man), Scott
himself also rested secure, until January, 1826,
when the house of Constable and Co. became bank-
rupt, at the close of that calamitous season which
pressed so heavily upon all branches of trade.   He
then, to use his own words, found himself called on
to meet the demands of creditors upon commercial
establishments, with which his fortunes had long
been bound up, to the extent of no less a sum than
£120,000.   How and why he was led into so deep
a confidence, and how far the prices received for
his works were connected with his commercial
transactions, has never, we believe, been clearly
explained, nor does it much concern the public to
know; the error, so far as his reputation is concerned (and the only charge against him was want
of prudence), he amply redeemed by the nobleness
of his conduct under this crushing misfortune; and
it has been truly said, that " the honour which rests
upon his memory for his gigantic exertions to pay
off this immense debt without deduction, is a far

nobler heritage to his posterity than the most princely fortune."

"On meeting his creditors, he refused to accept of any compromise, and declared his determination, if life was spared to him, to pay off every shilling. He ensured his life in their favour for £22,000; surrendered all his available property in trust (Abbotsford being rendered inalienable by the marriage articles of his eldest son); sold his town house and furniture, and removed to a humbler dwelling; and then set himself calmly down to the stupendous task of reducing this load of debt. The only indulgence he asked for was time; and, to the honour of the parties concerned, time was liberally and kindly given him. A month or two after the crash of Constable's house, Lady Scott died; domestic affliction thus following fast upon worldly calamity."

For five years after his pecuniary misfortunes, namely, from January, 1826, to the spring of 1831, Sir Walter continued his indefatigable labours; and in that period, besides several new works of fiction, he produced the History of Scotland, published in Lardner's Cyclopædia, Tales of a Grandfather, Letters on Demonology, and a number of smaller pieces. The Life of Napoleon was in part composed anterior to the calamity of which we speak; it was published in 1827, and, though read with interest, did not display the research and impartiality which the character of an historian requires. He also superintended a new edition of the Waverley Novels, with prefaces and illustrative notes; and the profits of all these works were so considerable, that, by the close of 1830, £54,000 had been paid off; all of which, except six or seven thousand, had been produced by his own literary labours. The copyright of the published novels was sold by Constable's creditors for £8400, half of which was assigned to Sir Walter by his creditors, in consideration of his assistance in furnishing prefaces and notes to the new edition.

But over-exertion in the evening of life, and under circumstances too well calculated to weaken the elasticity of his spirits, and to destroy the pleasure which he used to feel in composition, broke his constitution and brought on premature old age. In the autumn of 1830 he retired from his office of Clerk of Session. In the following winter symptoms of paralysis began to appear. Still he continued to labour until the summer of 1831, in the course of which mental exertion was strictly forbidden. He was advised to visit Italy in the following autumn, and even in his declining condition must have been gratified by the sympathy and the honour rendered to him. A passage to Malta in the Barham man-of-war was granted to him by the British government; and at Rome and Naples he was received with honours rarely paid except to royal blood. But his desire to return to his native land became irrepressible; and he hurried homeward, taking the route by the Rhine, with a rapidity which proved very injurious. He reached London in nearly the last stage of physical and mental weakness. Still the love of his native land was strong in death, and, after remaining some weeks in the metropolis, he was conveyed at his own earnest desire by sea to Leith, and reached Abbotsford July 11. After lingering two months, almost without consciousness, in the last stage of his most afflictive malady, he expired on the 22d of September, 1832. His body was laid in his family burial-place in the ruined abbey of Dryburgh on the Tweed.

Throughout the kingdom his death was regarded like the loss of a friend; and the general admiration of his talents, respect for his conduct, and sympathy for his misfortunes, was shown by the favourable reception of a project for raising a subscription to discharge the encumbrances existing on the Abbotsford estate, and to preserve it by entail in Sir Walter's family as a lasting memorial of his genius.

WILBERFORCE.

WILLIAM WILBERFORCE, whose name a heartfelt, enlightened, and unwearied philanthropy, directing talents of the highest order, has enrolled among those of the most illustrious benefactors of mankind, was born August 24, 1759, in Hull, where his ancestors had been long and successfully engaged in trade. By his father's death he was left an orphan at an early age. He received the chief part of his education at the grammar-school of Pocklington, in Yorksire, and at St. John's College, Cambridge, of which he became a fellow-commoner about 1776 or 1777. When just of age, and apparently before taking his B.A. degree, he was returned for his native town at the general election of 1780. In 1784 he was returned again; but being also chosen member for Yorkshire, he

chose to sit for that great county, which he continued to represent until the year 1812, during six
successive parliaments.   From 1812 to 1825, when
he retired from parliament, he was returned by Lord
Calthorpe for the borough of Bramber.   His politics were in general those of Mr. Pitt's party, and
his first prominent appearance was in 1783, in opposition to Mr. Fox's India Bill.   In 1786 he introduced and carried through the Commons a bill
for the amendment of the criminal code, which was
roughly handled by the Lord-chancellor Thurlow,
and rejected in the House of Lords without a division.

   At the time when Mr. Wilberforce was rising
into manhood, the iniquity of the Slave-trade had
engaged in a slight degree the attention of the
public.   To the Quakers belong the high honour
of having taken the lead in denouncing that most
unjust and unchristian traffic.   At the beginning
of the eighteenth century, during the life of Penn,
the Quakers of Pennsylvania passed a censure
upon it, and from time to time the Society of
Friends expressed their disapprobation of the de-
portation of negroes, until, in 1761, they completed their good work by a resolution to disown all
such as continued to be engaged in it.   In 1783 an
event occurred well calculated to rouse the feelings
of the nation, and call its attention to the atrocities of which the Slave-trade was the cause and
pretext.   An action was brought by certain under-
writers against the owners of the ship Zong, on
the ground that the captain had caused 132 weak,
sickly slaves to be thrown overboard, for the purpose of claiming their value, for which the plain-
tiffs would not have been liable if they had died a

natural death. The fact of the drowning was admitted, and defended on the plea that want of water had rendered it necessary; though it appeared that the crew had not been put upon short allowance. It now seems incredible that no criminal proceeding should have been instituted against the perpetrators of this wholesale murder.

Mr. Clarkson, in the course of his application to members of Parliament in relation this abominable traffic, called on Mr. Wilberforce, who stated that " the subject had often employed his thoughts, and was near his heart." He inquired into the authorities for the statements laid before him, and became not only convinced of, but impressed with, the paramount duty of abolishing so hateful a trade. Occasional meetings of those who were alike interested were held at his house; and in May, 1787, a committee was formed, of which Wilberforce became the parliamentary leader. Early in 1788 he gave notice of his intention to bring the subject before the house; but, owing to his severe indisposition, that task was ultimately undertaken by Mr. Pitt, who moved and carried a resolution, pledging the house in the ensuing session to enter on the consideration of the subject. Accordingly, on the 12th of May, 1789, Mr. Wilberforce moved a series of resolutions, founded on a report of the Privy Council, exposing the iniquity and cruelty of the traffic in slaves, the mortality which it occasioned among white as well as black men, and the neglect of health and morals by which the natural increase of the race in the West India islands was checked; and concluding with a declaration, that if the causes were removed by which that increase was arrested, no considerable inconvenience would result from discontinuing the importation of African slaves. Burke, Pitt, and Fox supported the resolutions. Mr. Wilberforce's speech was distinguished by eloquence and earnestness, and by its unanswerable appeals to the first principles of justice and religion. The consideration of the subject was ultimately adjourned to the following session. In that and in two subsequent sessions the motions were renewed.

In 1792 Mr. Wilberforce's motion for the Abolition of the Slave-trade was met by a proposal to insert in it the word " gradually ;" and in pursuance of the same policy, Mr. Dundas introduced a bill to provide for its discontinuance in 1800. The date was altered to 1796, and in that state the bill passed the Commons, but was stopped in the Upper House by a proposal to hear evidence upon it. Mr. Wilberforce annually renewed his efforts, and brought every new argument to bear upon the question which new discoveries, or the events of the times, produced. In 1799 the friends of the measure resolved on letting it repose for a while, and for five years Mr. Wilberforce contented himself with moving for certain papers ; but he took an opportunity of assuring the house that he had not grown cool in the cause, and that he would renew the discussion in a future session. On the 30th of May, 1804, he once more moved for leave to bring in his bill for the Abolition of the Slave-trade, in a speech of great eloquence and effect. He took the opportunity of making a powerful appeal to the Irish members, before whom, in consequence of the Union, this question was now for the first time brought, and the greater part of whom supported it. The division showed a majority of 124 to 49 in his favour ; and the bill was carried through the Commons, but was again postponed in the House of Lords. In 1805 he renewed his motion, but on this occasion it was lost in the Commons by over-security among the friends of the measure. But when Mr. Fox and Lord Grenville took office in 1806, the Abolition was brought forward by the ministers, most of whom supported it, though it was not made a government question in consequence of several members of the cabinet opposing it. The attorney-general (Sir A. Pigott) brought in a bill, which was passed into a law, prohibiting the Slave-trade in the conquered colonies, and excluding British subjects from engaging in the foreign Slave-trade; and Mr. Fox, at Mr. Wilberforce's special request, introduced a resolution pledging the house to take the earliest measures for effectually abolishing the whole trade: this resolution was carried by a majority of 114 to 15; and on the 2d of January, 1807, Lord Grenville brought forward a bill for the Abolition of the Slave-trade, in the House of Lords, which passed both Houses of Parliament. As, however, the king was believed to be unfriendly to the measure, some alarm was felt by its friends, lest its fate might still be affected by the dismissal of the ministers, which had been determined on. Those fears were, however, groundless; for, though they received orders to deliver up the seals of their offices on the 25th of March, the royal assent was given by commission by the lord-chancellor Erskine on the same day.

The rest of Mr. Wilberforce's parliamentary conduct was consistent with his behaviour on this question. In debates chiefly political he rarely took a forward part; but where religion and morals were directly concerned, points on which few cared to interfere, and where a leader was wanted, he never shrunk from the advocacy of his opinions. He was a supporter of Catholic Emancipation and Parliamentary Reform; he condemned the encouragement of gambling, in the shape of lotteries established by government; he insisted on the cruelty of employing boys of tender age as chimney-sweepers; he attempted to procure a legislative enactment against duelling, after the hostile meeting between Pitt and Tierney; and on the renewal of the East India Company's charter in 1816, he gave his zealous support to the propagation of Christianity in Hindostan, in opposition to those who, as has been more recently done in the West Indies, represented the employment of missionaries to be inconsistent with the preservation of the British supremacy in those countries. It is encouraging to observe, that, with the exception of the one levelled against duelling, all these measures, however violently opposed and unfairly censured, have been carried in a more or less perfect form.

As an author, Mr. Wilberforce's claim to notice is chiefly derived from his treatise entitled "A Practical View of the prevailing religious system of professing Christians in the higher and middle classes in this country, contrasted with real Christianity." The object of it was to show that the standard of life generally adopted by those classes in England not only fell short of, but was inconsistent with, the doctrines of the Gospel. It has been justly applauded as a work of no common courage, not from the asperity of its censures, for it breathes throughout a spirit of gentleness and love, but on the joint consideration of the unpopularity of the subject and the writer's position. The

Bishop of Calcutta, in his introductory essay, correctly observes, that the author, in attempting it, risked everything dear to a public man and a politician, as such—consideration, weight, ambition, reputation." And Scott the divine, one of the most fearless and ardent of men, viewed the matter in the same light: " Taken in all its probable effects," he says, " I do sincerely think such a stand for vital Christianity has not been made in my memory. He has come out beyond my expectations." Of a work so generally known we shall not describe the tendency more at large. It is said to have gone through about twenty editions in Britain, since the publication in 1797, and more in America ; and to have been translated into most European languages.

In the discharge of his parliamentary duties Mr. Wilberforce was punctual and active beyond his apparent strength ; and those who farther recollect his diligent attendance on a vast variety of public meetings and committees connected with religious and charitable purposes, will wonder how a frame naturally weak should so long have endured the wear of such exertion. In 1788, when his illness was a matter of deep concern, Dr. Warren said that he had not stamina to last a fortnight. No doubt his bodily powers were greatly aided by the placid and happy frame of mind which he habitually enjoyed ; but it is important to relate his own opinion, as delivered by an ear-witness, on the physical benefits which he derived from a strict abstinence from temporal affairs on Sundays. " I have often heard him assert, that he never could have sustained the labour and stretch of mind required in his early political life if it had not been for the rest of his Sabbath ; and that he could name several of his contemporaries in the vortex of political cares, whose minds had actually given way under the stress of intellectual labour, so as to bring on a premature death, or the still more dreadful catastrophe of insanity and suicide, who, humanly speaking, might have been preserved in health if they would but conscientiously have observed the Sabbath." (Venn's Sermon.)

In 1797 Mr. Wilberforce married Miss Spooner, daughter of an eminent banker at Birmingham. Four sons survive him. He died, after a gradual decline, July, 29, 1833, in Cadogan Place. He directed that his funeral should be conducted without the smallest pomp ; but his orders were disregarded, in compliance with a requisition addressed to his relatives by many of the most distinguished men of all parties, and couched in the following terms : " We, the undersigned members of both Houses of Parliament, being anxious, upon public grounds, to show our respect for the memory of the late William Wilberforce, and being also satisfied that public honours can never be more fitly bestowed than upon such benefactors of mankind, earnestly request that he may be buried in Westminister Abbey, and that we, and others who may agree with us in these sentiments, may have permission to attend his funeral." The attendance of both Houses was numerous. Mr. Wilberforce was interred within a few yards of his great contemporaries Pitt, Fox, and Canning.

THE END.

e Due

MAY 1 6 1949

Im The Story
personalised classic books

JANE
IN
WONDERLAND

LEWIS
CARROLL

"Beautiful gift...lovely finish.
My Niece loves it, so precious!"

Helen R Brumfieldon

★★★★★

UNIQUE
GIFT

FOR KIDS, PARTNERS
AND FRIENDS

Timeless books such as:

Kids

Alice in Wonderland · The Jungle Book · The Wonderful Wizard of Oz
Peter and Wendy · Robin Hood · The Prince and The Pauper
The Railway Children · Treasure Island · A Christmas Carol

Adults

Romeo and Juliet · Dracula

Highly
Customizable

Change
Books Title

Replace
Charactei Names
with yours

Upload
Photo to
inside page

Add
Inscriptions

Visit
Im The Story .com
and order yours today!